Christianity and Capitalism

Christianity and Capitalism

Perspectives on Religion, Liberalism and the Economy

Edited by
Bruce Grelle and David A. Krueger

C
S
S
R

Center for the Scientific Study of Religion
Chicago, Illinois

Studies in Religion and Society

Center for the Scientific Study of Religion

For a complete list of other publications in the
series, see the back of the book.

Cover photo by Chris Conroy, courtesy of C. Harrison, Conroy Company,
Newton, New Jersey.

Copyright © 1986, Center for the Scientific Study of Religion

Printed in the United States of America

Center for the Scientific Study of Religion
5757 University Avenue
Chicago, Illinois 60637

ISBN: Cloth: 0-913348-23-6
     Paper: 0-913348-24-4

Library of Congress Catalog Card Number: 85-73375

Table of Contents

Preface

Most of the essays in this volume were originally prepared for a conference entitled "Religion and the Economic Order: Historical Relations and the Normative Task". This conference was held at The Divinity School of the University of Chicago in April, 1984 and was sponsored by The Divinity School Association.

The conference's keynote address was delivered by Franklin I. Gamwell and was circulated in advance. Consequently, there are a number of references to his presentation by the other contributors to the volume. Likewise, the essays by Cornel West and W. Widick Schroeder are expanded versions of their critical responses to the presentations of Robert Benne and Douglas Sturm respectively. Thus, the interactive and dialogical nature of the conference has to a certain extent been preserved in the present volume.

This volume is not, however, merely a documentation of those conference proceedings. Rather, as even a casual reading will reveal, these essays are representative of the concerns and contours of much recent Christian ethical reflection on the economy.

The editors wish to thank various individuals for their participation in the activities which have culminated in the publication of this volume. We express our gratitude to Brad Hinze, Christine Firer Hinze, Don Matthews, Stephen Pope, Norma Schmidt, and Barry Stenger, all of whom were members of the conference planning group. Special thanks go to David Perry, co-chairperson of the conference. Special thanks go also to W. Widick Schroeder for his invaluable counsel on editorial matters and for the very generous amount of time and energy he devoted to this publication. We also thank Dean Franklin I. Gamwell for his support of the conference and for his encouragement in this publication. We thank James M. Gustafson, Robin W. Lovin, Stephen J. Holajter, and P. Travis Kroeker for their helpful comments on various sections of this volume. Finally, we owe our largest debt of gratitude to our contributors.

Bruce Grelle
David A. Krueger

Introduction

Christian Ethics and Economic Life

Bruce Grelle and David A. Krueger

Since its fledgling origins as an obscure sect within the Roman Empire, Christianity has been forced to consider the problem of its proper relationship to the larger social world. Within this broad context, much discussion in Christian ethics and in other disciplines has focused on Christianity's assessment of economic life.

Chrisitan theologians since Paul have been concerned with the proper use and value of wealth with respect to the Christian's aspirations toward salvation and the Kingdom of God. Prevalent in the Middle Ages was the question of the moral status of usury, not to mention the larger question of Christian participation in commercial life itself. In the twentieth century, debate within Christian ethics seems to have focused primarily on the relative moral merits of capitalism and socialism as social systems rather than on more particular problems such as the individual's use of wealth or the nature of one's vocation in the world.

That the relationship of Christianity and capitalism has exercised the minds of countless scholars is indisputable. Indeed, since Marx's claim that religion is simply the ideological counterpart of particular forms of economic and social relations, and since Weber's thesis regarding an "elective affinity" between a Calvinistic ethic and a capitalist political economy, numerous disciplines have joined Christian ethics in the fray over the question not only of what actually has been Christianity's historical association with capitalism but also of what that relationship ought to be.

On the current scene, questions about the proper ordering of economic life continue to cry out for serious moral reflection. Such questions are important not only for religious ethicists and other scholars but also for the larger public. Recent political debates in the United States, Great Britain, West Germany, France, and in other parts of the world have focused on the economic responsibilities of governments with respect to employment, education, and welfare. Debates have also revolved around questions of the relative merits and demerits of market mechanisms, centralized planning, and monetary, fiscal and industrial policies.

Within many academic and religious circles there exists a heightened interest in the extent to which religiously-based ethical convictions can provide perspectives for the evaluation and ordering of economic life. This discussion includes a wide spectrum of positions which range from trenchant condemnations of Western capitalism on the part of many liberation, feminist, and black theologians to the qualified Christian defenses of liberal "democratic" capitalism that have been articulated recently by such writers as Michael Novak, Richard Neuhaus, and Robert Benne. At the same time, John Paul II's *Laborem Exercens* is indicative of the sustained attention to economic matters that has characterized modern papal social thought. And, more recently, the National Conferences of Catholic Bishops in the United States and Canada have made their own important contributions to the current conversation. The essays in this volume should be read in the context of this history of Christian ethical reflection and as contributions to the ongoing discussion of the proper ordering of political economy for the service of human well-being.

The contributors to this volume are in direct conversation with one another. They bring a varied set of backgrounds and viewpoints to the conversation while sharing a common vocabulary and a common set of questions. What are the definitive characteristics of "capitalism" as a socio-economic system? What are the nature and legacy of "liberalism" as a theory and as a form of political economy? What is the relation between the "public" and "private" spheres of human life? How is "freedom" to be understood? Is it purely formal in character or does it entail some more substantive characteristics? What sort of distinctions can one draw between political life and economic life? What criteria, moral or otherwise, are most appropriate for measuring the efficacy of market systems of production and exchange?

In the course of addressing these and other questions, the contributors to this volume engage in a thoroughgoing exploration and articulation of alternative visions of human life in society. As is typical of the history of Christian social thought generally, these alternative visions emerge out of a sustained debate about the different ethical, economic, and ideological *implications* of what are, in many cases, similar theological and philosophical principles.

Yet, despite their differences, the essays in this volume all join in a rejection of the popular claim that religion is irrelevant to questions of economic life. This rejection puts them at odds with those who would view religion and ethics as merely private concerns with little or no relationship to various aspects of public life. It also distinguishes them from certain economists who claim that the logic of economic activity is relatively uninfluenced by spiritual and moral considerations.

Part One of this volume consists of two essays which present historical overviews of modern Christian attitudes toward capitalism. John T. Pawlikowski articulates the major features of modern Roman Catholicism's approach to economic questions as they have emerged from the papal social encyclicals, the Second Vatican Council, recent Latin American ecclesiastical documents, and the American Catholic community. His primary focus is on the development of certain key themes such as private property, the principle of subsidiarity, and the concept of "a preferential option for the poor." David Krueger surveys major twentieth century Protestant approaches to economic life, focusing especially on their definitions and evaluations of modern capitalism. Taken together, these two essays provide a relatively broad picture of the field of Christian social ethics as it has addressed economic issues in the modern period. This picture provides a general context within which to situate the constructive arguments contained in Part Two of this collection.

Part Two begins with an essay by Franklin I. Gamwell which attempts to define the terms within which religious evaluation of the economic order might take place. Several features of his argument provide touchstones for the discussions of the other authors. Gamwell's characterization of modernity in terms of the autonomy of the individual, his focus on liberalism and its conceptions of freedom, and his distinction between private and public-regarding purposes and associations are recurrent themes that surface at various points and in various ways throughout this volume.

The theme of liberalism, for example, is central in some way to all the essays. Indeed, there are many respects in which this volume may be viewed as a collection of meditations on the present and future viability of this tradition—on the extent to which various aspects of the tradition of liberalism ought to be preserved, reformed, or rejected. Yet as Gamwell points out, there are distinctions to be drawn even within the tradition of political liberalism itself. Thus, he identifies a difference between "established" and "reformed" liberalism while others have distinguished between "deontological" and "utilitarian" liberalism (Sandel 1982, 1-4), and still others (as noted in Grelle's discussion of Weber) have distinguished between "humanist-cultural" and "economic" liberalism. In view of all this, one way to read the present volume is with an eye toward which aspects of the liberal tradition are being invoked, defended, or criticized in each of the essays.

In the essays by Robert Benne, W. Widick Schroeder (and Daniel Rush Finn in Part Three), for example, it is possible to identify a number of themes that have been central to a certain classical version of economic and political liberalism. Basic to this perspective is a positive evaluation—on both economic and ethical grounds—of market systems as efficient satisfiers of individual subjective preferences. Another important feature of this perspective is the desire to keep the political and economic orders distinct—particularly with regard to the mechanisms of political and economic decision-making.

Yet these sorts of positions depend for their cogency upon larger ideological, institutional, and even metaphysical frameworks which include certain conceptions of equity and efficiency, certain rules of property and legal systems that enforce those rules, and a certain understanding of human nature and of the relationship between the individual and society.[1] It is this larger ideological and institutional framework of liberalism that provides a primary focus for Gamwell, Cornel West, Douglas Sturm, (and Kay Warren in Part Three).

In addition to various versions of liberalism, the influence of other traditions of social thought is also apparent. Concerns with the nature of distinctions between public and private and with the notion of the common good that characterize a number of the essays show the influence of pragmatism, neo-Aristotelianism, and the natural law tradition of Roman Catholic social thought. The tradition of Western Marxism is represented by West and also informs the essays by Sturm and Warren. The tradition of process thought is evident in the essays by Schroeder, Gamwell, and Sturm. The reader will likely detect other influences as well.

Another way to approach the essays in the second section is to engage in a straightforward polemical reading that focuses on the debates between the critics (Sturm, West) and the defenders (Benne, Schroeder) of liberal capitalism. Regardless of what themes one chooses to focus upon or of what interpretive approach one takes, however, the essays that comprise Part Two are indicative of the content and parameters of recent Christian ethical reflection on the economy.

Finally, the inclusion in Part Three of interpretations from orthodox economics, anthropology, and social theory reflects the widespread recognition that the ethical evaluation of economic life is necessarily an interdisciplinary enterprise. An endless array of technical fields of knowledge bring perspectives to bear on such difficult economic issues as employment and welfare policy and the role of multi-national corporations in the Third World. Indeed, the wide diversity of opinion evidenced in this volume and in Christian ethics generally is due, in part, not only to the complexity of the issues at hand but also to the fact that the Christian ethicist is forced to make choices regarding the use of these specialized fields of knowledge.

With this interdisiplinary character of economic ethics in mind, Daniel Finn suggests the relevance of "orthodox" economics ("that majority opinion within economics stretching from conservative monetarists to liberal Keynesians") for ethical reflection. In the process, Finn provides a succinct history of methodology in economics and articulates major presuppositions and theses which have important implications for normative evaluations of social policy options. While Finn is generally sympathetic to the potential value of orthodox economics for practical moral reasoning, he is careful to highlight aspects which ought not to be appropriated uncritically.

The relevance of social theory for religious ethics is the topic of Bruce Grelle's essay. The socio-historical relations between Christianity and capitalism have been a pre-eminent concern for such outstanding social theorists as Weber, Sombart, Troeltsch, and Tawney, and this body of work continues to be central to contemporary discussions in Christian social ethics.

The volume concludes with an essay by Kay Warren which demonstrates the relevance of perspectives from anthropology for work in economic ethics. Warren describes the impact of social and economic change on various post-colonial Third World peasant communities. Her essay is significant not only for its characterization of the impact of Western capitalism on "traditional" cultures, but also for its challenge to liberalism's claim that autonomy is the distinguishing feature of modernity and, as such, ought to be embraced as normative for moral agency. A sensitivity to such cross-cultural questions is particularly important in view of an increasing awareness of global economic interdependence and in view of the more specific theses put forward by such writers as Braudel (1981-1984) and Wallerstein (1976, 1980, 1983) regarding capitalism as a world system.

In sum, the essays in this volume may be regarded as a recent installment in the long history of Christian ethical reflection on economic life. The issues raised and the positions outlined by the various authors provide a relatively thorough and balanced introduction to the diversity of Christian perspectives on the economy. We hope they will serve to stimulate further discussion on this important topic.

Notes

1. For a discussion of the "functional prerequisites" and ideological underpinnings of market systems of exchange see Barnard Barber (1977) and Walter A. Weiskopf (1977).

Part One

Christianity and Capitalism:
Historical Perspectives

CHAPTER I

Modern Catholic Teaching on the Economy: An Analysis and Evaluation

John T. Pawlikowski, O.S.M.

INTRODUCTION

The American Catholic Bishops' pastoral letter on the American economy, together with similar statements by the Canadian Catholic hierarchy and Pope John Paul II in the course of his many pastoral visits worldwide, have elicited a new interest in the Roman church's teachings on economic issues. These public reflections of the last decade do not represent, however, a sudden new intrusion by Roman Catholicism into national and international economic developments. Rather they are integral to a process launched in the last century with the formation of the Fribourg Union in Europe and the subsequent crystallization of its thought in the first social encyclical *Rerum Novarum* in 1891.

This chapter attempts to outline the general thrust of that process as it emerges from official Catholic documents coming from Roman sources. This is by no means the full story. Many individual Catholic theologians, ethicists and policy planners as well as various national hierarchies have played key roles in its maturation. But Popes and Councils still set the basic tone for Catholic teaching. And it is on their statements that this essay shall concentrate.

THE THOMISTIC LEGACY

There is little doubt that the theological vision of Thomas Aquinas profoundly shaped the thought of the church on social questions for many centuries. In the synthesis developed by Aquinas, the primary focus was placed on the duties of a person to society rather than on the rights an individual could claim on the basis of inherent human dignity. All social duties were seen as a consequence of the social functions which a given individual fulfilled. This outlook located the basis of social policy in an agreed-upon set of duties that were part and parcel of the major institutions and functions of the state. Persons finding themselves in these offices automatically acquired a certain set of social responsibilities. David O'Brien and Thomas Shannon in their volume *Renewing the Earth* (1977, 21-22) describe the medieval situation in these words:

What held the society together was a theory of social obligation that sprang from the very nature of society and was understood from a theological point of view as related to a hierarchically ordered universe ultimately ruled over by God. Consequently, Aquinas and other medieval philosophers and theologians did not have a theory of individual or social rights; they focused on the duties incumbent upon individuals because of their social obligations. This clearly implied that social obligations took priority over individual desires or wants. As a result, claims against society were made in terms of clearly specified social responsibilities that were proper to various roles within the society.

Making social duties the cornerstone of social thought had the effect of maintaining organic unity within medieval society. The responsible fulfillment of role-designated duties by each member of society guaranteed social tranquility. In the medieval vision the discussion of social policy was largely limited to the discussion of the *a priori* duties and responsibilities assigned to every social office and function in the community. Under such conditions the only conceivable infringement of human rights would be for the state to somehow impede a person's performance of designated societal duties.

This brief description of pre-modern church attitudes is important for understanding why Catholicism came to the struggle for human rights in the economic sphere rather late and with some difficulty. For the medieval social vision died very slowly and grudgingly. The Enlightenment, with its heightened sense of the individual's self-worth apart from and beyond any particular social calling, made indirect inroads. So did the challenge presented by Marxism and other forms of European socialism. These movements were beginning to have an effect in the latter part of the nineteenth century and the beginning of this century not only in academic circles but among the working class where a much greater sense of human dignity was beginning to surface. This new self-awareness was starting to make the working class, Catholics included, seriously question their assigned status in the prevailing economic sphere. Many were tempted by the Marxist vision and abandoned their faith. As such departures from Catholic practice continued to increase within the working classes, the Vatican felt itself under strong pressure to somehow respond in a constructive fashion. The birth of the social encyclicals, beginning with Pope Leo XIII's *Rerum Novarum* in 1891, was its response.

RERUM NOVARUM

Its Origins in the Fribourg Union—The publication of *Rerum Novarum* was in many respects a startling event when one considers the previous history of Catholicism and the personal background of Leo XIII. No historical precedent existed in the Roman church for such a decree. And Pope Leo himself was allied with conservative, aristocratic forces in Catholicism which were trying everything imaginable to fend off the assault upon their economic hegemony by the newly organized working class.

A question may therefore legitimately be posed regarding the ultimate motivation for this first in a distinguished series of social encyclicals. Why did *Rerum Novarum* break tradition and come forward with a strong defense of the rights of the workers that paved the way for active participation by Catholics in unionizing efforts not only in Europe but in North America as well? A close reading of the encyclical will show that it does not represent as much of a departure from traditional Catholic theology as is sometimes claimed. This is due in large part to the fact that those basically responsible for framing the argument, the Fribourg Union, were able to couch their affirmation of workers' rights in fairly traditional scholastic language. This enabled the Pope to accept a viewpoint which below the surface was far more radical than his own theological instincts.

The path that led to the issuance of *Rerum Novarum* began with a prophetic address to the upper classes of Paris in 1868 by the future Cardinal Mermillod. He tried to sensitize the ruling elites to the awful conditions faced by many in the working class whom he described as abandoned and exploited. He coupled this with a clear warning that the newly founded workers' movement would escalate into a raging torrent that might engulf all the structures of the established political order unless the Catholic Church could find ways of channeling this worker outrange into more constructive outlets. This same concern was articulated by several other Catholic leaders in Europe such as Frederic Ozanam, Augustin Cochin and Maurice Maignen. Their views were generally met with hostility by the Catholic elites, both clerical and lay.

The events of 1870-71 proved to be decisive in the development of a new social consciousness in Catholicism. The Franco-Prussian war and the worker insurrection known as the "Commune de Paris" had the potential of totally destabilizing Europe. Both events made it increasingly clear to Catholic leaders that they must respond meaningfully to the deteriorating conditions of European workers or risk mass conversion to socialist doctrine. Sparked by this realization, Catholic social thinkers in a number of European nations devoted themselves with renewed vigor to the development of a social doctrine identified with the struggles of the working classes.

In France these traumatic events of the 1870s profoundly affected two military officers named Albert de Mun and Rene de La Tour du Pin. They came to know each other while in prison together during the Franco-Prussian war. Their conversations elicited a shared resolve to devote their lives to the resolution of social conflict once their incarceration had ended. Together with Maurice Maignen they eventually founded the "Committee for the Formation of Catholic Workers' Clubs in Paris." The "L'Oeuvre des Cercles" quickly attracted considerable attention throughout France. They were able to break down many long-standing social barriers by bringing together wealthy patrons and groups of workers from a given geographic location. While still exhibiting a degree of paternalistic concern towards the workers, these clubs bred new recruits for the Catholic social movement. Several of the influential members of the Fribourg Union were won over through their involvement in "L'Oeuvre des Cercles."

Though it encountered stiff opposition in sectors of French Catholicism, "L'Oeuvre des Cercles" continued to prosper and eventually garnered support from kindred groups in other parts of Europe. Cardinal Mermillod became the focal point of one such group. In 1881 Mermillod was summoned to Rome by Pope Leo XIII to serve as a consultant on church-state issues. This papal call had been instigated by Count Franz Kuefstein of Austria and Abbe Villeneuve from New York state and included the establishment of a new Vatican-supported study circle on economics. Mermillod soon assumed a central role in the deliberations of this group. Though their accomplishments over a two year period have been described as "meager" (see Paulhaus 1980, 68), they began the effort of relating dominant themes of Thomistic thought to the new social conditions of Europe and thus paved the way for the eventual acceptance of the ideas espoused in *Rerum Novarum*. Additionally, Mermillod and Kuefstein went on from this experience to central participation in the Fribourg Union.

The leaders of the Fribourg Union first gathered in 1884. Within a firm commitment to a resolution of the social crisis of the time and a fierce loyalty to Catholic teaching and papal authority, they pledged to study together the nature of work, property and society itself in light of Thomistic thought. The Union was also aware that study alone, as important as it was, would not by itself change the condition of the working class. So they likewise committed themselves to pursue the establishment of international legislation that would reflect the spirit of their intellectual conclusions.

Mermillod assumed the spiritual leadership of this essentially lay Catholic body. Their yearly meetings from 1885 to 1891 brought together a wide variety of Catholic thinkers from every corner of Europe. Though they shared a basic commitment to certain social ideals, their political philosophies varied considerably from support for aristocratic traditions to endorsement of the new democratic trends then emerging.

In the course of their deliberations several questions assumed high priority for the Union members. The first of these revolved around the just wage and the role of state intervention in securing it. The Fribourg Union statements clearly argue that work is more than a commodity. It represents a *personal* act of the worker. Through faithfulness to one's work a person acquires a moral right to a salary that will provide adequate subsistence for the person's family. The Union offered no hard and fast scheme for determining a just wage. It should be determined, they argued, through a contract between employer and workers which would take into consideration all production costs. Generally speaking the Union did not look kindly upon direct state intervention to ensure a just wage. Its membership strongly inclined towards freely negotiated contracts. This implied that the workers would have the opportunity to unionize for collective bargaining. Only when the contractual relations failed to provide for the basic subsistence of the workers did the state have the responsibility to step in. The greatest possible latitude was to be given to private initiative.

On the question of state intervention and the realization of a just wage the

Fribourg Union took a middle course among the options seeking attention at the time. They were more interventionist than the liberals but stayed clear of the socialists by insisting on the subsidiary and limited nature of this intervention. *Rerum Novarum* espoused this position in its entirety.

With regard to the highly disputed question of private property, the Union again steered a middle course. The right to private property was strongly reaffirmed. Special emphasis was given to the inviolability of this right in rural areas—a clear rejection of the socialist position. Having affirmed the right, the Union thinkers then introduced a series of modifications of the right. The right of each person to subsistence was underscored, even to the point of eventually terming it a "primordial" right. This theme clearly signalled a repudiation of the liberal perspective which had elevated individual rights to private property to the pinnacle of social morality. But the full implications of the Union's perspective were never spelled out. A measure of ambiguity remains, as it does in *Rerum Novarum*, regarding the right of poor people to seize the property of the rich out of desperation or the right of the state to seize private property, with or without compensation, when it judges that such property is not being used for the common welfare.

Through its years of existence the Fribourg Union took up the issue of capitalism itself. At times, the group gave support to some stringent critiques of capitalism by its members. Henri Lorin's view, for example, that capitalism was based on egotism and usury and hence constituted what we would term today a "sinful social structure" in need of total replacement, won enthusiastic approval at one point. But the critique of capitalism was never carried to term. Instead, the Union devoted its attention to the creation of a more moderate social model. It was called the "regime corporatif." This social system was defined by the Union in 1886 as "the mode of social organization which rests on the grouping of men according to their common natural interests and common social functions, and which results necessarily in the public and distinct representation of these different organisms" (Fribourg Union 1886).

It was the fervent hope of the Union that this social model, rooted in the organic tendencies of medieval political thought, would provide the answer to the social chaos plaguing Europe which it ascribed primarily to Enlightenment rationalism, Protestantism (which in the mind of the Fribourg theologians had undermined authority and introduced rampant individualism) and capitalism. Ultimately, then, Fribourg came down on the side of social reform rather than social revolution. And it did so by developing a social model that tried to "restore" values deeply embedded in the scholastic tradition. Here lay the grounds for its appeal to a fundamentally conservative pope and his aristocratic colleagues. As Norman Paulhaus has correctly stated (1980, 79), the Union's purpose in proposing the establishment of a corporative system "was simply to reform the contemporary socio-economic order and rid it of its worst defects. The medieval *spirit*, not its institutions, served as the 'old wine' which they now tried to pour into 'new wineskins' ".

The society envisioned by the Fribourg Union depended on the reemergence of living organisms which would serve as the building blocks of a society dependent on natural groups of people organized in accord with their professional duties, rights, interests and, above all, social functions. Hence, the medieval vision in which duties prevailed over rights was not totally overturned. What was added, and what proved crucial, was the realization that for such a system to remain viable under modern conditions, these natural and permanent groupings must be given some form of legal status in order to insure the protection of the rights of all. A corollary to this was the belief that these groupings must be free to express their views and have public representation in the political domain. This perspective laid the groundwork for a Catholic commitment to the principle of union organizing. Implicit, but central, to the Fribourg Union's vision of the "regime corporatif" was the rejection of class struggle. This is a crucial point to raise today, given the Vatican's recent attacks on liberation theology for seemingly "sanctifying" class struggle. The present position continues to reflect a strong birthright of modern Catholic social thought.

This brief overview of the genesis of the Fribourg Union's social Catholicism is crucial for any understanding not only of its child, *Rerum Novarum*, but for the directions taken by later Catholic social teaching. The Fribourg Union had clearly established certain parameters for the Catholic commitment to social reform that have tended to remain firm and consistent through much of this century: no rejection of private property; no support of class struggle; no formal endorsement of capitalism which in many ways undercuts the organic model of society inherited from medieval thought; a preferential option for the rights of the workers because it is their class whose allegiance the church stands to lose; and the firm support of unionization based on a fresh interpretation of the classical organic model. The trunk of this social vision remains firmly implanted in medieval thought with the Enlightenment, Protestant individualism, and capitalism viewed more as enemies rather than friends of labor. In recent years the attack on Protestantism has totally subsided, and with Paul VI some definite openings towards socialism were to be seen. But in many ways the spirit of the Fribourg Union still energizes contemporary Catholic social teaching.

The teachings of the Fribourg Union first received papal approbation in January, 1888 when Mermillod and several other Fribourg leaders met with Leo XIII. In a memo to the Pope, they strongly played up the anti-Protestant motif in their work, maintaining that the sufferings of the working classes were attributable in large measure to the Reformation's abandonment of traditional church teachings. This unfair characterization of Protestantism no doubt contributed to the Union's favorable hearing in the Vatican. The ultimate sanction for their work came with the actual issuance of *Rerum Novarum*. Paradoxically, by the time of the encyclical's publication the movement had virtually fallen into disarray and would make no subsequent productive contribution to Catholic social thought.

A careful reading of *Rerum Novarum* will reveal a close affinity between the

Fribourg Union and Leo XIII on most major points. One of the best summaries of *Rerum Novarum* is to be found in John XXIII's later encyclical, *Mater et Magistra*. John highlights the following principles as pivotal to the spirit of *Rerum Novarum*:

> He (Pope Leo) first and foremost stated that work, inasmuch as it is an expression of the human person, can by no means be regarded as a mere commodity. . . .
>
> Hence, its remuneration is not to be thought of in terms of merchandise, but rather according to the laws of justice and equity.
>
> Private property, including that of productive goods, is a natural right possessed by all, which the state may by no means suppress. However, . . . he who uses his right in this regard must take into account not merely his own welfare but that of others as well.
>
> The State . . . can by no means disregard the economic activity of its citizens. . . . Nor may the State ever neglect its duty to contribute actively to the betterment of the living conditions of the workers.
>
> . . . the State should see to it that labor agreements are entered into according to the norms of justice and equity, and that in the environment of work the dignity of the human being is not violated either in body or spirit.
>
> There is affirmed the natural right to enter corporately into associations, whether these be composed of workers only or of workers and management; also the right to adopt that organizational structure judged more suitable to meet their professional needs.
>
> Workers and employers should regulate their mutual relations in a spirit of human solidarity and in accordance with the bond of Christian brotherhood. For the unregulated competition which so-called *liberals* espouse, or the class struggle in the *Marxist sense*, are utterly opposed to Christian teaching and also to the very nature of man (John XXIII in Gremillion 1975, 147-148).

In light of the description of the main themes of the Fribourg Union given above, the intimate connection between its thought and *Rerum Novarum* should be quite evident.

Its Impact on American Catholicism.—Turning to the American scene for a moment, *Rerum Novarum's* organic model of society inherited from the Fribourg Union never exercised much influence over Catholicism in the United States. Where it had its most profound effect was in labor organizing. Though some American Catholic leaders such as Archbishop John Ireland and Cardinal Gibbons had endorsed union activities, especially the Knights of Labor, prior to the encyclical, union-organizing was suspect in the eyes of many Catholics. The encyclical dramatically changed that. It opened the doors to a period of deep involvement by the American Catholic Church in the betterment of working class living conditions. This aspect of American Catholicism is too little known. But it has been acknowledged by some commentators on American life such as James Hastings Nichols, whose general perspective is not especially friendly towards the Roman church. Nichols has called it the best social doctrine of any church in the United States (see Greeley 1967, 217). Several labor reformers, such as Terence Powderly, first Grand Master of the Knights of Labor, and "Black John" Mitchell of the United Mine Workers, were Catholics. It was in the improvement of the conditions of the American worker that Catholic social action had its greatest impact on American society. As a result, the American Catholic working class has never been alienated from the church to the same degree as its European counterpart. Labor historians have shown that Catholic influence helped to account for the moderate social philosophy and policies of the American Federation of Labor and for the absence of a political labor party in the United States.

But American Catholicism's strong support of unionization efforts was not based simply on pragmatism. Though the theorists of social ethics in American Catholicism are not quite as well known as their counterparts in American Protestantism, their views were decisive in shaping the U. S. church's response to the social encyclicals. No person was as crucial in this regard as Msgr. John A. Ryan. As professor of moral theology at the St. Paul Catholic seminary and subsequently at the Catholic University of America, he combined papal teaching, natural law theory and an abiding appreciation of the American social experiment into a social model that emphasized state intervention on behalf of the rights of the working class. Some of his detractors believed he stood very close to the borders of outright socialism. This Ryan basically denied. But when he assumed in 1920 the directorship of the Social Action Department of the Catholic Bishops' Conference (a post he held until 1945), he was able to use his theoretical model as a basis for strong personal and institutional support of New Deal reforms. Ryan convinced a large part of the American Catholic hierarchy that the program of social reconstruction offered by the unionization movement and later by Franklin Delano Roosevelt was fundamentally in line with the social teachings of Leo XIII and Pius XI.[1]

Concluding Observations—Before leaving *Rerum Novarum*, an earlier point needs to be repeated. After a close examination of the text and context of the encyclical, one receives the distinct impression that the overriding concern in the mind of Leo XIII was not the human rights of the workers of Europe *per se*, but the fear that they would be lost by the Catholic faith if the Marxist unions remained the only viable option for their frustrations. Thus, I believe we need to admit that the encyclical's defense of the working class is really a by-product of the classic Catholic concern for preservation of what is looked upon as the one true faith. This was not the principal orientation of the Fribourg Union, though it admittedly was a concern. But one must honestly wonder whether their doctrine of the dignity of the worker would have received papal approbation if Marxism had not proved the threat it did. While I do not wish to downplay the ultimate impact that the encyclical produced both in Europe and North America, it did not represent a major theological departure for Catholicism with respect to the foundations for social policy.

QUADRAGESIMO ANNO: REAFFIRMATION AND NEW PERSPECTIVES

Forty years later, Pius XI brought out the second major social encyclical on the anniversary of *Rerum Novarum*. It repeated many of the same themes of the earlier document: the dignity of labor; the rights of workers to organize and even to participate in some measure in ownership, management and profit; the belief that communist and even more "moderate" socialist economic philosophies are absolutely incompatible with Christianity.

Pius XI also added some new dimensions to the thought of his predecessor. Economic concentration had become a far more threatening reality than in Leo's time. And he squarely addressed this issue. Economic power, he claimed, had passed over into the hands of a few who "are frequently not the owners, but only the trustees and directors of invested funds, who administer them at their good pleasure" (*Acta Apostolicae Sedis* 1931, 185). "Economic power," the Pope went on, "has been substituted for the free marketplace. Unbridled ambition for dominance has replaced desire for gain; the whole economy has become harsh, cruel, and relentless in frightful measure" (*Acta Apostolicae Sedis* 1931, 211). In commenting on this section of *Quadragesimo Anno* in his own encyclical, *Mater et Magistra*, John XXIII adds that "Thus it happened that even public authorities were serving the interests of more wealthy men and that concentrations of wealth, to some extent, achieved power over all peoples" (John XXIII in Gremillion 1975, 150).

Subsidiarity: A Central Theme—Quadragesimo Anno also introduced a theme that would become central to Catholic social teaching in subsequent years and which now has become a matter of some dispute in contemporary Catholic attitudes towards economic matters. I refer to the principle of *subsidiarity*. Though the principle has roots in *Rerum Novarum*, Pius XI gave it its classic formulation:

> Just as it is wrong to take away from individuals what by their own ability and effort they can accomplish and commit it to the community, so it is an injury and at the same time both a serious evil and a perturbation of the right order to assign to a larger and higher society what can be performed successfully by smaller and lower communities. This is a fixed and unchangeable principle most basic in social philosophy, immovable and unalterable. The reason is that all social activity, of its very power and nature should supply help to the members of the social body, but may never destroy or absorb them (Pius XI in Higgins 1980, 85).

Commenting on the principle, David Hollenbach (1979, 156-157) summarizes the thrust of this linchpin of modern Catholic social teaching as follows:

> The principle states that government intervention is justified when it truly provides help ("subsidium") to the persons and smaller communities which compose society. More importantly, however, the family, the neighborhood, the church, and both professional and labor groups all have a dynamic life of their own which must be respected by government. There are legitimate claims rooted in the dynamics and structure of these groups.

Historically, one must acknowledge that this principle was not merely the fruit of theological reflection but equally a response to the thrust toward centralization inherent in the various forms of socialism, Marxism in particular, that Catholicism viewed as basic challengers not only to its social doctrine but to its faith perspective as well. Today the principle has become somewhat of an ideological football in discussions of Catholic outlooks on economic questions. On the far right, a 1976 Wanderer Forum issued a resolution calling upon the church to keep in mind the principle of subsidiarity which in this group's mind dictates that social and political action be taken at the lowest and most decentralized level possible. The principle has thus become the backbone of the conservative Catholic attack on the liberal welfare state and on any form of governmental intervention in the economy. Within the more left-leaning Catholic peace and justice movement, where socialism of some color is generally a preferred substitute for capitalism, the principle has largely fallen into disuse. Its anti-socialist origins discredit it far too much. In recent years both Andrew Greeley (1984, 487-492), and John Coleman (1982, 102) have faulted the Catholic left for what they feel is an unfortunate abandonment of this classic Catholic social principle.

One of Catholic America's leading commentators on economic affairs over the past several decades, Msgr. George Higgins, has recently come to the defense of the principle of subsidiarity. In this context he criticizes what he sees as its misguided application by Catholic conservatives. It would be false, he argues, to say that this principle automatically sanctifies voluntary associations over state institutions or simply implies that "government is best which governs least." He adds:

> On the contrary it means that, while government should not arbitrarily usurp the role of individuals or voluntary organizations in social and economic life, neither should it hesitate to adopt such programs as are required by the common good and are beyond the competence of individual citizens or groups of citizens (Higgins 1980, 92).

The meaning of "subsidiarity," Higgins feels, must be more precisely defined. It never meant to imply that the state's role was to be deemed as of lesser importance in the overall operations of a society than the contributions made by freely associated groups devoted to human welfare. "*Subsidium* means aid, help," he says. "The principle of subsidiarity is concerned with the relationship of the state to other societies, not with the nature of the state itself" (1980, 92).

Higgins has provided some important nuances in our understanding of this classical Catholic social principle. He has helped rescue it from abuse by the conservative elements in the American Catholic church who wish to use it primarily as an axe against government intervention of any kind. But he has not solved all the problems connected with the principle.

I have a certain sympathy with the directions in which Higgins takes the principle of subsidiarity. Yet I am convinced that the classical interpretation does in fact lean somewhat more in the anti-government intervention thrust than he allows. While this may be considered simply overcompensation against government centralization which was viewed as the "enemy" position by the

Catholic leadership, in my judgment it does lessen the intrinsic value of this principle. I believe the classical interpretation has solid foundations in the biblical notion of the dignity of the individual person. The process of distinguishing the person from the community was a hallmark of the progressive movements in Second Temple Judaism that served as the basic context for Jesus' teachings. But the principle too easily lends itself to misinterpretation (see Pawlikowski 1982, 76-135).

It might be best to de-emphasize this principle today in favor of a greater stress on the principle of *participation*. This principle may be far more crucial to the preservation of the individual human dignity that stands at the core of the gospel. It can be applied in both capitalist and socialist societies (e.g., it has been central to the vision of the Solidarity movement in Poland). What would be critical is the degree to which people affected by decisions have some input into those decisions. This is a key point made in the first draft of the American Bishops' pastoral letter on the U. S. economy. In this document participation seems a far more central ethical theme than subsidiarity: "Justice demands the establishment of minimum levels of participation by all persons in the life of the human community" (U. S. Bishops 1984, 351). This fruitful debate over the principle of subsidiarity's value and meaning needs to continue.

PIUS XII: NEW BEGINNINGS

The war years immediately following the publication of *Quadragesimo Anno* left the church leadership little time for comprehensive reflection on economic questions. But in a series of Christmas radio addresses Pius XII made some points which were to serve as an important resource for future efforts by John XXIII, Paul VI and the II Vatican Council (see Yzermans 1961). One finds within them some notable turns. A new orientation is emerging. Concern for the faith and dignity of European workers, while important, is now seen to be insufficient. The horrible realities of World War II have convinced the Pope of the need for a comprehensive reconstruction of the social order.

We must appreciate the profound implications of this call for a new social order on the part of Pius XII. The Christmas addresses clearly put to rest any attempt to preserve the old social barriers and aristocratic privileges in Europe that the Fribourg Union and the earlier social encyclicals tried to some degree to preserve. A subtle revolutionary spirit is to be found in these messages. Nothing short of a fundamental rethinking and redesign of the international economic order can bring about human dignity for all peoples, a dignity which is their birthright and whose ultimate source is God.

More specific themes in the Christmas addresses include the following: (1) the economically advantaged nations have the primary responsibility to build a new economic order devoid of the disequilibrium of previous systems; (2) the religious dimensions of human existence cannot be fully grasped without an understanding of how profoundly economic realities shape life for good or ill;

(3) no analysis of the roots of war is complete without an appreciation of its economic causes; and (4) the centrality of the principle of subsidiarity is reaffirmed.

In short, these Christmas addresses, while they do not carry the same weight as the encyclicals and conciliar documents, provided the seedbed for a new approach to economic matters which is continuing to emerge in Catholicism. They are overlooked far too frequently in treatments of Catholic social teaching. The more we examine them the more decisive they appear.

THE ERA OF THE II VATICAN COUNCIL

The onset of the II Vatican Council and the papacy of John XXIII brought some further developments in Catholic perspectives on economic questions. I will highlight four: (1) private property; (2) the role of government; (3) internationalization; and (4) pluralism.

John XXIII's *Mater et Magistra* (1961) opens with an interesting analysis of the tradition's treatment of private property since Leo XIII. John emphasizes that the use of property has been increasingly socialized in Catholic thinking in the seventy years that have elapsed since *Rerum Novarum*. This is due in large part to the heightened fact of interdependence among the peoples of the world. This new "multiplication of social relationships," this "daily more complex interdependence of citizens," has become a major feature of our age which John XXIII is convinced the church cannot ignore in addressing economic matters (see Gremillion 1975, 155-156).

John XXIII begins his own teaching on economic issues by reasserting a classical Catholic theme, private property. But it is clothed in somewhat new garb. He speaks of "private initiative," rather than private property as such, and immediately follows with the assertion that public authorities have the obligation of ensuring an effective output of goods and that these goods are to be used for the benefit of all citizens (Gremillion 1975, 154). It appears that *Mater et Magistra* has elevated government intervention in the use of property to a moral plane equal to that of private initiative, and this on a continuing (not a last resort) basis. This would seem to warrant a major governmental role if the principle of human sustenance is to be realized on a global level. Government, though, should not totally destroy private initiative, for this would result in economic stagnation. On this point *Mater et Magistra* is quite clear. *Rerum Novarum* and *Quadragesimo Anno* both placed limiting conditions on private poverty. But the decision about limits was laid more in the lap of the individual believer. To a significant extent that decision-making has now been transferred to the state. This is a development of great consequence.

This same approach to private property surfaced in the document *Gaudium et Spes* (*The Church in the Modern World*) issued by the II Vatican Council. The Council Fathers failed to reaffirm any direct link between private property and the natural law. This is significant, for it opened the door for Catholic participation in more socialistic models of government. While *Gaudium et Spes* attached great importance to the access "of both individuals and communities to some control over material goods," it insists that

> The right of private control, however, is not opposed to the right inherent in various forms of public ownership. . . . By its very nature, private property has a social quality deriving from the law of the communal purpose of earthly goods (Gremillion 1975, 306-307).

The leading Catholic social commentator Joseph Gremillion (1975, 33) offers an incisive summary of developments under John XXIII:

> . . . John clearly and definitely carries over the Church's inherited teaching on property into the aggiornamento era he is launching. But in so doing he arouses the Church to a reality more basic than the permanence of property: The Church of Vatican II is "inheriting" a society in process of radical transformation, compared with that of past generations, because of socialization, the multiplying complex of relationships, and interdependence among groups and nations. . . . In Church teaching, the *common good* is not the glib phrase of a political campaign. It forms the bedrock of Catholic social doctrine, more fundamental than property, because its goal and measure is man and his perfection.

Regarding the role of government intervention, we can see from the discussion of private property that its moral legitimacy was broadened. As was noted earlier, Leo XIII, (faced as he was with a very doctrinaire form of European socialism,) was very cautious about endorsing any major role for government in economic affairs. Forty years later, Pius XI showed some relaxation on this score. He placed greater emphasis on governmental action as *one* means of coming to grips with the social and economic problems facing the world in the 1930s. On balance, nonetheless, reserve was the dominant tendency with respect to governmental intervention in both their encyclicals.

The era of John XXIII took a decided turn towards an enhanced role for government. The economic problems that had come to the fore since the early social encyclicals had assumed such complexity that this Pope saw no realistic solution to them without strong government action. While voluntary groups retained a vital stake in the solution, John urged a new partnership between them and the government and even claimed that government was at times required to act on its own initiative if economic justice is to be achieved. With the development of the internationalization focus, Catholic attention has shifted away from almost exclusive concern with the condition of Catholic workers in Europe and North America to the poor of the world held in economic oppression by unjust global economic structures. John XXIII and the II Vatican Council brought First World Catholics into extensive dialogue with Third World Catholicism for the first time. Thus, the focus of.this period, and especially of the years that immediately followed, was not so much on maintaining the dignity of the worker (though that remained a concern), but of suggesting ways in which the basic economic structures of the global community could be revamped to provide at least basic sustenance for the impoverished millions in the Third World. John XXIII never suggested a wholesale abandonment of the prevailing capitalist system, but he did launch the call for a major overhaul that went beyond the reformist impulses that dominated the early encyclicals. Paul VI and the 1971 Synod of Bishops, as well as numerous regional statements, subsequently intensified this theme.

The motif of pluralism is the final hallmark of the new era of social teaching introduced by *Mater et Magistra* and the II Vatican Council. In John's thought there is not the explicit and harsh rejection of all forms of socialist economics as contrary to Christian faith. There is also greater recognition that economic schemes must be related to the specific conditions prevailing in different countries. The church cannot endorse one scheme for all lands. The attempt to push the so-called "organic" model inherited from the Fribourg Union had ended. At Vatican II the Bishops in *Gaudium et Spes* deliberately refrained from speaking about a Catholic social doctrine because of its ambiguity. Vatican II at least implicitly stated that Catholicism has no settled teaching on economics nor any complete program for securing economic justice. The church must remain open and flexible on these matters.

THE PAPACY OF PAUL VI: THE VISION GROWS MORE RADICAL

With the papacy of Paul VI, the themes set forth by *Mater et Magistra* and *Gaudium et Spes* were pushed with great vigor. On the point of pluralism the respected Dominican theologian, M. D. Chenu, O.P., has argued that Paul VI in many ways overturned the methodology of earlier official Catholic statements on social questions. That method is now more inductive than deductive with far greater stress given to pluralism. The church is no longer viewed as bound to a social system supposedly based on natural law. Nor can we speak of Catholic social "doctrine," but only of Catholic social teaching or the social teaching inherent in the gospel. Paul VI's *Octogesima Adveniens*, issued on the eightieth anniversary of *Rerum Novarum*, unabashedly makes this point:

> If today the problems seem original in their breadth and their urgency, is man without the means of solving them? It is with all its dynamism that the social teaching of the Church accompanies men in their search. If it does not intervene to authenticate a given structure or to propose a ready-made model, it does not thereby limit itself to recalling general principles. It develops through reflection applied to the changing situations of this world, under the driving force of the Gospel as the source of renewal when its message is accepted in its totality and with all its demands (Gremillion 1975, 505).

It should also be noted that this pluralistic approach to economic problems which focused on the local church's particular situation also stems from the ecclesiological change brought about by the II Vatican Council. Paul VI alludes to this in *Octogesima Adveniens*. Under the conciliar vision, the local church assumes a much greater responsibility for providing the moral guidelines for its particular economic and political situation.

Another crucial dimension of Paul VI's thought is the explicit recognition that economic problems are clearly political in nature. They cannot be solved without meaningful political change and greater participation in political decision-making. *Octogesima Adveniens* says:

> It is true that in the term "politics" many confusions are possible and must be clarified, but each man feels that in social and economic fields, both national and international, the ultimate decision rests with *political power*. The passing to the political dimension also expresses a demand made by the man of today: a greater sharing in responsibility and in decision making. . . . In order to counterbalance increasing technocracy, modern forms of democracy must be devised, not only making it possible for each man to become informed and to express himself, but also by involving him in a shared responsibility. Thus human groups will gradually begin to live as communities (Gremillion 1975, 507-508).

Intimately related to the pluralistic thrust advocated by Paul VI is the question of whether this may include Christian commitments to socialist, even Marxist, options. Paul addressed this question directly in *Octogesima Adveniens*. He strongly criticizes the ideologies behind many socialist movements and warns Christians about the tendency to idealize socialism while overlooking the genuine limitations of concrete socialist movements. He is also less receptive than John XXIII to Marxism. It would be "illusory and dangerous" he thinks, for Christians to employ Marxist analysis in economic affairs, especially to promote class struggle in the name of achieving greater economic justice. But having issued this sober warning Paul VI opens the door for some cooperation in the promotion of economic justice between Catholics and socialists (*Octogesima Adveniens*, #31).

Another prominent feature of Paul VI's thought, related to his modest opening to socialism, is his significant restriction on private property. He goes well beyond the positions of Leo XIII and Pius XI in this regard. His other major economic encyclical, *Populorum Progressio,* speaks of the right of state expropriation of certain pieces of private property which are underused or poorly used or whose present use causes hardship for the people or is detrimental to the interests of the country. He also calls unacceptable the practice of the rich of transferring their wealth outside their home country "without care for the manifest wrong they inflict on their country by doing this" (#24).

Populorum Progressio coupled this acknowledgment with a comprehensive critique of contemporary international economic structures. It likewise spoke out against any "renewal of liberal ideology . . . in the name of economic efficiency." Hence it was seen by many, including many Catholics, as the strongest and most direct attack on the capitalist system yet tendered by an official Catholic document. While many Catholics, especially those in the financial world, took strong exception to what they considered a virtual endorsement of socialism, other Catholics, especially those in the Third World, took it as their justification for personal involvement in anti-capitalist movements.

THE 1971 ROMAN SYNOD

The spirit of *Populorum Progressio* (1967) was re-echoed in the 1971 Synod of Bishops' Document, *Justice in the World*. While lacking the same authority as an encyclical or a conciliar document in traditional Catholic theology, it nonetheless served to undergird the direction Paul VI had taken in 1967. Representative bishops from throughout the world rallied to the Pope's side. Their document strongly supported the right of development among the "have-not" nations "in the face of international systems of domination" (#13). It also reaffirmed participation as a key right of all people in the economic sphere and clearly introduced the notion of social-structural sin into official Catholic ethical vocabulary. Conservative and left-leaning Catholics tended to react to this document in much the same ways as each did to *Populorum Progressio*.

THE PONTIFICATE OF JOHN PAUL II: A THEOLOGY FOR ECONOMIC ACTIVITY

The pontificate of John Paul II has again ushered in some change of approach to economic questions. At the same time some reaffirmations of previous themes are also evident.

John Paul II's first encyclical, *Redemptor Hominis*, while not specifically on social questions, laid some necessary groundwork for his subsequent reflections in *Laborem Exercens*. Gregory Baum captures an essential thrust of *Redemptor Hominis* when he interprets the Pope as insisting that all social commitment is founded in the church's Christological vision. As Baum (1979, 55) understands it, the Pope is saying that

> Because of God's act in Jesus Christ the Church must respect the dignity of persons, defend their rights as human beings, and summon people to involve themselves in political action so that these rights will be respected. In other words, the Church's concern with human rights is not part of a humanitarian mission, based on natural law, related to its essential supernatural mission in a subordinate manner. The Church's solicitude for human well-being is in fact an exercise of its supernatural mission founded upon its Christological doctrine.

John Paul II appears to see a historical dimension in the notion of divine grace. This grace is not merely the source of personal unity between creature and Creator but an enabling force that renders men and women responsible historical agents for the transformation of life on this earth. Put another way, says Baum, in *Redemptor Hominis* "The spiritual is historical. The divine summons empowering people to enter into holiness does not thereby lift them out of their historical situation and make them ready for an invisible world, but leaves them in their historical place and appoints them to be agents of Christ in their troubled societies" (1979, 56).

For John Paul then, the human dignity of the worker rather than the faith of the worker becomes the primary focus of change in the economic sphere from the Catholic perspective. Even more, working for economic justice, or for any other form of justice, becomes a way of manifesting Christological reality to the world, of making visible the human dignity inherent in the "Word-made-flesh" theology. We have come full circle from Leo XIII's concern that continuing economic injustice might erode the faith of the European working classes. We are back to a link between faith and economic justice (not so strongly stressed by John XXIII and Paul VI), but one that is integral rather than consequential.

John Paul follows much the same track in the more recent *Laborem Exercens.* But direct applications are made to the economic realm. Richard McCormick (1982, 92-95) has described this encyclical as an ongoing philosophical meditation on human work in its varied dimensions.

Two themes in particular emerge as central in John Paul's vision. The first is the centrality of work to the whole social question. Work is considered in two respects. The first is quite traditional—exploitive working conditions are immoral. The immorality becomes more pronounced when one considers the dignity of the human person in light of the Incarnation. Any economic system, capitalist or collectivist, that reduces work to a mere instrument is to be condemned. This viewpoint also implies the priority of labor over capital. While the direct way of stating this concept may be somewhat unique to John Paul, it is consistent with the tradition that has prevailed since Leo XIII.

The second major point made by John Paul is the more creative one—work is considered not only for its potential to de-humanize, but as the means whereby the human person assists in the sanctification of creation. Here *Redemptor Hominis*'s "spiritual is the historical" theme highlighted by Gregory Baum is applied to the realm of economics. Work becomes a vehicle for exercising human co-creatorship. Michael Novak (1982a, 93-94) describes this papal theology as "radical," for it argues that "it is in sharing in the creativity of the Creator that the human subject fulfills his vocation."

The creation theology of *Laborem Exercens* has elicited considerable controversy. Novak, in support of the Pope's position, sees in it a firm endorsement of some principal themes of democratic capitalism. For John Paul, Novak believes, the person as individual graced by God becomes the central focus of any economic system. This seems to undercut any basis for class struggle and to reject any exaggerated contrast "between oppression and liberation in favor of the contrast between the absence and the presence of creativity" (Novak 1982a, 86). Novak likewise feels that this creation theology justifies capital as the material embodiment of labor and underscores private ownership, rather than nationalization or collectivization, as the fruit of individual work.

George Higgins (1982, 3), while also in praise of the encyclical, sees it much more as a challenge to Western capitalism, including its American expression. He sees the Pope's endorsement of unions and his call for new forms of profit-sharing, co-management, and co-ownership of productive property as clearly rejecting some "sacred" capitalist themes. While Novak is right in emphasizing the centrality of the individual person in *Laborem Exercens*, his further conclusions seem highly overdrawn. When he interprets the following sentence from the encyclical as an endorsement of private property in the capitalistic sense, my sympathy goes to Higgins: "We can speak of socializing only when the subject character of society is ensured, that is to say, when on the basis of his work each person is fully entitled to consider himself a part owner of the great workbench at which he is working with everyone else" (Novak 1982a, 84).

In the above quotation the Pope seems to be endorsing democratic socialism more than democratic capitalism. Indeed, the key to understanding this may be the Solidarity Movement's experience in Poland. In his volume on the movement's philosophy, Fr. Jozef Tischner (1984, 44-49) of the Papal Theological Faculty in Cracow and a scholar personally close to John Paul II argues that Solidarity espoused a moderate form of socialism with many of the features of co-ownership and co-management advocated in *Laborem Exercens*.

The Pope has taken several decisive steps in *Laborem Exercens*. I think Novak is partially correct in seeing it as a move away from Paul VI and the 1971 Synod statement. The focus is definitely placed far more on the human person rather than on the sinful social structures highlighted by Paul VI and the Synod. International economic institutions are not critiqued in the same direct manner they were during Paul VI's papacy, though in subsequent addresses John Paul has returned to this issue. His Canadian addresses are a good example of this.

One could argue, I think, that the current round of Vatican attacks on the economic views of liberation theology is evidence that John Paul is attempting to tone down many of the implications drawn from Paul VI's two encyclicals and from the Synod document by Catholics in the Third World. Rather, he seems to be advocating a model emerging from the Polish experience which he believes could reform both Western and Eastern economies towards greater justice. But contrary to Novak, John Paul continues the unchanging Catholic critique of capitalism. Capitalism continues to be judged as hostile to many central beliefs of the Catholic faith. While no Pope has called for its total dismantling (Paul VI might come closest to this), neither have they called for its universal introduction as an economic condition of justice.

The Protestant ethicist Stanley Hauerwas is especially harsh on two aspects of *Laborem Exercens*. He argues, first, that the theology of co-creatorship has no biblical basis. On the contrary, though, I would contend that this dimension of the encyclical, along with its tying of human dignity to the Incarnation, represents one of the encyclical's most enduring contributions to Catholic social theology.

With Hauerwas' second critical point I have far more sympathy, though I believe he overstates it. Hauerwas believes that John Paul's creation theology is overly romantic and stands in danger of making work demonic, "an idolatrous activity through which we try to secure and guarantee our significance, to make 'our mark' on history." In some sections it seems to suggest that "John Paul II would prefer a society of happy peasants and self-initiating artists, but such a society is not only impossible, it is not even desirable" (Hauerwas 1982, 94-95). There is a danger that John Paul has moved too far away from the vision of Paul VI and the Synod. The harsh realities brought about by present-day international economic structures are ignored far too much. While the Solidarity model may have some relevance for the Third World, it may not be totally applicable. It is also interesting to note that *Laborem Exercens* seems to move towards a specifically Catholic economic model for society in the spirit of the early encyclicals and away from the pluralistic thrust of John XXIII, the II Vatican Council and Paul VI.

Laborem Exercens, in its desire to correct certain "false" signals from Paul VI, may be giving out some of its own. Novak's interpretation of parts of it is a case in point. In my judgment it tips too much back towards the individual basis of economic life—to the neglect of the communal. John XXIII, Vatican II and Paul VI were more incisive in this respect. The encyclical also fails to recognize adequately that economic justice will not be achieved without a certain measure of struggle and even expropriation. I would support John Paul's rejection of *class struggle* in its pure sense as contrary to the gospel spirit of reconciliation and to what my colleague at the Catholic Theological Union, Donald Senior, terms Jesus' most scandalous teaching: enemy love. The Pope here continues a traditional position of the modern social encyclicals. But he seems to be writing off struggle as a necessary tactic. In so doing, willingly or not, he may be buttressing the economic status quo, because it is highly unlikely that economic power will undergo redistribution with enhanced participation solely on the strength of new models. Power in some form will be necessary to bring these ideas to concrete fruition. *Laborem Exercens* evades this issue far too much. Whatever my criticisms of *Laborem Exercens*, it has provided us with the ultimate criterion for judging all economic systems—the dignity of the human person.

Laborem Exercens also challenges a term becoming more popular in some economic circles and picked up by some ethicists: *human capital.* When economists such as Theodore Schultz (1971) use it, they are admittedly taking a step forward in stressing the human contribution essential to authentic economic development. Nevertheless, they leave the impression that human creativity is a commodity—a view that does not easily mesh with *Laborem Exercens's* stress on *inherent* human dignity as the heart of any economic system.

PREFERENTIAL OPTION FOR THE POOR

No treatment of Catholic teaching on the economy today would be complete without some discussion of the preferential option for the poor. It legitimately might be described as the most radical Catholic principle relative to the economy. It also brings to light the increased importance of the Latin American Catholic experience for the worldwide church. For it was in Latin America, where in many places the institutional church historically exhibited a kind of "preferential option for the rich," that the concern for the poor first emerged in such a dramatic fashion as a focal point of Catholic identity. The first beginnings of this are to be seen in the documents coming from the meeting of the Latin American bishops held at Medellin, Columbia, in 1968. These documents strongly reaffirm the bishops' support for the directions taken by Pope Paul VI in *Populorum Progressio*. The bishops were saying that their experiences in working with the poor in Latin American buttress the papal viewpoint given in that document. The spirit and content of these documents were tremendously influential on the message from the 1971 Roman Synod about deep structural injustices in the international economy.

Paul VI's *Octogesima Adveniens*, a papal letter issued in 1971 on the occasion of the eightieth anniversary of *Rerum Novarum*, picks up on this theme: "In teaching us charity, the Gospel instructs us in the preferential respect due the poor and the special situation in society" (#23). But it was in the meeting of the Latin American bishops at Puebla, Mexico, in 1978 that the term "option for the poor" clearly emerged as a central category for assessing economic systems (see Eagleson and Scharper 1979, 264-267). Pope John Paul II seemed to endorse this perspective in his visit to Brazil a year later. Both the American Bishops' pastoral on the economy and its Canadian counterpart view this theme as wholly consistent with a biblical perspective.

There is little doubt that this notion of a "preferential option for the poor" will remain a central point of discussion in Roman Catholicism. Some Catholic scholars such as Donal Dorr (1983) argue that this option for the poor is not simply an invention of more radical Catholic circles in Latin America. He insists that concern for the marginalized and those suffering economic deprivation has been present without interruption in official Catholic social teaching since the time of Leo XIII. There is a measure of truth in his claim. The earlier encyclicals gave a certain priority to the working classes who, though not destitute in the same measure as millions in the Third World today, were in a constant struggle to secure minimal sustenance. But the present form of this option, as expressed in Latin America in particular, is tied to a call for a major transformation of the social order which simply was not present in the thought of either Leo XIII or Pius XI. Hence I believe it represents a somewhat more radical turn in Catholic teaching than Dorr would have us believe. Yet there is some possibility of tracing it back to Scripture itself, especially to Jesus' pronounced concern for the "Am Ha Aretz," the people of the land. Little doubt exists in my mind that this concern was central for Jesus, though some Jewish groups of the time such as the Pharisees may have shared this concern with him (see Pawlikowski 1982, 105).

Arguments against a "preferential option for the poor" have been put forth by several Catholic leaders. Michael Novak (1984) has been among the most prominent critics. He would contend that while we certainly must concern ourselves as Christians with the plight of the poor, such prioritizing of the poor obfuscates the real issues and can easily lead to a simplistic anti-capitalistic/pro-socialist mentality and/or support for the "small is beautiful" economic philosophy. As Novak sees it, the central theological issue for Catholicism relative to the economy is the one raised by Pope John Paul II in *Laborem Exercens*: co-

creational responsibility. How can we create sufficient freedom for human creativity in our economic systems so that we may finally solve the problems of
unemployment and poverty? All the "preferential options for the poor" that fail
to achieve such a solution will simply leave the victims of poverty in their
degraded state.

While Novak's rejection of a "preferential option for the poor" is definitely
far too severe, his point about the need to focus on what is necessary to create
a viable economic system that will ultimately eliminate the need for such an
option must be taken seriously. His solution is far from adequate; but the danger
of which he warns—jumping to simplistic solutions as a result of the option—
is a real one. One also wonders, in countries like the United States, Canada
and Australia where the Catholic Church has not been traditionally identified
with the ruling economic elites, whether the term facilitates or hinders the
discussion of genuine economic development for all people.

FINAL OBSERVATIONS

From the above discussion it is clear that official Catholic teaching on economic issues has experienced both consistency and evolution in the past century.
How it will develop in the future will depend on whether Third World Catholicism recaptures some of the influence it was beginning to exert under Paul
VI. This may occur through the election of a Pope from that region. In my
view, to remain vital and meaningful this teaching must stress the notion of
participation far more than subsidiarity, maintain the pluralism of economic
models endorsed by John XXIII and Paul VI, incorporate John Paul II's sense
of Incarnationally-based human dignity (modified by a fully communitarian
sense) as the center of ethical evaluation of economic systems, further refine
Laborem Exercens' sense of co-creatorship, and deal more directly and realistically
with appropriate forms of power for bringing about a greater sharing of human
wealth. While Catholic social teaching must stand ideologically above both
capitalism and socialism, it must be prepared to work for reform within both
existing systems. It must reject any marriage offers from either side. This does
not mean that I wish the Catholic leadership to resurrect the organic model of
the Fribourg Union or to canonize the Solidarity model. The Church must
continue to push for the realization of some basic human values in both capitalist
and socialist countries. But it should not simply stop there. It may, as *Laborem
Exercens* did, suggest some concrete structures that could fit into either model.
It must not preclude criticism of deficiencies of the present-day international
economic structure which make poverty the primary face of humanity in our
world. Maintaining such a course will not prove easy. Only in such a way,
though, can Catholic social teaching make a genuine, permanent contribution
to the humanization of the economy, and not simply become the spiritual pawn
of this or that system.

Notes

1. On Ryan's influence, see Charles Curran (1982, 26-91), Andrew Greeley (1967, 216-246) and John Coleman (1982, 85-97). Ryan's most notable and systematic works are *A Living Wage: Its Ethical and Economic Aspects* (1906), and *Distributive Justice* (1916, revised 1927, 1942).

CHAPTER II

Capitalism, Christianity, and Economic Ethics: An Illustrative Survey of Twentieth Century Protestant Social Ethics

David A. Krueger

This chapter surveys the contributions of major twentieth century Protestant thinkers on questions of economic life in general and capitalism in particular. It is important to note at the outset of this survey that there are a number of significant differences between Protestant social ethics and Roman Catholic social teaching. Many of these differences are best understood in terms of the differences between Protestant and Roman Catholic ecclesiologies.

While it is true that the post-Vatican II Roman Catholic Church has experienced an increasing amount of theological and ethical diversity and an increasing collegiality, encyclicals and papal letters have remained the locus of moral authority. Protestant ethics exhibits no such organizing source. While the various Protestant traditions have their own classic figures, confessional documents, and other sources (e.g., scripture) for ordering their ethics, they have, on the whole, exhibited a great deal of theological and ethical pluralism. The formal authority of official pronouncements varies, depending upon whether a given denomination has a congregational, presbyterian, or episcopal form of polity. As a result of these differences, in order to gain perspective on modern Protestant economic ethics one must focus both on individual thinkers and on the pronouncements of various Protestant ecumenical bodies.

Unfortunately, a survey of this kind can do justice neither to the breadth and richness of the field nor to the total lifework of any one figure or tradition.[1] Rather, the aim is to select particular figures and movements which have been most influential and which best illustrate the diversity of perspectives within Protestantism.

After discussing a number of prominent North American and European theologians who have devoted considerable attention to issues of economic life, I consider the contributions of the Protestant ecumenical movement. While the modern ecumenical movement has been an important forum for Protestant ethical reflection on major social issues, its pronouncements, like those of individual theologians, do not purport to speak authoritatively for the church as a whole in the way that Papal statements and Roman Catholic church councils do.

WALTER RAUSCHENBUSCH: THE SOCIAL GOSPEL

Most prominent of Protestant responses to the economic and social conditions of American industrial life in the early twentieth century is that of Walter Rauschenbusch, a leading figure in the Social Gospel Movement and professor of church history at Rochester Theological Seminary. Rauschenbusch's most seminal works are *Christianity and the Social Crisis* (1907), *Christianizing the Social Order* (1912), and *A Theology for the Social Gospel* (1917). As a movement, the Social Gospel argues that Christianity must be reinterpreted and applied to the modern world in light of the fundamental human demand of sociability and wholeness of life. The most fundamental ordering principle for Rauschenbusch and the Social Gospel is the doctrine of the Kingdom of God. This theological motif is characterized as an immanent human telos, initiated by Jesus, to be realized within history by his followers, and defining the constitutive features of social righteousness.

For Rauschenbusch, biblical history functions normatively for interpreting the present situation and for making moral choices. Within that biblical history, three elements are crucial—(1) the eighth-century prophets, (2) the "social aims of Jesus", and (3) the primitive churches (1907, chs. 1-3). With such a foundation, Rauschenbusch is able to make a prophetic denunciation of numerous economic and social conditions of his day, e.g., disparities in the distribution of wealth, the perceived selfishness and greed of profit-taking which is necessarily detrimental to the common good, and a spirit of possessive individualism as exemplified by private property. Coupled with such a denunciation is the proffered alternative of the Kingdom of God, announced by Jesus Christ. Defined as (1) a realm of love and (2) a commonwealth of labor (1917, 54-55), the Kingdom of God involves service to the common good and "the organized fellowship of humanity acting under the impulse of love" (1917, 155). Rauschenbusch intuits such religious demands to require the wedding of Christianity with modern historical trends toward democracy (both political and economic) and socialization of the economy.

Such a social ethic is notable for its optimistic portrayal of human nature (with its conviction that Christian love can directly transform individuals and social structures) and for its reduction of a social ideal (the Kingdom of God) into a particular political and economic program. Such capitalist institutions as private property and profit-taking, which feed upon self-interest, are considered inherently inimical to the religious demands of the historical realization of the Kingdom of God. It is no wonder, then, that Rauschenbusch would infer the compatibility of a socialist political economic program with the ideals of the Social Gospel.

PAUL TILLICH: THE CASE FOR RELIGIOUS SOCIALISM IN THE CONTEXT OF
EMERGENT NAZI GERMANY

Paul Tillich's thought provides the most prominent and comprehensive attempt among early twentieth century European theologians to address issues of economic life from a socialist perspective.[2] Tillich's most systematic articulation of an economic ethic is found in *Die sozialistische Entscheidung*, translated in English as *The Socialist Decision* (1977). Written in 1933, Tillich's exposition of "religious socialism" is set in the context of the foreboding developments of the National Socialist movement in Germany. Seeing Germany at a critical turning point in history, Tillich advocates democratic socialism as the only viable political option which could avoid the impending destruction of Germany and of Europe by the Nazi rise to power. Tillich also defends democratic socialism, rather than liberal capitalism, as the proper political economic expression of the ontological and ethical elements of prophetic Christianity.

As John Stumme has noted, Tillich's special contribution to the discussion of socialism was to place it within a theological perspective (1977, xix). Insofar as Tillich considers the concrete political economic goals of democratic socialism to be coherent with, if not logically deduced from, constitutive features of his theology, his position can be defined as "religious socialism". In particular, Tillich grounds his theological discussion in his understanding of human nature and argues that there are two roots of human experience—(1) *being* (existing for oneself) which is grounded in the origin ("whence") of human existence, and (2) *consciousness* (standing critically over against oneself) which is grounded in the demand, expectation, and unconditional possibility ("whither") in human existence. Given these two constitutive features, the telos of human life becomes maximal fulfillment of each person's being (1977, 105ff) defined in terms of freedom. Justice within human relationships, then, consists of the recognition that other human beings must be accorded equal dignity in light of their same quest for maximal fulfillment (1977, 6).

With this understanding of human nature, Tillich examines forms of political economy in order to determine which is most instrumental to the above notion of human fulfillment. Capitalism is rejected for what Tillich sees as its inevitably self-destructive consequences. Rather than promote maximal fulfillment of "being", it removes individuals (the proletariat) from the creative origins of life and causes their complete objectification. Constitutive of capitalism is the "bourgeois principle" which involved "the radical dissolution of all conditions, bonds, and forms related to the origin into elements that are to be rationally mastered." Such objectification effected through the forces of free competition involves not only persons (the proletariat) but nature as well, both becoming merely instrumental to the purposes of the powerful (the bourgeoisie) (1977, 48, 53, 67). Inherent within capitalism and coupled with this process of objectification is liberalism's idea of harmony which assumes that the free play of often conflicting social forces will result in social progress. Tillich claims that the actual result of a free market economy is "class rule and imperialistic war, the crisis of the proletarian masses and their utter insecurity" (1977, 58, 89).

Thus rejecting capitalism, Tillich argues that socialism is the political-economic solution which fulfills the requirements of human nature and which is consistent with the demands of prophetic Christianity. Socialism will overcome the objectification of capitalism's autonomous economic rationality by substituting the "deliberate planning" of a centralized political economy for the institutions of the competitive free market. Through economic centralization, Tillich believes economic power formerly held by private enterprises (including "landed estates, heavy industry, major manufacturing concerns, banking, and foreign trade") will be democratized and "placed into the hands of society as a whole." As a result, technology will be placed under human control for the service of all humanity (1977, 161), the result of which will be "the best possible supply of economic goods for all" (1977, 90), and "an equal share in social power and economic profits" for all (1977, 53).

Tillich acknowledges that such a social telos assumes nothing less than "a new form of human being and of society as a whole" (1977, 63), "[I]t [socialism] presupposes a radical transformation of human nature, and in the last instance— since human nature constantly grows out of nature as such—a transformation of nature and its laws" (1977, 111). While ultimately democratic insofar as it strives to fulfill the demands of human nature for all individuals, Tillich assumes that the movement to a socialist society will require an undemocratic leap which surrenders majoritarian control to the hands of the dictatorship of the proletariat, a submission which "occurs as a free choice and is to prevail only for a limited time" (1977, 60).

Tillich argues that bourgeois society tends to alter and increase human needs to the extent that productive enterprises cannot respond efficiently and quickly enough to such desires (1977, 154ff). On the other hand, he believes that centralized planning will more adequately satisfy universal human needs by basing investments on "actually existing needs" which will remain relatively constant. Hence, in its broadest brushstrokes, Tillich's socialist political economy is one in which needs "can be satisfied through a well-organized, centrally controlled economy without market fluctuations and economic crises even when the goad of unlimited possibilities for profit and the lash of the threat of economic disaster are absent" (1977, 157).

Tillich contends that socialism is the form of political economy that is most coherent with prophetic Christianity. Indeed, Tillich argues that only a wedding of socialism and Protestantism can insure the creative possibilities of each. Arguing against the atheistic materialism of Marxist socialism, Tillich claims that traditional theological symbols and notions of prophetic Christianity (e.g., the emphasis on eschatological fulfillment, the tension between origin and ethical demand, the priority of time over space, notions of human fulfillment) provide substance for and correctives to the secularist socialism of his day. By positing the religious nature of socialist belief (e.g., that humans are not objects but essentially beings with creative spirit who reach for fulfillment), Tillich can suggest how questions of ultimacy begged within socialist thought are resolved through central Christian symbols. At the same time, socialism provides ways in which Protestantism can translate "religiously symbolic languages of the past into the secular consciousness of the present" (1977, 147).

Whether or not Tillich's rejection of capitalism and his wedding of prophetic Christianity with a socialist political economy are defensible on his own theological grounds is subject to debate. Clark Kucheman, for instance, argues that Tillich's empirical reading of capitalism, as interpreted through Marxist economic analysis, is empirically false, and if corrected, would lead him to affirm free market capitalism as the form of political economy most coherent with his theology (1966, 165-183).

In a rejoinder, Tillich hedges on Kucheman's challenge by suggesting both that the Marxist model does not fit certain types of societies such as the United States and also that the central aim of religious socialism was the denunciation of dehumanization and the correlative movement toward social and economic justice (1966, 189-191). It remains an open question, therefore, how Tillich would assess the ability of capitalist economies over the past half century to fulfill the demands of justice.

EMIL BRUNNER: ETHICS AND ECONOMY WITHIN THE ORDERS OF CREATION

Though responding to the same European situation, Emil Brunner developed an economic ethic which diverges radically from Tillich's religious socialism. For many years a professor of theology at the University of Zurich, Brunner's most seminal works for social ethics include *The Divine Imperative* (1937) and *Justice and the Social Order* (1943).

Brunner's thought consists of a theological emphasis on the "divine command" with a social ethic focusing on "orders of creation." The result is an economic ethic which embraces essential aspects of a capitalist economic order while at the same time condemning certain capitalist practices with a virulence that matches Rauschenbusch's and Tillich's.

Like Karl Barth's, Brunner's theology attempts, above all else, to preserve the sovereignty and freedom of God. Consistent with this objective, Brunner claims that "[t]he Good is simply and solely the will of God" (1937, 56). God's will for humans—the "divine command"—"can only be perceived by him to whom God speaks His Word, in faith" (1937, 111). Unlike traditional Thomistic natural law ethics, the will of God is not considered to be accessible to humans in the form of abstract universal first principles from which practical conclusions can be logically deduced. Rather, Brunner argues that the Divine Command must reassert itself anew in every moment—it is "absolutely concrete" (1937, 117, 122).

While Brunner's theology, in good Protestant fashion, ably protects against any form ·of natural theology which would employ an *analogia entis* (arguing analogically from knowledge of human being to divine being), it does assert that the divine will for human life is partially embodied in structures of human life whose patterns permit agreement on courses of human action (Lovin 1984, 13ff).[3] "In its *form* the will of God is stamped upon that which exists" (1937, 125). Brunner calls these structures or forms "orders of creation." They provide general patterns and "constants" which must be acknowledged as God-given and as the context within which "God's command for the actual moment reaches us" (1937, 125). Those orders include marriage and the family, the economy (work and civilization), government, culture, and the church.

As is the case with other figures and movements within twentieth-century Protestant ethics, love plays a prominent role in Brunner's ethic both as the animating principle in the ethic of persons and as the *ultimate* goal of the various orders. In the personal sphere of mutual relations of persons, where the "I" encounters the other as "Thou", love reigns supreme. Such love recognizes no claims or rights; it neither differentiates nor delimits (1943, 50). Rather it gives freely and unconditionally to the other. On the other hand, life in society requires criteria which differentiate and delimit what things belong to what persons. Love, therefore, cannot function directly as an ordering principle. Such a task falls to justice which gives to each his or her due. Social and economic justice, in accord with the divine will, are based upon the "primal order" of things. Such a primal order refers to certain universals which give each person the law of its being, specifies one's proper relationships with others, and forms the basis for each person's rightful and "fitting" due (1943, 89). "The law of justice points to an order of being in virtue of which there is allotted to every creature its sphere, its scope, its freedom and its limitation" (1943, 48).

Brunner's theological anthropology affirms that humans are both equal and unequal in essential respects. Social justice requires a recognition of this fact by the social order. Because all humanity is created in the image of God, all persons possess an essential equality of dignity which dictates that social justice respect certain inherent equal rights owed to all alike (e.g., freedom of religion, freedom of movement, the right to obtain livelihood from work, the right to adequate development). On the other hand, Brunner also thinks it self-evident that there exists an essential inequality of kind and function among humans and that such inequality (rather than equality) forms the basis for human community. "Community can only exist where there is difference . . . [and] presupposes reciprocal giving and taking . . ." (1943, 41).

Each order of creation, then, becomes an occasion for the exercise of vocation in which the neighbor is supplied with something of value and in which relationships of mutuality are developed—be it between husband and wife in marriage, producer and consumer in the economy, or governor and governed in the polity. Consequent to this understanding of human nature and human relationships is a model of society based on the metaphor of an organism composed of unequal parts (1937, 404ff; 1943, 154). To deny such inequalities of function and their commensurate rights is not only to argue against the divinely created orders of creation but is to attack the practical possibilities for human flourishing in community.

As noted above, while the *ultimate* goal of the orders is love of neighbor, justice, and not love, is the actual ordering principle for attaining such an end. The similarity here to Christian Realists such as Niebuhr and Bennett is evident. Because sin pervades the various orders, Brunner asserts that the will of God is not expressed *directly* through creation but only "indirectly" (1937, 126). Sin hinders but does not completely obliterate the human capacity to discern rationally the "constants" of creation which order proper human relationships (1943, 90ff). Hence, the moral agent is faced with the precarious process of moral discernment—one must attempt to "glimpse" the divine intentions of the creator within creation's sinful state. At the same time one must recognize God the Redeemer's imperative to perfect creation. The result is a tension-filled ethic with both conservative and transformative aspects.

For Brunner, the general purpose of the economic order is "to provide the individual and the community with the material goods which are necessary for life" (1937, 397-8, 402ff). Economy is based upon the human activity of labor which requires cooperation and exchange among workers. Brunner defines the economic order as "the process by which material goods, needed to support life, are produced, distributed, and consumed" (1937, 396). Consistent with the above claims about human inequality, community within the economic order is established through relations among functional unequals—various kinds of workers—who provide labor of various kinds within an organic whole. Such work becomes a God-given calling for service to the neighbor (1937, 386ff). Indeed, the first question for the Christian who considers the economic order is "How can I serve within it?" (1937, 401).

Like most theological ethicists of this century, Brunner argues that there is not a "Christian economy" (1937, 402). Nevertheless, he mentions a number of "guiding lines" and general criteria which articulate, in general terms, the kind of economic order which he thinks would be consistent with Christian convictions.

Like papal social thought and Protestant ecumenical ethics, Brunner rejects the two polar extremes of individualism and communism. On the one hand, radical individualism is rejected for its understanding of the individual as self-sufficient and the community as merely instrumental to the desires of individuals. One implication of such a social theory, Brunner thinks, is an understanding of private property which asserts the owner's unconditional right of disposal— a notion which Brunner usually includes within his description of capitalism. On the other extreme, Brunner rejects totalitarian communism which subsumes the individual into purposes of the community, making the individual merely instrumental to the good of the community. Implicit in such a social theory is an understanding of property which rejects completely the validity of private disposal of property (1937, 404ff; 1943, 176ff). Within these two extremes is a social theory consistent with Brunner's understanding of the orders of creation whose goal is the "mutual limitation of the individual and the community, the moulding of individuality within the intimate life of the community" (1937, 405).

Brunner's ethic, unlike Tillich's, does not argue that justice requires a classless, egalitarian economic order. To the contrary, economic justice requires that functional differences result in differences in distribution of wealth and income. At the same time, though, Brunner is quick to acknowledge that the facts of sin and egoism often make actual inequalities excessive. Likewise, the sorts of economic incentives used to prompt human effort often become inimical to the claims of justice and contradictory to the imperative of service to the neighbor (1937, 403; 1943, 156). Hence, while justice may require some amount of redistribution so that the weak might be supported by the "power of the community," such "artificial adjustment" is only a *regulative* idea and not a *constitutive* principle of the economy itself (1937, 404). Brunner also rejects "economic democracy" as a viable possibility due to his beliefs about the organic nature of the economic order (1943, 173-75).

Consistent with this social theory is the critically regulative principle of "property-in-community" which affirms the right of private property established in creation (1943, 148ff),[4] but which rejects any claims to unconditional use by owners (1937, 404ff).[5] Additional characteristics of a just economic order include the absence of monopolies (1943, 168) and provision of a living wage (1943, 172).

While the reader might think that the foregoing account suggests an *explicit* affirmation of a modern capitalist political economy on Brunner's part, such is not the case—especially given Brunner's description of capitalist theory and practice in *The Divine Imperative*. There, Brunner judges capitalism as unqualifiedly "unjust and wicked" (1937, 416). Capitalism is defined both as an attitude (a qualitative conception of value, rational calculation, and unchecked individualism) and as a pattern of community (in which labor is degraded to a mere commodity) (1937, 417ff). Such excessive and degrading dependence of the working class on the capitalist class to exercise unconditional power over the terms of work robs labor of its dignity and constitutes "the real sin of capitalism" (1937, 422). Brunner also defines capitalism as "unchecked and unlimited individualism" (1943, 175) which necessarily entails an understanding of private property which includes its unconditional right of disposal independent of any moral criteria imposed by the community (1943, 79).

Brunner claims that the exercise of the Christian vocation of service to the neighbor is impossible in such a system (1937, 423). Indeed, such a system is not an order at all but anarchy and "a perversion of the divine oder of creation"— a perversion against which the Christian is obliged to fight (1937, 426). Brunner's condemnation of capitalism sounds much like that of Rauschenbusch and Tillich. Indeed, his language seems excessively strong for an ethic which has been known generally for its conservative tenor.

While the Brunner of 1937 assumes the necessity for a new economic order, he is vague about its exact characteristics or the process by which it will originate. Clearly, though, it would not consist of the proletarian transformation and ideal to which Tillich subscribed. However, by 1943, Brunner exhibits more clarity and less radicalism in his thoughts about the shape of a new economic order. In *Justice and the Social Order,* he argues that the solution to the injustices of capitalism is not to be sought in the alteration of the conditions of ownership but in the community's limitation of the right to disposal of property according to the requirements of justice. "It is not the capitalist himself who is the enemy of economic justice, but the irresponsible capitalist." The realization of responsible ownership, he proposes, will require various amounts of political legislation. A shift to public ownership would remain only as the *ultima ratio* in special cases (1943, 170ff). Finally, Brunner envisions such an order as including large doses of economic planning along with private property and some dependence upon free market mechanisms (1943, 180ff). The implications and extent of such political control are left unspecified and unanalyzed. In sum, one can argue that in spite of Brunner's strong criticisms of capitalism, both in its theory and practice, his evaluations and prescriptions (especially his later ones) nevertheless affirm essential aspects of modern capitalism (e.g., a strong emphasis on private property, free markets, and differentiated earnings).

JOHN BENNETT: "CHRISTIAN REALISM"

Following in the wake of liberal Protestantism and the Social Gospel Movement was the redevelopment on the North American scene of neo-orthodox "Christian Realism". With a host of disciples in its camp (Reinhold Niebuhr, John Bennett, and more recently Paul Ramsey), Christian Realism exhibits both similarities to and differences from its predecessors. While the priority of the love commandment as the essential starting point or "principle" for social ethics remains, its application in Bennett's ethic is only indirect. Similarly, while the Social Gospel's "turn to the social" is continued (i.e., the recognition that social questions or problems demand social structural solutions), it is not assumed that social structural remedies will provide permanent solutions to the problem of sin which resides in the human heart. Hence, Christian Realism rejects the Social Gospel's understanding of human nature which assumes that human action can approximate quite fully the demands of love. It also rejects the facile belief that the ideals of the kingdom of God could be reasonably approximated.

While most Christian Realists have treated economic issues in some fashion, John Bennett's work is especially noteworthy not only because his thought embraces the major tenets of the movement, but also because Bennett exhibits a long-standing interest in economic issues. Bennett is worthy of examination not only for his attention to ethical method in matters of economy but also for the changes over time in his ethical assessment of capitalism.

Bennett has been prominent not only as professor of social ethics and later as President of Union Theological Seminary in New York but also for his involvement in American and international ecumenical circles. In both contexts he has demonstrated his ongoing preoccupation with issues of economic life. Bennett's most notable writings include *Social Salvation* (1947), *Christian Ethics and Social Policy* (1946), *Christians and the State* (1958), *Christian Values and Economic Life* (1954), and *The Radical Imperative* (1975). Secondary literature on Bennett is extensive.[6]

Bennett asserts that the primary source of guidance for Christian ethics is "the Biblical revelation with Christ as the center." This entails a focus on the ethical supremacy of self-giving love (1975, 30-34). While love acts as a radical imperative to seek social structural chnages, it does not act as a strict first principle from which specific legislation or policies can be deduced in necessary fashion (1975, 47). Rather, Bennett argues that Christian practical moral reasoning must include two middle terms—intrinsic values and "middle axioms"— in order to infer the demands of love for concrete social situations. Hence, while Bennett and Rauschenbusch both understand God's relationship to the world in terms of love, Bennett's conviction that sin is a permanent feature of human existence results in an altered conception of human agency in which the freedom to love is tempered by the tendency toward sin.

First, Bennett infers from the imperative of love four general intrinsic values— human welfare, freedom, order, and justice. Provision of these values becomes the normative criterion for judging all political and economic systems.[7] Second, Bennett argues for the use of "middle axioms" which include provisional goals, means, and rules which attempt to concretize intrinsic values in a specific historical period and with reference to concrete situations. They are more concrete than universal ethical principles but less specific than programs that include legislation and political strategy (1946, 77). First proposed by J. H. Oldham in a preparatory volume for the Oxford Conference of 1937, middle axioms are "an attempt to define the directions in which, in a particular state of society, Christian faith must express itself. They are not binding for all time, but are provisional definitions of the type of behavior required of Christians at a given period and in given circumstances" (1937, 210). Hence, while Christian practical moral reasoning does not provide a blueprint for a "Christian society", it does provide some sense of direction for social decisions in light of more general values and convictions which, while grounded in the Christian faith, are generally shared in common morality itself. In this respect, Bennett's willingness to move the terms of the debate to those shared by Christians and non-Christians alike shows a certain affinity to major strains in modern papal social thought.[8]

Bennett offers two middle axioms for application to decisions about economic life. They are (1) "That the national community acting through government in co-operation with industry, labor, and agriculture has responsibility to maintain full employment" and (2) "That the national community should prevent all private centers of economic power from becoming stronger than the government" (1946, 81). Such axioms have extrinsic value—they have value not in themselves but only insofar as they are instrumental to the realization of intrinsic values. Furthermore, they are changeable specifications of those more general, universalizable values.

Bennett's own deliberations on the compatibility of various economic institutions and practices with the imperative of Christian love show considerable changes of opinion over time. Early in his career, Bennett, still heavily influenced by the Social Gospel, was strongly critical of capitalism, attacking its egoism, concentration of economic power, and concurrence of wealthy privilege and poverty of the masses (1947; 1936). He opted instead for the possibilities for justice and human well-being seemingly inherent in socialism. Later, with the advent of the New Deal and post-World War II affluence, Bennett moved away from the affirmation of socialism and gave conditional approval to capitalism in the form of a mixed economy (a market economy with state intervention). In *Christian Values and Economic Life* (a volume of the "Ethics and Economic Life Series" sponsored by the National Council of Churches), Bennett applauded the "free enterprise" system for its propensity to promote the following values and states of affairs: (1) the value of productivity, (2) numerous centers of power, and (3) cultural freedom (1954, 247). At the same time, Bennett advocated a political strategy of pragmatic experimentation with regard to the appropriate mix of private initiative and state intervention in the economy. The ethical task of such experimentation is the delicate weighing of values, both extrinsic (e.g., productivity, efficiency) and intrinsic (well-being, freedom, justice, order), toward the end of maximizing their combined value (e.g., 1954, 220-221).

Thirty years later, in *The Radical Imperative*, Bennett exhibited yet another, although less dramatic, shift. Criticizing the too facile assumption of the "Ethics and Economic Life Series" that economic growth would naturally alleviate poverty, he again invoked the need for pragmatic experimentation and renewed debate about economic institutions which avoid rigid ideological categories. Seemingly more critical of capitalism, Bennett again isolated "structural flaws in free enterprise systems"—the incompatibility of profit-taking and provision of social needs, and also the danger to the community of "vast private economic empires" (1975, 150-151, 154).

WALTER MUELDER: COMMUNITARIAN PERSONALISM

Walter Muelder's writings illustrate the application of yet another prominent school of American religious thought—"communitarian personalism"—to economic life. Muelder was for many years dean of the Boston University School of Theology and, like Bennett, an active participant in the ecumenical movement. His most notable publications include *Religion and Economic Responsibility* (1953), and *Foundations of the Responsible Society* (1959). He has borrowed heavily from the thought of Boston Personalists such as Edgar Brightman (as did Martin Luther King, Jr. a generation later) who considered personality as the central quality both of ultimate reality itself and of finite selfhood and as the highest law of ethics. Personality, for Muelder, is the result of life in community (1983, 7). Theologically speaking, Christian monotheism requires that the most comprehensive unit within which the "person-in-community" is to be evaluated is the entire world community (1953, 218, 225). "The metaphysical religious postulate is that a purposive intelligent God is the ultimate creator of all values and that reality is a meaningful whole" (1953, 28).

In terms of social ethics, Muelder contends that communitarian personalism implies the same social ideal to which Bennett and the ecumenical movement gave allegiance—"the responsible society" in which individuals fulfill their rights and duties in society under the sovereignty of God. Muelder's ethic, like those which preceded, gives primary emphasis to love, defined as "the affirmation of personality of complete good-will" and "a voluntary commitment to fellowship". Wishing to distinguish his own understanding of love from that of Christian Realists such as Reinhold Niebuhr, Muelder criticizes Niebuhr's theological anthropology as being incoherent in its conflicting accounts of individual human nature and collective human behavior. Niebuhr, he claims, "did not adequately deal with the redemptive forces that can be released into history by committed human beings and by the immanence of *Agape* in human nature and history" (1983, 12). As shall be seen, though, this conceptual difference does not seem to result in different constructive projects.

Muelder distinguishes religion from economy in terms of the distinct values to which each refer. While religious values are necessarily inclusive, intrinsic, and ultimate, economic values are strictly instrumental (1953, xi, 4). The purpose of economics, then, "is to help men make intelligent decisions regarding the means of community life . . ." (1953, 29). Work, as participation in the economic order, becomes a religious vocation for which Muelder offers three evaluative principles: (1) personality (What does a particular job do to the people who engage in it?), (2) community (What does it do to significant interpersonal relations and to structural relations in the whole community?), and (3) ultimate meaning (What does it do to each person's sense of ultimate significance and concern for God's purpose in one's life?) (1983, 362).

In light of Muelder's global frame of reference and his view of the instrumental nature of the economy, the goal of economic life is to fulfill the economic needs of the entire human community. In spite of an allegiance to democratic socialism early in life,[9] Muelder's elaboration of the responsible society follows that of Bennett and the ecumenical movement (see below). Within the polar extremes of *lassez-faire* capitalism and Marxist communism, the responsible society experiments with varying degrees of political control over economic life.

> Tension between government operation and regulation, on the one hand, and private economic power, on the other, can never be resolved on any a priori basis. . . . Only proximate and provisional answers can be given to the shifting focuses of personal and group desires and power alignments (1959, 140).

Notable topics for which Muelder provides substantial treatment within his framework of communitarian personalism include property, agricultural policy, consumption, social welfare, the vocation of management and labor, collective bargaining, and the world economy (1953; 1959).

J. PHILIP WOGAMAN

J. Philip Wogaman, professor of Christian ethics at Wesley Theological Seminary, is the final and most contemporary figure to be treated in this survey. His volume, *The Great Economic Debate: An Ethical Analysis* (1977), is important for its attempt to develop general terms for Christian ethical debate about the economy. Wogaman attempts to provide not only general theological ethical criteria but also a comprehensive "mapping" of major systems of political economy to which those criteria are to be applied. Wogaman's main purpose, then, is to suggest how Christian ethical criteria permit the Christian to choose from among major systems of political economy.

In general theological terms, Wogaman argues that ethics must be grounded theologically such that it answers questions of "ultimate meaning." For Wogaman, that theological foundation is a Christological one which claims that Jesus Christ, who relates to humans with boundless love, conveys the true nature of human relationships. This Christology assumes additional facts about the world: (1) that all individuals are part of the family of God, (2) that there is an essential equality which supercedes every form of inequality, and (3) that physical goods and well-being are good instrumentally insofar as they provide conditions for higher human purposes (1977, 41-47).

In light of these theological convictions, Wogaman posits five "normative criteria" by which to judge various theories of political economy.

(1) "Does the ideology take material well-being itself seriously as a basis for human fulfillment?" (2) "Is it committed to the basic unity of the human family and does its view of economic life measure economic success in terms of the economic undergirding of mutual love in the life of community?" (3) "Does it include belief in the value of each individual human being and is it committed to individual freedom and opportunity for individual creative development and expression?" (4) "Does it consider human beings to be equal in a sense that is more basic than any inequalities, and does this guide the formulation of economic objectives and policies?" (5) "Does it take the universality of human sinfulness seriously and does it make realistic provision for the effects of self-centeredness in its proposed policies?" (1977, 51-53).

With such normative criteria, Wogaman sets out to evaluate five generic kinds of political economy: Marxist socialism, lassez-faire capitalism, social market capitalism, democratic socialism, and economic conservatism. Wogaman himself opts for democratic socialism as most consistent with Christian normative convictions.

In spite of his attempt to provide comprehensive terms for a theological economic ethic, Wogaman's project suffers in two respects. First, he does not always provide clear descriptions of the various political economies about which Christians must make choices. This makes it difficult to distinguish the options he proposes and to know what aspects of each he affirms and rejects.[10] Second, Wogaman is often inconsistent and haphazard in referring back to the five normative criteria which he initially proposes as critical benchmarks for evaluating forms of political economy.

PROTESTANT ECUMENICAL ETHICS

Anyone conversant with developments within the modern ecumenical movement knows the difficulty of making generalizations about either the method or content of its social ethics. On the international scene, for instance, whatever consensus might have existed two or three decades ago in terms of the development of the concept of "the responsible society" now seems to have vanished. With the emergence of indigenous liberation theologies in Asia and Latin America, for example, one finds an irreducible pluralism of methodologies, empirical assessments, and constructive proposals with regard to issues of economic life. Presented with this diversity of perspectives, I shall limit my discussion to two components of Protestant ecumenical social ethics which give special attention to the economy and to the assessment of capitalism—"The Ethics and Economic Life Series" of the National Council of Churches, and the development of "The Responsible Society" motif prominent in the early life of the World Council of Churches.

The National Council of Churches: "The Ethics and Economic Life Series"— Prominent among North American ecumenical evaluations of economic issues has been the "Ethics and Economic Life Series", initially sponsored by the Federal Council of Churches and continued by the National Council of Churches of Christ in the U.S.A. in the early 1950's. An ambitious project, funded by the Rockefeller Foundation and initially producing six volumes published by Harper, it was an attempt to fulfill the need for "a more careful and realistic investigation of economic life in its relation to spiritual and moral values" (cited from the Foreword to each volume).

Bringing together a host of scholars, the project is notable for its general commitment to interdisciplinary inquiry and, in particular, to its considerations of both ethical analysis and technical, economic analysis. While usually unthematized, regular appeal is made to economic literature. Reflecting back on the project thirty years later, John Bennett captured an essential aspect of the role of economic expertise in ethical evaluation of economic life.

> I learned from them [the economists] better than I would have been able to learn from fellow theologians or students of ethics what unexpected problematic by-products may result from the best-intentioned policies. That is one thing on which economists seem to be experts (1975, 151).

As noted above, the project is defined in part by the general conviction that ethical evaluation of economic questions requires considerations both of ethics and of economics. Ethics by itself might provide worthy ideals for economic life without necessarily knowing how to accomplish them in terms of economic policy, and without necessarily having an accurate "description" of the economic realities to which those ideals and policies must refer. On the other hand, economics by itself, has no recourse to the ends and purposes of life to which its knowledge of empirical realities and procedural means ought to be directed. Hence, while the project seems to proceed implicitly with the notion that both ethics and economics serve as correctives for the deficiencies of the other, James Gustafson is correct in asserting that they "remain rather unconnected in some of the material" (1971, 76). Of the six volumes in the study, three are full-length monographs, and three are anthologies. *Goals of Economic Life* (1953), edited by the economist A. Dudley Ward, is an attempt to articulate the values, goals, and purposes which have been prominent in the American economy and to evaluate their validity from a number of disciplinary perspectives, most notably economics, political science, and Christian ethics. Kenneth Boulding, in *The Organizational Revolution: A Study in the Ethics of Economic Organization* (1953), treats the nature, causes, effects, and ethical implications of the "organization revolution" in both economic (agriculture, industry, labor) and political life (the increasing bureaucracy of the nation state). The economist Howard Bowen, in *Social Responsibilities of the Businessman* (1953), treats the issue of the moral and social responsibilities of business managers. In an argument quite advanced for his day, Bowen argues against a laissez-faire business philosophy focusing on short-term profits to the exclusion of any concern for the social interest. He argues rather that both moral responsibility and the long-term success of American business dictate that managers account for social implications (harms) of business practices. The reader conversant with contemporary debates about corporate social responsibility will find many proposals which have only recently become accepted as standard corporate practices (e.g., public interest directors, the social audit). *American Income and Its Uses* (1954), edited by Elizabeth Hoyt, treats ethical issues related to affluence and consumption. Written by economists, it not only presents empirical data on aspects of affluence (e.g., altered notions of "welfare", the effect on family life, changes in patterns of income distribution) but moves to the ethical level by challenging the facile assumption prevalent in post-World War II American society that increases in material consumption are necessarily instrumental to human welfare. The only work which is strictly empirical, *The American Economy—Attitudes and Opinions* (1955), edited by A. Dudley Ward, presents summary findings of a statistical survey which attempts not only to describe the economic values which pervade the American work force but also to isolate what individuals perceive as moral problems in their daily economic activities. An interesting period piece which documents work attitudes in the early 1950's, the study is notable for its rather optimistic picture not only of general worker satisfaction but also of the long-term economic future of the United States.

Finally, *Christian Values and Economic Life* (1954), the only volume edited by a theologian (John Bennett), is useful not only for its attempt to summarize the findings of preceding volumes but also for its more explicit attention to ethical analysis. While previous volumes contain concluding essays by Christian ethicists (Bennett, Reinhold Niebuhr, Walter Muelder), these contributions are often only indirectly related to the contributions by economists and others. This volume concludes with summary essays by both the economist Howard Bowen and Bennett which focus on broader questions about the relation of ethics and economics. Taken together, their treatments are interesting for their points of convergence. Bowen, the economist, is able to posit, almost intuitively, the dependence of economics on ethics and religion in the discernment of its proper ends and purposes. He asserts that the first task of ethics "is to discover the basic values or goals that ought to be achieved through economic life" (1954, 191-192).[11] Bennett, on the other hand, admits no universal formula by which ethics ought to go about that task, realizing the importance of economic expertise in the translation of ethical ideals into economic policy. While the volume, and indeed the entire series, is helpful as far as it proceeds, some readers might wish to know how the various disciplinary approaches might converge or diverge on their prescriptions for concrete economic problems (e.g., employment policy, government intervention in various aspects of the economy).[12]

The World Council of Churches and "The Responsible Society"—Thorough assessment of the social teaching of the World Council of Churches (WCC) on issues of the economic order and of capitalism is elusive. Lacking the ecclesiastical authority and arguable coherence of papal social thought, WCC social teaching is characterized not only by pluralism at the level of theological foundation but also at the level of social analysis and practical prescriptions. Given the voluminous quantity of social pronouncements that have emerged from six General Assemblies, countless smaller conferences and projects on various issues of ethical concern, and from the large number of study materials prepared in conjunction with those events, any comprehensive treatment is far beyond the scope of this survey, if not in itself impossible. Secondary literature is extensive.[13]

While the primary literature lends itself to numerous methods of analysis (chronological, theological, topical), for the present purposes I shall focus my treatment on the theme of "the responsible society", a concept which not only dominated early ecumenical social teaching in general but also provided the theoretical framework for defining the proper purposes of the economic order per se and for judging the performance of capitalism in particular. Secondly, I shall briefly trace a shift in WCC documents away from the model of "the responsible society" toward a more critical stance showing affinities with liberation theology and stressing radical change of international economic and political structures.

"The Responsible Society"—Walter Muelder and others trace the roots of the

concept of "the responsible society" to earlier expressions of the modern ecumenical movement. As a theme, "the responsible society" is a conceptual response to the ongoing question plaguing twentieth century Protestant churches
of how to state norms adequate for economic and political life. This ecclesiastical
concern to contribute to solutions of modern social problems reaches back not
only to the Stockholm Life and Work Conference of 1925 but also to the official
formulation of "The Social Creed of the Churches" in 1908. Its most evident
precursor is found in the 1937 Oxford Conference on Church, Community and
State.[14] Central is the recognition that Christians of good conscience exhibit
differences of judgment and conviction regarding the proper ordering of economic life, particularly with regard to the relative merits of private enterprise
and social ownership of the means of production (Oldham 1937, 92-97). These
differences are conditioned by varying circumstances and political persuasions.
The report is notable not only for its attempt at social analysis but also for its
explicit concern for how the "Christian message" provides criteria for judging
economic life.

Emerging formally at the First General Assembly of the World Council of
Churches at Amsterdam in 1948, the concept of "the responsible society" functions as a normative criterion by which to make critical evaluations of the two
competing post-war social systems, communism and capitalism (Grenholm 1973,
34; Muelder 1959, 18). It shows a certain consensus about criteria of political
and economic evaluation in spite of pluralism at the level of theological foundations (e.g., Barthians, Protestant natural law theologians).[15]

Grounded in the metaphor of responsibility (of human to God and human
to human), "the responsible society" is defined in Section III of the Assembly
Report, "The Church and the Disorder of Society", as

> . . . one where freedom is the freedom of men who acknowledge responsibility to justice
> and public order, and where those who hold political authority or economic power are
> responsible for its exercise to God and the people whose welfare is affected by it (World
> Council of Churches 1948, 51).[16]

Implicit in its full formulation is a rejection both of totalitarian communism
(with its rejection of political and economic freedom) and laissez-faire capitalism
(with its tendency toward economic injustice) (World Council of Churches
1948, 54). While the political side of "the responsible society" is clear in its
affirmation of the basic freedoms of Western liberalism, its economic aspect is
less clear. Its thrust seems to be toward the advocacy of a mixed economy which
avoids a concentration of economic power and which guarantees the provision
of equal opportunity (Bock 1974, 69-70). Emerging out of the matrix of ethical
principles and concrete situations (Muelder 1959, 16), "the responsible society"
was a "call to find a social arrangement maintaining in dynamic equilibrium
freedom, order, and justice, while barring the way to anarchy and tyranny"
(Bock 1974, 70; also Duff 1956, 191).

A dynamic moral standard developing over time, "The responsible society" was reaffirmed, amplified and eventually brought under radical criticism as an adequate social ethical paradigm at later assemblies and conferences. The Second Assembly at Evanston in 1954 asserts that "the responsible society" is not a specific "Christian" alternative to capitalism or communism but merely "a criterion by which we judge all existing social orders and at the same time a standard to guide us in the specific choices we have to make" (World Council of Churches 1955, 48). It is further defined as a society with both private ownership of the means of production and increased state responsibility for the economy.[17] Evanston is notable for its concern to relate the ideal of "the responsible society" to the newly emerging concerns and problems of the less developed countries of the Third World. Implicit, though, is the assumption that their development could proceed more or less according to the model of the western industrialized nations.[18]

"The Responsible Society" and the Emergence of the Paradigm of "Liberation"—With little alteration at the Third Assembly at New Dehli in 1961, the paradigm of the responsible society first received serious challenge as the dominant social ethical paradigm for evaluating the political and economic orders at the World Conference on Church and Society at Geneva in 1966.[19] Characterized by some as a sea change in ecumenical ethics, the Geneva Conference, entitled "Christians in the Technical and Social Revolutions of our Time," upheld certain aspects of "the responsible society" while including several reservations which qualified and radically called its adequacy into question. Notable is a developing pessimism regarding technology and capital transfer as sufficient for economic development and political and economic justice. With the emergence of "the theology of revolution" juxtaposed against "the theology of the responsible society", a call is sounded for a "fundamental restructuring of the world economy" as a prerequisite for proper human development (World Council of Churches 1967, 86). The Conference is characterized by its careful attention to contemporary policy debates and the specificity of its prescriptions and judgments. This specificity has received trenchant criticism from some quarters (cf., Ramsey 1967; Lefever 1979).[20]

Two years later, the Fourth Assembly at Uppsala is even more emphatic in its insistence that the ideals of "the responsible society" could not be achieved on a world-wide basis within the confines of current economic and political structures. Rather, radical structural change was advocated within less developed countries, developed countries, and in the international economy (The Uppsala Report . . ., 46). Finally, the Fifth Assembly at Nairobi in 1975 is clear in its use of "liberation" as the dominant paradigm by which to view the political and economic orders.[21] Nairobi, then, signifies both the overthrow of "the responsible society" as the dominant model for evaluating social life and the rise of "liberation" as its major competing metaphor by which to evaluate questions of economics in general and of capitalism in particular. This splintering of the earlier consensus only serves to reiterate the radical pluralism and ambiguity of teaching authority that exists in Protestant social teaching in general and in its economic ethics in particular.

CONCLUDING REMARKS

The task of summarizing the state of twentieth century Protestant economic ethics is a difficult one. Generalizations are elusive. While a few summary comments are in order, they do not purport to be exhaustive or systematic in their analysis of the literature.

First, one notices a general and principled rejection by all parties of an extreme form of capitalism, variously labelled as "laissez-faire capitalism," "radical individualism," and "individualistic capitalism." For the thinkers treated above, this form of economy seems to function both as a theoretical ideal type and as a summary description of the actual state of economic life in early twentieth century Europe and North America. It is this type and state of economy against which all the Protestant ethicists cited here have waged trenchant criticism. Indeed, even such diverse thinkers as the conservative Brunner and the more radical Rauschenbusch and Tillich understood the major flaw of laissez-faire capitalism in the same terms—a degrading and thorough-going dependence of one class of workers (the proletariat) on another (owners of capital). Differences emerge, though, in the extent to which the various figures think such a state of affairs is a necessary condition of a capitalist economy. Thinkers such as Rauschenbusch and Tillich, who think it is, propose socialist alternatives which imply radical systemic change. Others, such as Brunner, Muelder, and (until more recently) the ecumenical movement, do not, opting for reformist solutions which retain essential aspects of a capitalist economic order (e.g., private ownership of the means of production, varied dependence on a free market) but which envision various degrees of political intervention (e.g., in the redistribution of wealth and income). This latter trend seems to prevail in most documents of modern papal social thought as well, although some would contest such an interpretation.

Differences in the economic ethic of those surveyed depend in part upon different understandings of the role of love and the role of equality in social life. While all those surveyed assign love a central place in Christian ethics, differences are immediately evident in the ways in which love functions to order institutional life in society. Those who argue that love has only an "indirect" effect on economic life (e.g., as mediated through justice, middle axioms, or institutional "orders") tend to favor less radical political economic proposals than those who see a more "direct" role for love in the organization of economic life. Another way to distinguish the manner in which various thinkers understand the role of love in social life is to order those distinctions in terms of their understandings of sanctification. In relation to this issue the important question becomes, "To what extent can humans reflect the gracious love of God under the conditions of sinful existence?" While the generalization might not hold in each case, it is fair to conclude that those who respond optimistically tend to favor more revolutionary and radical methods of social and economic intervention and eschew more limited reforms.

In addition, one's understanding of equality (and inequality) affects the presumptive abilities of various forms of economy to fulfill requirements of justice. Brunner, for instance, whose understandings of human nature and human community are grounded in the (presumably) essential givenness, and hence justice, of inequality of kind and function, infers that justice in the economic order implies considerable degrees of inequality in power and distribution of wealth and income. Hence, while he may condemn capitalism for creating *excessive* inequality, the fact itself that capitalism seems to entail unequal distribution of wealth and power is not morally reprehensible. Other thinkers, though, who infer from Christian theology and ethics a greater presumption in favor of equality, argue that economic justice requires a more egalitarian distribution of wealth and power. In such an argument, capitalism tends to be rejected in a principled way in favor of socialism.

Notes

1. Noticeably absent from this survey are such figures as Karl Barth, European political theologians such as Metz, Protestant liberation theologians such as Jose Miguez Bonino, and those contributors to this volume whose ethical assessments of the economic order are presented in their own words and which therefore do not require treatment in this survey.
2. For a critical appraisal of Tillich's social thought see Ronald Stone (1980).
3. Robin Lovin (1984) convincingly demonstrates that Barth, in his lifelong debate with Brunner on the knowledge of God, skillfully kept Brunner on the defensive regarding the freedom of God. The unfortunate consequence of this polemic was that Brunner was unable to devote sufficient attention to defending his own position regarding our knowledge of humanity. For Barth's and Brunner's public debates on this matter see Baillie (1946).
4. Brunner's thoughts on private property indicate a shift from *The Divine Imperative* to *Justice and the Social Order*. In his earlier text, Brunner is ambivalent about private property, claiming it is "neither affirmed nor denied" by Christian affirmations (1937, 404). By the time of *Justice and the Social Order*, though, Brunner thinks that private property has clear theological warrants, and argues that it is a right established in creation, scripturally based, and necessary for freedom (1943, 148 ff., 160, 59 respectively).
5. The reader conversant with modern papal social thought will note the similarity here to the papal tradition's distinction between right of property and right use.
6. Notable works on Bennett include David H. Smith (1970); Carl-Henric Grenholm (1973); Robert Lee (1969); and Edward Long Jr. and Robert Handy (eds.) (1970).
7. "In public life, Christian love has been related to the existing situation by means of general human values or principles, the recognition of which is much broader than is the acceptance of the claims of Christian love. I refer to such values as peace or order, justice, freedom, and what I shall call the material conditions of human welfare" (1956, 31; see also 1954, 208-9; 1966, 38).
8. Notable examples include the use of Thomistic natural law in earlier papal documents and the emphasis on "signs of the times" in documents of the Second Vatican Council and the Aggiornamento generally.
9. Muelder campaigned for Norman Thomas in 1928, 1932, and 1936.

10. This lack of clarity is found especially in his attempts at describing and distinguishing "social market" capitalism and "democratic socialism."

11. An interesting and extensive body of literature written by twentieth century economists who don the ethicist's cap and who, implicitly or explicitly, are interested in the relationship of economics to philosophy and/or theology is commended to the reader. See for instance Boulding (1970), Galbraith (1970; 1972), Heilbroner (1970b; 1980), Knight (1976), Knight and Merriam (1945), Munby (1956; 1961; 1969), Schumpeter (1975), Silk (1976), Viner (1978).

12. With an additional grant from the Rockefeller Foundation, the project was later extended and included the following publications: Walter Wilcox (1956), John A. Fitch (1957), and Victor Obenhaus (1965).

13. See Duff (1956); Grenholm (1973); Bock (1974); Lindquist ((1975); Norman (1979); Lefever (1979).

14. See especially Section Three ("Report of the Section on Church, Community and State in Relation to the Economic Order") in the official report of the conference (Oldham, 1937).

15. Barthians such as J.H. Oldham, W.A. Wisser't Hooft, and Roger Mehl espoused an act-deontological ethic defined in terms of obedience and response to God acting in history. Modified natural law ethicists such as William Temple, John Bennett, and Heinz-Dietrich Wendland espoused a teleological ethic which assumes significant continuity in moral knowledge accessible to Christians and non-Christians alike (cf. Grenholm 1973, 40-55). Nevertheless, both camps were proponents of "the responsible society". Duff characterizes these two camps, respectively, as an "ethic of inspiration" and "ethic of ends" (1956, 93-96).

16. *The Message and Reports of the First Assembly of the World Council of Churches* (1948).

17. *The Responsible Society in a World Perspective* (1954), a preparatory study for the Evanston Assembly.

18. See Section III of *The Christian Hope and the Task of the Churches* (1954), a preparatory volume containing background material for the Evanston Assembly.

19. Relevant to the topic at hand is a preparatory study for the Conference entitled *Economic Growth in a World Perspective*, Denys Munby (ed.) (1966).

20. Especially relevant is Section I of the Official Report entitled "Economic Development in a World Perspective" in *World Conference on Church and Society (Official Report)*, (1967).

21. See the work commissioned by the WCC's Commission on the Churches' Participation in Development and intended as a preparatory volume for Nairobi, Richard D.N. Dickinson (1975).

Part Two

Christianity and Capitalism:
Perspectives from
Contemporary Christian Ethics

CHAPTER III

Freedom and the Economic Order: A Foreword to Religious Evaluation

Franklin I. Gamwell

The purpose of this essay is to propose some terms within which religious ethics might pursue an evaluation of the contemporary American economic order. Any such evaluation involves, explicitly or implicitly, the affirmation of political principles, and, therefore, I will discuss the economic order in relation to political theory. It is widely agreed that American political history may be included, at least in large measure, within the tradition of political liberalism. Accordingly, I will, in order to limit the scope of this discussion, attend to the alternatives within that political tradition. In other words, I will assume that some form of liberal economic order is ethically justifiable, so that the appropriate form of liberalism and the correspondingly appropriate form of the economic order are the questions for which terms will here be proposed.

I

It has often been said that the economic order is a distinctively modern problem. Generally, this claim means that moral and political deliberation about the economy as such were not possible until extensive social differentiation of economic activities appeared in the modern age. I will first discuss this claim in order to relate the differentiation of the economic order to the emergence of political liberalism. More importantly, I will suggest that the sense in which the economic order is a modern problem is complex, because the same character of modernity which is reflected in economic differentiation also sets the conditions within which moral and political deliberation are properly pursued.

Although modernity is not easily defined, there is widespread agreement that its distinguishing characteristics include the pervasive commitment to autonomy in thought and practice. In part, this agreement is only verbal, since "autonomy" is used with diverse meanings. Still, it is commonly understood that the modern affirmation should be distinguished from the heteronomy of belief and action characteristic of medieval Christianity and feudalism. For present purposes, then, I offer a minimal definition of autonomy, such that all other definitions, whatever their differences, should be consistent with or include this one: the commitment to autonomy maintains that principles of authentic belief and practice are validated by appeal to human experience and reason as such. By virtue of this appeal, the affirmation of autonomy may also be called the humanistic affirmation and, by either name, is distinguished from heteronomy, in which truth and value are defined authoritatively by some inherited tradition or institutional order, e.g., Christianity or feudalism. This definition is minimal because it leaves open to further argument the substantial character of authentic belief and practice, and the conclusion of this argument may be termed the affirmation of autonomy in its complete or substantial sense. However much is left to further argument, the merit of even the minimal meaning is suggested by its consistency with what has surely become one of the most apparent marks of modernity, namely, the affirmation that appropriate formulations of belief and forms of practice are not imposed upon passive recipients by inheritance but are the creations of active subjects and are, therefore, open at least in principle to recreation or change.

The differentiation of economic activity and the emergence of political liberalism may be understood as expressions of the affirmation of autonomy. For present purposes, I intend here nothing more than the historical observation that these developments did not occur until this affirmation replaced the heteronomous authorities which controlled medieval civilization. Economic differentiation did not appear until the authority of feudal social organization, in which economic activity was diffused with kinship and other non-economic institutions, declined. Liberalism did not emerge until the authority of medieval religious and political forms was undermined. Also, the two developments were related. The new economic order was advanced by the political liberty of those who were its principal creators, and they were among the most important advocates of political liberalism. It might be argued further that the affirmation of autonomy in its minimal meaning is a necessary condition for economic differentiation and political liberalism. I take such an argument to be included in Max Weber's monumental investigation of western societal rationalization, and, although I will not pursue the matter here, I am inclined to think that such an argument in some form is sound. But even if these two developments are necessarily expressions of the humanistic affirmation in its minimal meaning, it remains another question whether they express this affirmation in its complete sense. They will fail to do so precisely insofar as they are not in truth justifiable by humanistic appeal.

The relevant task of modern moral and political deliberation, then, is to evaluate the contemporary economic and liberal political order by just such an appeal. Accordingly, the affirmation of autonomy sets the terms for a religious evaluation that seeks to be fully modern. To be sure, many have insisted that a religious ethic cannot be fully modern, because religious claims necessarily contradict the humanistic affirmation. As I have defined it, however, humanism is not transparently areligious or even atheistic. Its contradictory is heteronomy, and whether religion or theism is necessarily heteronomous is a question the answer to which is open to considerable controversy. I will not seek to enter that debate here. But I am persuaded that the modern affirmation is irreversible, so that contemporary religious ethics is not credible unless its judgments are defended by humanistic appeal. On this point, there is some dissent in the recent literature relating Christian ethics to the economic order. Both Philip Wogaman's volume, *The Great Economic Debate*, and Robert Benne's work, *The Ethic of Democratic Capitalism*, pursue extensive conversation between religious ethics, modern philosophy and social science. If I read them rightly, however, both finally justify their normative judgments by exclusive and, therefore, heteronomous appeal to characteristic convictions of the Christian faith. It is not only legitimate but also necessary for Christians to ask about the meaning of their own constitutive convictions and to do so in relation to, among other things, the economic order. In the modern world, however, it is not sufficient to know what those convictions are and what they prescribe; credibility also involves the further question of whether those convictions are true and whether those prescriptions are justified, and this further question is properly answered only by appeal to autonomous principles of thought and practice. It may be objected that I have arbitrarily endorsed the standards of modernity as those appropriate for contemporary religious ethics. But I hold that there is no alternative once the affirmation of autonomy has appeared. Arbitrariness then is the absence of appeal to human experience and reason as such, so that such an objection is itself plausibly advanced only on humanistic grounds.

I will simply assert my conviction that ethics is peculiarly religious when it seeks to defend on humanistic grounds a comprehensive principle of evaluation, where "comprehensive" is used in the strictest sense to mean a principle in terms of which the worth and importance of all things may be assessed. For present purposes, at least, I take comprehensiveness in this sense to be included among the distinguishing characteristics of religious conviction. This definition is informed in part by the following statement of Clifford Geertz: "Sacred symbols thus relate an ontology and a cosmology to an aesthetics and a morality; their peculiar power comes from their presumed ability to identify fact with value at the most fundamental level" (Geertz 1973, 127). Equally, however, this understanding of religious ethics is consistent with Tillich's definition of religion as "ultimate concern," to which all other concerns are subservient, and Reinhold Niebuhr's insistence that religion relates human existence to "the totality of things conceived as a realm of meaning" (Niebuhr 1942, 44). Moreover, comprehensive evaluation is, in my judgment, the implication of Christian theism, for which the divine reality is the creator and redeemer, not only the source but also the end of all things. A humanistic defense of religious ethics is beyond the scope of the present essay, but the plausibility of the enterprise might be suggested by the following consideration: Evaluative distinctions imply evaluative comparisons, so that nothing less than a comprehensive evaluative comparison can identify the worth or importance of anything at all. I take this to be Niebuhr's claim is saying that self-consciousness or self-transcendence "*forces* human beings to relate their action in the last resort to the totality of things conceived as a realm of meaning" (Niebuhr 1942, 44; emphasis added). I will return to the distinguishing character of religious ethics in my concluding comments.

The previous discussion has sought to clarify the claim that our economic order is a distinctively modern problem in order to relate that problem to political liberalism and to the conditions for convincing ethical evaluation. We may now say that economic differentiation and political liberalism are, historically considered, expressions of the distinctively modern affirmation of autonomy and, moreover, that this affirmation defines the proper appeal in ethical evaluation. Given the assumption that some form of liberal economic order is ethically justified, I will now proceed in the following way: I will seek to distinguish specifically economic purposes and the summary political question regarding them. I will then seek to clarify the alternative answers to this summary question that are available within political liberalism. I will close with some comments regarding religion and these liberal alternatives.

II

Unfortunately, the nature of economic purposes is too often taken for granted or summarily treated rather than theoretically pursued. As a consequence, familiar definitions do not suffice. It is often said, for instance, that economic association consists in exchange transactions, with or without money. Absent some greater specification, however, this definition does not differentiate economics as an aspect of the social order. For all human relationships may be discussed as exchange transactions. Citizens exchange consent for the just governance of state officials; intellectuals exchange ideas; lovers exchange affection. We want for some statement about the *kind* of exchanges found in the economic order. Alternatively, it is said that economic association, with or without money, allocates scarce resources to satisfy competing human ends. As with the previous definition, however, this too is excessively inclusive. All human purposes require resources that are scarce, at the least because human time and energy is so. Again, we require specification regarding the *kinds* of ends for which specifically economic association allocates relevant scarce resources.

In order to achieve a more specific understanding, I will focus upon the qualifying phrase, "with or without money," which is generally found in familiar definitions. "With or without" obviously implies that the use of money is not a *necessary* condition of economic associations. I suggest, however, that we so understand economic relationships that the use of money is always a consistent condition, i.e., economic exchanges or transactions always *permit* the use of money. This suggestion makes decisive a practice which is indisputably essential to the modern differentiation of the economic order. Whatever might be said about economic activity in the absence of money, it is impossible to imagine the modern economic order or anything like it without the specialization of production and distribution which the use of money allows. There are, to be sure, complicated questions about what money is, what counts as money, and what functions money serves, most of which are beyond my competence. For my purposes, however, most of these questions may be begged by stipulating simply that money is a "medium of exchange" (Samuelson 1967, 262) or an item used to make payments (see Heilbroner 1970b, 308). The relevant point, then, is that money is, in the first instance, not itself something for which people engage in exchanges or itself something for which one makes payments. It is strictly instrumental in character. To say this does not deny that people may and do seek to possess money for its own sake, nor that such possession, at least in substantial amounts, may have political and other economic consequences. Whatever secondary relationships people may have to money or as a result of money, these arise because money is in the first instance a strictly instrumental medium of exchange, and this primary sense is the one which I intend when I suggest that economic relationships are those consistent with the use of money.

The consequence of this formulation is that interaction is specifically economic only if or insofar as human association is not itself the common end of the individuals involved. Insofar as the association itself is commonly pursued, the use of a strictly instrumental medium of exchange is inconsistent, because the association cannot be in the same respect both instrumentally and intrinsically important. Thus, I propose to distinguish between private-regarding association, in which association is not its own end, and public-regarding association, in which association is its own end, and I take this to be an application to associations of Aristotle's familiar distinction between production and practice. Strictly speaking, the distinction proposed here is analytic with respect to institutions, because at least some may be public-regarding in one respect and private-regarding in another. For instance, political association may be public-regarding, because definition and creation of our common life is itself our common purpose; but the same association may be private-regarding insofar as we salary our public officials for their participation. Nonetheless, the distinction may also serve to identify differentiations within the social order, depending upon the specific or controlling purposes of particular institutions. Thus, universities are, properly speaking, public-regarding institutions, at least if we may agree that their distinguishing or controlling purpose is nothing other than the scholarly conversation. In contrast, manufacturing institutions are private-regarding, at least if we may agree that their distinguishing or controlling purpose is the manufacture of some non-human thing and the distribution of the income therefrom.[1]

If the use of money makes an interaction private-regarding, it is also true that any private-regarding interaction is consistent with the use of money. Thus, the economic order is the organization of private-regarding relationships or associations in a society. However generous this understanding may seem, it is nonetheless sufficiently specific to identify the kinds of exchanges or the kinds of ends which distinguish economic organization from other associational purposes. The exchanges are private-regarding, and, accordingly, the ends are private, as opposed to the common pursuit of human association itself. Moreover, we may now say that the differentiation of the economic order means nothing other than the creation of institutions whose distinguishing or controlling purposes are private-regarding in character.

Given this formulation, the summary political question regarding economic organization may be stated as follows: Under what conditions and to what extent should private-regarding associations occur within the social order? Because an answer to this question necessarily relates the economic order to other aspects of the larger community, such answers, in their most general expressions, belong to political theory. I will now pursue this question by seeking to clarify the answers found within the Western liberal tradition.

We are generally accustomed to a rough distinction between nineteenth and twentieth century liberalism, in accord with which the former emphasizes minimal government and maximal independence of individuals and their voluntary associations, while the latter compromises this independence through governmental interventions in pursuit of equality and welfare (see Wolff 1968, Lowi 1969). In some respects, nineteenth century liberalism persists in twentieth century American politics under the name "political conservativism." Several scholars, however, further complicate the matter with the claim that these two types together illustrate only one of two forms of political liberalism. J. David Greenstone, for instance, argues that liberalism has been "dipolar," at least within American political history. One pole is "interest liberalism," which is characterized by "utilitarian politics that seeks to maximize rights, interests and preferences" (Greenstone 1982, 6). This tradition traces its intellectual heritage to Hobbes, Locke and the classical utilitarians; has generally dominated American political life; and has frequently been thought to exhaust the liberal tradition (see Hartz 1955, Kariel 1977, Unger 1975). So-called nineteenth and twentieth century types are generally distinguished, implicitly or explicitly, *within* the pole of interest liberalism. In addition, Greenstone insists, the liberal tradition includes a second pole which appears as a minority report, "a politics of humanitarian reform that emphasizes individual self-development, that is, the capacity to master certain *substantive standards* of excellence" (Greenstone 1982, 6). This alternative, he continues, has been expressed in New England Puritanism and in certain reform movements of the last two centuries; it found one of its eminent political representatives in Abraham Lincoln and one of its eminent philosophic representatives in John Dewey.[2]

Of course, if both of these two poles are indeed forms of liberalism, they must have something in common which identifies the liberal tradition as such or inclusively. I propose to define political liberalism generically as the humanistic view that all relationships or associations within the social order should seek to maximize the freedom of all individuals. Politically speaking, in other words, the affirmation of autonomy implies the principle of freedom. This definition leaves unspecified precisely how freedom is properly understood and, therefore, suggests that different poles of liberalism might be distinguished by fundamentally different understandings of freedom.

III

I will discuss in due course the minority pole of Greenstone's dipolar liberal tradition, but I focus attention for the present upon the dominant form, which "seeks to maximize rights, interests and preferences" and which I will call "established political liberalism." We may approach the understanding of freedom characteristic of this form with the help of Charles Lindblom and John Dewey. "In the early development of . . . liberalism," Lindblom writes, "it was a movement to enlarge and protect the liberties first of nobles and then of a merchant middle class. . . . As the movement came gradually to be associated with ideals of popular rule in the late eighteenth century, it maintained its preoccupation with liberty, to which popular rule was, however, never more than a means" (Lindblom 1977, 163). Dewey concurs: "Born in revolt against established forms of government and the state, the events which finally culminated in democratic political forms were deeply tinged by fear of government, and were actuated by a desire to reduce it to a minimum so as to limit the evil it could do" (Dewey 1954, 86). When the movement achieved expression in political theory, Dewey continues, individual liberty was protected by insisting upon the priority of individuals and their purposes to the formation of society. "The obnoxious state was closely bound up in fact and in tradition with other associations, ecclesiastic . . . economic, . . . , and, by means of the church-state, even with unions for scientific inquiry and with educational institutions. The easiest way out was to go back to the naked individual, to sweep away all associations as foreign to his nature and rights save as they proceeded from his own voluntary choice, and were guaranteed by his own private ends" (Dewey 1954, 88). In short, established liberalism may be understood as the affirmation that human interests or ends are constituted solely by choice. In rejecting what it took to be the heteronomous purposes defined by inherited institutions, established liberal theory insisted that autonomy would be affirmed only if the interests of the individual were bound neither by history nor by nature but solely by the self's own election. Thus, Greenstone is right in calling this a politics based upon preferences.

Because the material character of individual interests is solely preferential, it follows that freedom is formal in character, i.e., the social telos of maximal freedom for individuals implies nothing about the proper purposes for which freedom is exercised. Freedom is the capacity to pursue preferences, and the social telos is mutual non-interference with respect to this capacity. Many established liberals take mutual noninterference to mean simply the absence of constraint or coercion, although others insist that, under some conditions, the duty to aid or assist is included or implied. The absence of coercion does not mean that coercion is never legitimate. On the contrary, there should be coercion precisely insofar as this is required to prevent or to compensate for illegitimate coercion. As both Greenstone and Dewey suggest, in other words, established liberal theory requires some understanding of individual rights in accord with which one person's exercise of freedom is limited by the legitimate freedom of others, and for this reason such theory includes an endorsement of the state as that association which both specifies rights and, where necessary, coerces to protect them. But the proper purpose of government never includes decisions regarding the ends for which freedom should be exercised, because those are constituted solely by individual choice, i.e., freedom is formal in character.

We are now in a position to clarify the established liberal answer to the summary political question regarding economic organization: Under what conditions and to what extent should private-regarding associations occur within the social order? In a general way, the answer may be formulated directly: private-regarding associations, as all associations, should occur under conditions of freedom in the formal sense and, consistent with these conditions, should be maximized. The second half of this answer (namely, that private-regarding associations should be maximized) is implied by the first (namely, that freedom is formal in character). Because freedom is simply the absence of interference, the ends of good human association are, by definition, other than the association itself. With respect to his or her preferences, the autonomous or "naked" individual of established liberalism is independent of his or her communities. Accordingly, the telos of the social order is to maximize private-regarding associations, consistent with the conditions of freedom in the formal sense. I will call this the priority of private-regarding associations in established liberalism, and this means that all other relationships, including especially political associations, are teleologically subservient to free economic exchanges.

Given that human interests are private by definition, it might be thought that all associations are private-regarding by definition. There is one sense in which this is true. Since the most inclusive telos of the social order is to serve private interests, all institutions properly contribute in some way to this inclusive purpose, and this is what I mean by the priority of private-regarding associations. So to leave the matter, however, begs questions of differentiations within the social order and, most especially, the difference between specifically economic and specifically political associations. Thus, I proposed earlier that "private-regarding" and "public-regarding" be used to identify specific or distinguishing purposes. Given this stipulation, we may speak of established liberal political association as public-regarding in character. In seeking to define the rights of individuals, for instance, the distinguishing purpose of the democratic process is nothing other than human association itself, for common definitions as such are a kind of human association. I have already said that the ends of human association are, because freedom is formal, other than association itself. Within established liberalism, then, the point to be stressed is that public-regarding associations never serve human interests directly. Since those interests are necessarily private, public-regarding associations only set the conditions for or are in some way instrumental to the creation of free, private-regarding exchanges. Thus, democratic political participation in the established liberal order is never itself the pursuit of happiness but solely a duty to which we all are bound in order that conditions might be designed in which our economic activity might be maximized. "Politics is," as an old saying has it, "a burden."

Capitalism, I suggest, is a theory of economic organization which holds that private-regarding relationships should be predominantly non-governmental. Historically speaking, this theory developed coincidentally with and in the context of established liberalism. If, with Lindblom, liberalism as a movement initially sought to protect the liberties of first nobles and then a merchant class; and if, with Dewey, liberalism as a political theory asserted the priority of private purposes to associations; capitalism developed the related claim that such liberty is best protected and such priority honored if economic relationships are predominantly independent of government. The capitalist thesis may also be expressed in terms of the established liberal principle of freedom. Given that the social telos is maximal freedom in the formal sense, government is limited to activity required to specify and protect rights to such freedom, and the capitalist thesis is that such activity is sufficiently minimal that the economic order is predominantly non-governmental.[3]

"Predominantly" is an imprecise term, but in truth there is no way to specify exactly to what extent the established liberal government is properly involved in private-regarding associations. As a result, there is room for considerable debate on this matter within the controlling framework of capitalism—say, with respect to taxation, income distribution, or the government ownership of enterprises deemed essential to the national defense or the general welfare. Nonetheless, the conviction that economic organization should be predominantly non-governmental has some implications which generally characterize the capitalist thesis. The two most important are the affirmations of private property and of the competitive market. The former generally precludes governmental ownership of the means of private-regarding production or government purchase of products, so that capitalism implies an economic order constituted in the main by non-governmental enterprises that are consumer directed. Competition is a characteristic implied by the established liberal principle of freedom. If the economic order is predominantly non-governmental, buyers and sellers to which there are not significant alternatives constitute a constraint upon voluntary association. It is worth noting that governmental activity is a necessary condition for both characteristics of the capitalist order, and this illustrates the earlier point that established liberalism is not anarchism. Property rights are governmentally defined, and competitive markets are governmentally protected. Moreover, it is generally recognized that government must so define the rights to private property as to protect individuals from the indirect consequences of associations in which those individuals do not voluntarily participate. These consequences are variously called "neighborhood effects" or "externalities" and are frequently illustrated by the environmental hazards posed for the larger community by certain production or consumption patterns. However, capitalism is committed to the judgment that governmental activity required to correct or compensate for externalities is not so extensive as to compromise the predominantly non-governmental character of the economic order.

A great deal of recent debate regarding specific conditions of the American economic order can be more or less understood within the context of established political liberalism and in relation to the capitalist thesis. I add the qualifier, "more or less," because the debate includes many who are far more empirical than they are theoretical in their modes of thought. Accordingly, the political principles informing parties to the debate are often as implicit as they are explicit, and the implicit principles are not always theoretically coherent. Still, there is a large range of debate within which participants are on the whole committed, at least implicitly, to the convictions of established liberalism. Disagreements within this context may be roughly characterized by a continuum which runs from the more complete affirmation that economic relationships should be non-governmental to the more complete affirmation that these relationships should be governmentally constituted. At some point in the movement from the one to the other, the thesis that private-regarding relationships should be predominantly non-governmental is abandoned or repudiated, and it is in this sense that the debate may be understood in relation to the capitalist thesis. Thus, one may speak of more complete capitalists, less complete capitalists, less complete socialists, and more complete socialists.

Because the debate takes place within established liberalism, the varying positions result from varying judgments regarding the kinds and extent of governmental activity that is required to protect rights to freedom in its formal sense. I do not have the competence to review the range of issues in relation to which these varying judgments are expressed, but I will seek briefly to illustrate the point.

Many of the issues debated concern the externalities or neighborhood effects of non-governmental, private-regarding relationships. As I have noted, the capitalist thesis asserts that requisite governmental activity to prevent or compensate for these externalities is sufficiently limited so that the predominantly non-governmental character of the economic order is preserved. Others, however, now doubt that this is so. If one includes among such externalities the systemic effects of inflation and/or unemployment; the effects upon patterns of human settlement, including especially problems of urbanization; and the consequences upon the natural environment; some judge that governmental activity is required of such kind and measure that a more or less socialist economic order is implied.[4] A second set of issues within the established liberal debate concerns the economic and political consequences of non-governmental concentrations of wealth and institutional power. Most especially, there is contention about large economic corporations. Some insist that size must be judged relative to the markets in which these institutions exist and, by that standard, judge that the American economy is "workably competitive" (see,e.g., Friedman 1962, ch. 8; Benne 1981, 104-18). Others claim, in varying measure, that large corporations enjoy control over markets and, moreover, undue influence within the body politic, such that rights to freedom of both consumers and citizens are more or less severely violated and government ownership or extensive supervision in many industries is prescribed (see, e.g., Galbraith, 1973).

Whatever more specific issues are identified, however, the inclusive issue within the established liberal debate concerns the distribution of economic resources and benefits. In the last analysis, the only social issue for established liberalism is that of distribution. Since freedom is the capacity to pursue private preferences and associations are instrumental to those pursuits, the question of proper associations is the issue of who gets what resources and benefits. Even specifically political rights (of suffrage, of speech, etc.) may be understood in these terms, because political association is instrumental to maximizing free, private-regarding relationships. Accordingly, contention within established liberalism regarding systemic externalities or the concentration of non-governmental wealth or institutional power may be reformulated as disagreements about the effects of differing economic arrangements upon the distribution of resources.

In substantial measure, these disagreements are empirical in character, reflecting disparate readings of contemporary economic conditions. But empirical disagreements do not exhaust the debate, which also reflects alternative judgments regarding the principles of appropriate distribution. Established liberalism has always ached under this problem, because the telos of maximal freedom in its formal sense does not specify the character of legitimate freedom. On the contrary, the principle is vacuous in the absence of an independent definition of rights. The claim of more complete capitalists that individuals have a right to whatever resources and benefits they command within competitive markets is simply one possible definition; it is, as any other, consistent with but not entailed by the telos of maximal formal freedom. Other positions insist upon a fairly generous understanding of equal economic opportunity which implies considerable governmental activity to compensate for accidental inequalities. Still others advocate such equality of economic distribution as to raise into doubt whether private-regarding relationships can be predominantly non-governmental. The distinction between nineteenth and twentieth century liberalism, which I earlier mentioned in passing, turns upon such differing principles of distribution.

IV

If the preceding comments at least suggest the range of positions that are possible with the established liberal context, they do not compromise the common affirmation which those positions share, namely, that private-regarding associations are teleologically prior in the social order. This affirmation comes, as it were, with the territory, i.e., identifies the established liberal context. For many political historians, the dominance of this context in American political life during the past century explains in part the massive economic achievements which the country has enjoyed. More importantly, the continued political power of established liberalism is confirmed for some by the apparent dominance of economic institutions and economic goals in a time of perceived economic plenty, such that social purpose continues to be so largely designed to achieve maximal economic growth. Recently, this apparent dominance has been subject to increasing criticism. Some argue that American society faces a present or impending crisis, because the pursuit of maximal private-regarding associations eventually destroys the democratic political community upon which the established liberal order itself depends. In his justly famous aphorism, Reinhold Niebuhr said that "man's capacity for justice makes democracy possible," just as "man's inclination to injustice makes democracy necessary" (Niebuhr 1944, xiii). When interest is widely thought to be preferential, the argument runs, the capacity for justice erodes, because the preferential view of interest is inconsistent with a moral affirmation of the interests of others (see Sullivan 1982; Sandel 1982). Be that as it may, several thinkers have claimed that a social order in pursuit of maximal private advantage is inconsistent with the best possibilities of human existence. The human spirit is compromised and the democratic ideal impoverished, this claim has it, when relationships to the natural world and, especially, to other human individuals are designed to maximize preferential satisfactions.

When evaluation of the American economy implicitly or explicitly attends in some such way to the extent of private-regarding associations, the debate is no longer contained within established liberalism. To the contrary, the established liberal understanding of freedom is now itself called into question. I redirect attention, then, to the minority report within Greenstone's dipolar liberal tradition. Consistent with his characterization of this alternative as "a politics of humanitarian reform," I will call it "reformed liberalism." It is most often found in proposals for a "communitarian" political theory, and, as this name implies, the decisive issue involves the proper understanding of the relation between individuals and their communities.

Reformed liberalism has found no more persuasive advocate than John Dewey, and I will appropriate his thought as paradigmatic of the position. Dewey's critique of established liberalism centers on its implicit or explicit assertion that individuals are independent of their human associations, and, in contrast, he insists that individuality is socially constituted. Each individual is "a *distinctive* way of behaving in conjunction and *connection* with other distinctive ways of acting" (Dewey 1954, 188), by which Dewey means that each person has the possibility of greater distinction precisely insofar as he or she is more fully related to more distinctive others. Thus, the individuality of each properly consists in activity which is maximally constituted by the distinctiveness of others and seeks in turn maximally to contribute to others. Robert Horowitz has written that Dewey's inclusive philosophical purpose was "to further the realization of democracy in every sphere of life" (Horowitz 1963, 746), and, for Dewey, the democratic ideal is nothing other than the telos of maximal human association. "Every way of life that fails in its democracy limits the contacts, the exchanges, the communications, the interactions by which experience is stretched while it is also enlarged and enriched. . . . The task of democracy is forever that of creation of a freer and more humane experience in which all share and to which all contribute" (Dewey 1951, 394). Dewey would applaud, then, the following citation from his contemporary, Alfred North Whitehead: "One general end is that these variously coordinated groups should contribute to the complex pattern of community life, each in virtue of its own peculiarity. In this way individuality gains the effectiveness which issues from coordination and freedom obtains power necessary for its perfection" (Whitehead 1961, 67).

As these citations suggest, Dewey's correlative formulation of individuals and associations is or at least implies a material as opposed to formal understanding of freedom, i.e., the social telos of maximal freedom for all individuals now implies a certain character to the purposes for which freedom is properly exercised. Freedom is itself socially constituted and, therefore, includes but is not exhausted by non-interference; greater freedom is the capacity for greater individuality and is, therefore, the function of more enlarged and enriched associations. "Liberty is that secure release and fulfillment of personal potentialities which takes place only in rich and manifold associations with others: the power to be an individualized self . . . enjoying in its own way the fruits of association" (Dewey 1954, 150). Accordingly, the proper exercise of freedom aims to maximize the distinctiveness communicated among humans. The affirmation of autonomy does not mean that interests are solely constituted by choice; on the contrary, the absence of heteronomy releases humans to recognize and choose in accord with the nature of human existence, and Dewey's formulation illustrates the criterion that forms of liberalism are distinguished by differing understandings of freedom.

Because interests are not solely a matter of preference, it follows that the priority of private-regarding associations in the social order is inconsistent with reformed liberalism. Since democracy is the pursuit of distinctive individuals who maximally inherit from and contribute to their communities, and since whatever is communicated among humans is insofar public, we may say that the inclusive social telos is to maximize the public world. Accordingly, private-regarding or economic relationships are now relativized by or made subservient to this telos. In response to the question, "To what extent should private-regarding associations occur within the social order?" the answer is now, "To whatever extent is required to maximize the public world." Identifying the proper extent is a task for political debate and decision, because that determination depends upon particular conditions, but this does not gainsay that the political debate properly appeals to a non-economic telos. We require, said Dewey, "a form of social organization that should include economic activities but yet should convert them into servants of the higher human capacities of individuals" (Dewey 1963, 31-32).

To be sure, a considerable measure of human communication occurs within specifically economic organizations, especially among those who are more responsible for the making of decisions. By definition, however, this communication is limited by the private-regarding purposes of the organization. Accordingly, the creation of the public world is maximized when human communication or association is its own end, that is, in public-regarding associations. For Dewey, such associations pursue "the values of intellectual, esthetic and companionship life" (Dewey 1963, 88), and I take the relevant purposes to include friendship, art, education, politics and religion. But however these purposes are specifically identified, public-regarding associations now become teleologically prior. To maximize the public world is to maximize public-regarding associations—and, by implication, in the long run.

Nothing which has been said implies a disparagement of economic activity or economic organizations. Indeed, Dewey judged that the possibilities of human association in America are so great precisely because economic achievements have been so impressive. The creation of the public world, in other words, requires private preconditions. The pursuit of enlarged human community requires time and energy that are unavailable without biological health and a substantial provision of material security, and the fact that such a massive measure of the human race must devote virtually all of life to the pursuit of life itself is also a measure of how far short of its possibilities the human adventure remains. For the same reason, there is a prima facie case for economic activity that is technologically as efficient as possible. Even with release from biological and material concerns, however, public-regarding associations wait upon conditions that private-regarding associations must provide, e.g., universities and museums must be built, transportation and communication services must be developed and maintained.

Within the context of reformed liberalism, the conditions under which private-regarding associations should occur wait in part upon empirical considerations, such that judgments are informed by the particular situation of a given society and the telos of the maximal public world. Given the extent to which individuals in contemporary American society spend their time and energy in specifically economic associations, for instance, some have advanced proposals for "economic democracy," in the sense that major economic institutions become worker-controlled. The purpose is to make economic relationships themselves occasions for enhanced human community. Of course, worker-controlled enterprises are not as such inconsistent with capitalism, in the sense that private-regarding relationships are predominately non-governmental, and whether the economic order should be capitalist is also in part an empirical question. Since the reformed liberal understanding of freedom includes the absence of coercion, there is a prima facie case for free markets of the kind which capitalism advocates. But this endorsement is subject to the following qualifications: (1) free markets are affirmed insofar as the distribution of resources and benefits effected through the market is acceptable; (2) free markets are affirmed insofar as it is proper to permit social organization in pursuit of private preferences. The first qualification is required because economic resources and benefits are preconditions for public-regarding association, and the second is required because the social telos is not the maximal satisfaction of preferences but the maximal public world. It may be that these two qualifications spell the doom of a capitalist economic order in contemporary America. Although I am not prepared to argue the case, I will briefly suggest some reasons peculiar to reformed liberalism which weigh in this direction.

The first reformed liberal qualification upon competitive markets prescribes that the distribution effected must be acceptable. Given impressive affluence, and given that individuals cannot significantly pursue human association for its own sake without substantial private preconditions, the telos of maximal public-regarding relationships implies the attempt to provide such preconditions for all. The public world is enhanced when more individuals of distinction contribute to it. Thus, the distribution permitted through the competitive market must not compromise the required measure of economic equality. It may be, as some have suggested, that private preconditions can be established by governmental redistributive mechanisms that do not alter the predominantly non-governmental character of the economic order. But the inequality of income and, especially, wealth in American capitalism seems to be so excessive and so persistent as to recommend doubt on this point (see Thurow 1980, ch. 7; Heilbroner 1966, 27-28). This doubt is, in my judgment, increased if one believes that substantial economic inequality compromises the genuinely democratic character of non-economic, especially political, associations.

But if that point remains unclear, the more telling qualification upon market organization is the second: competitive markets are recommended only insofar as it is proper to permit social organization in pursuit of private preferences. If it is true, as some have argued, that capitalist economic organization is inherently expansive, then the limitation upon economic association which reformed liberalism implies will itself imply something other than capitalism. Waiving that summary judgment, however, more specific considerations may lead to the same conclusion. The question of externalities assumes added importance within the reformed context. The relevant effects of private-regarding relationships upon the environment, both natural and human, include not only issues of survival and economic rights but also the most appropriate settings for human communities; if the former do not the last may well require extensive governmental supervision of economic activity. Moreover, the control of large economic institutions may become decisive. If it is true that such organizations presently dominate the American social order, then it is probably true that these organizations will, in the absence of major governmental activity to the contrary, prevent the supremacy of public-regarding purposes. The dominant institutions of a society will, absent major resistence, bend social purposes to their own. I do not think, as some do, that these considerations dictate massively decentralized economic institutions; the economic capacities of large organizations make that change undesireable, even if it is possible. But I do suspect that the prescribed task of relativizing private-regarding purposes to public-regarding ones will require a governance of economic corporations—and, more generally, of the economic order—such that something other than capitalism, in the sense that I have defined, is implied.

Be that as it may, the burden of the present essay lies elsewhere. I have sought to show that a liberal assessment of the economic order waits upon a prior choice between established and reformed poles of the liberal tradition. The first holds to the priority of private-regarding associations and the second to the priority of public-regarding associations. If the inclusive public problem for established liberalism is the appropriate distribution of economic resources and benefits, the inclusive economic issue for reformed liberalism involves the preconditions for the maximal public world, and this difference is the consequence of different convictions regarding human individuality and human freedom. Although I have not presented sufficient reason to choose the one or the other, I am in a position to suggest that religious ethics must take its side with the minority report. At least this follows if, as I stipulated earlier, religious ethics is distinguished by a comprehensive principle of evaluation. The established liberal claim that human interests are solely matters of preference is necessarily the claim that these purposes cannot be evaluated. They are, as it were, neither good nor bad, such that principles of evaluation must exclude them. But, then, there is no comprehensive principle of evaluation. Stated in relation to Christian theism, established liberalism asserts that "divine reality" may be the source but is not the end of human existence, since human ends are constituted solely by individual choice—and this implies that there is no divine reality at all in the Christian sense. At least to first appearances, the unity of all things in their creator and redeemer is more readily consistent with the view of socially constituted individuality which I have identified with reformed liberalism. Equally, the affirmation that autonomy is the capacity to choose in accord with the nature of human existence is more readily consistent with the view that a theistic source and end of human existence may be defended on humanistic grounds. Within liberalism, in other words, it is this substantive affirmation of autonomy which may also be, in Tillich's term, theonomous. If we must choose between established and reformed liberalism, then, there is reason to seek a comprehensive formulation of the latter in order to achieve a convincing religious evaluation of the economic order.

Notes

1. For the present, I offer this distinction as one to be assessed by its usefulness in the succeeding discussion of liberalism and the economic order. But I believe that it is useful in that discussion because it can also be defended as a distinction important to ethical and political theory.
2. Elsewhere, I have discussed at greater length the two principal forms of liberalism and the secondary distinction between nineteenth and twentieth century types. See Gamwell (1984).
3. To this argument in terms of freedom, some may object that another defense for capitalism has traditionally been offered. Ever since Adam Smith mentioned the "invisible hand," the advocates of capitalism have argued that competitive markets maximize the efficient allocation

of resources in the economic order. Because each offers exchange where his or her offer is most dear and seeks exchange where the other's offer is cheapest, the collective consequence is to produce and distribute goods and services of such kind and in such quantities also maximize the preferences satisfied by available resources. Correspondingly, non-competitive markets misallocate resources by producing too much of some goods and/or services and too little of others. It is this argument (or, rather, far more sophisticated versions of it) which justifies the fascination of economists and social theorists with the competitive system of prices. It may be questioned whether acceptance of this argument entails capitalism in the sense that I have described. Charles Lindblom, for instance, claims that competitive economic enterprises might be governmentally rather than privately owned and be fully consistent with "efficiency pricing"; alternatively, government directed rather than consumer directed competitive markets are conceivable (see Lindblom 1977, 93-106). Be that as it may, the argument for capitalism in terms of efficient resource allocation may be reformulated in terms of freedom. Competitive markets are most efficient because individuals are there most free to enter or refrain from economic relationships in accord with their preferences. It is also worth noting that the claim regarding efficiency assumes an appropriate distribution of the resources with which individuals enter the market. Competitive capitalism maximizes preference satisfaction, if it does, *given* the distribution that obtains. In the established liberal formulation, this qualification is addressed by stipulating that rights to freedom must be protected, i.e., the question of appropriate distribution is answered as a part of the specification of these rights.

4. For a discussion of these problems, see Heilbroner (1976). It should be noted, however, that Heilbroner's analysis suggests evaluative principles which are other than those of established liberalism.

CHAPTER IV

Capitalism with Fewer Tears

Robert Benne

My title is a shameless borrowing from an essay by James Luther Adams entitled "The Protestant Ethic with Fewer Tears" in which he suggests that with proper modifications some of the virtues of the Protestant ethic are perennially viable. But even closer to my intents is the title of a book written by Irving Kristol—*Two Cheers for Capitalism* (1978). It expresses directly the thesis that I will argue. I believe there is much to say for the contributions of capitalism to the combination of democracy and capitalism. Contrary to what many Christian ethicists argue, I believe that a market economy is not an enemy of democratic practice, but rather an ally. I do not think that democracies can flourish without being coupled to economies with a good measure of free market characteristics. Thus, two cheers for capitalism, not three cheers which would indicate the kind of thorough enthusiasm that is inappropriate for any historical achievement of humankind.

On the other hand, my chosen title suggests that there are tears associated with capitalism. I do not need to chronicle all the reasons for tears. I mention two to which I will later return. Market systems have a tendency to reflect and sometimes magnify the inequalities of the initial starting points of participants in the system. This seems to be true in both the domestic and international realms. Market systems do not reward people well if they cannot respond to what those systems demand. Those who contribute little or nothing receive little or nothing in return. The capitalist economic system on its own does not generally address the plight of the worst-off. Second, there seems to be an imperialist tendency in capitalist economic arrangements toward imposing rational economic calculus and practice into areas of life that are best not ordered according to that approach. This leads to a "commercialization" of society and culture, or, in the words of Franklin I. Gamwell, the predominance of private-regarding activities over public-regarding.

These two problems are a genuine source for tears and therefore cannot and should not be swept under the rug. I believe that both of these challenges, as well as other serious ones, can be creatively addressed within the possibilities and potentialities of a dynamically developing democratic capitalism. This will take leadership better than we presently have in Washington, but which is nevertheless available in this society. At any rate, the tears associated with democratic capitalism should not lead to the conclusion that it ought to be replaced by some sharply different political economy in which most economic decisions concerning production and consumption are made politically—either by the state or by some process of "economic democracy" legally mandated by the state. Such approaches, it seems to me, would lead to a society far less attractive than ours.

Before we proceed further, it will be useful to define "capitalism," since I find that the word means too many things to too many people. To illustrate with a ridiculous extreme, a Marcusian Marxist from the University of Texas whom I was debating defined capitalism as any economic system that makes people work. According to him, all extant systems are capitalist and need to be abolished. Less distorted, but yet seriously flawed, are those that call semi-feudal Latin American economies capitalist. They are not. Rather, I define "capitalism" as an economic system that relies on a workably competitive market as the dominant mode of making economic decisions; on private ownership of the means of production; on economic freedom to enter the market as producer and consumer, investor or laborer; and on a legal order that protects voluntary and peaceful exchange and that attempts to maintain the competitive nature of the system. Further, it relies on a rational and systematic pursuit of profit as a primary spring for economic action. Incidentally, it is important to note that private ownership merely affirms that ownership is non-governmental. It leaves the door open for many kinds of ownership and management, including that by employees whose incidence I hope will increase in this country.

I make a moral defense of that kind of economic system with two further provisos. First, that it is combined with constitutional democracy. Market systems can be combined with authoritarian governments of the right (Taiwan) and the left (Hungary), but neither meet the criteria of a desirable and just society. Second, I defend the market economy as an apt partner for democracy only if the economy is workably competitive, i.e., if the pricing system of the market is actually responding to realities of supply and demand. This second proviso is already included in my definition of capitalism but I mention it again to emphasize its importance. Many rejections of capitalism are based on the belief that there is no such thing as a competitive market system, that what is called a market system is a noncompetitive monopolistic or oligopolistic system under the domination of private economic powers (Benne 1981, 96-104). My judgment is that there is indeed a workably competitive market system in this land and that competition is probably increasing rather than decreasing as the scope of markets widens, technological innovation increases and consumers become better informed (Benne 1981, 105-122).

One more preliminary comment is in order regarding the religious grounding of my argument for democratic capitalism. In his essay, Gamwell reads me as giving a *Christian* defense of democratic capitalism in the sense that I make arguments based upon revelatory-particularist grounds. It is as though I am constructing a Christian economics. This, I think, is a misreading of my position. On the contrary, I am usually chastized by Christian readers for not being biblical and theological enough. They claim I rely too much on Reinhold Niebuhr's anthropology and Rawl's Kantian political philosophy, neither of which is directly biblical or theological in the sense of being dependent upon special revelation.

I tend to agree more with these latter critics than with Gamwell. The arguments I make here are "from below," based on our general, common humanity and historical experience. True enough, my normative principles are broadly Western in that they draw from both biblical and classical sources. But I see no way of avoiding that kind of particularism, either for myself or for Gamwell.

Arguments on social ethical matters based on our common human reason and historical experience—arguments from below—fit my Lutheran orientation. Debates about the relative merits of political and economic systems deal with penultimate matters on the basis of penultimate criteria. This does not mean that political and economic matters are unimportant; they may be matters of life and death. All social systems, though, are caught up in ambiguity. The central and essential message of the Christian faith transcends all socio-political systems. Its central symbols should never be confused with the achievements of extant social systems or with movements toward ideal ones. If the central message of Christianity is, as I believe it to be, justification by grace through faith on account of Christ, which is characterized by God's gracious gift and our receptivity, then every effort at political and social justice is of a different order than the redeeming act of God in Christ. There are no redemptive human politics.

Thus, we are discussing matters about which Christians of intelligence and good will can differ. They are not items of *status confessionis*, beliefs essential to the faith. Such a viewpoint, I hope, enables me to be both humble and bold. Humble in that I realize that arguments from below are powerfully conditioned by our relative knowledge, by our place in time and space, and by the inexorable pressure of our own interests. But bold in the sense that my salvation is not dependent on the rightness of my argument. I can be wrong without being damned.

I. PRINCIPLES

Normative criteria for a practically and morally adequate political economy are: (1) that it is efficient, producing sound economic growth; (2) that it is as decentralized as possible, inhibiting concentrations of power; and (3) that it aims at the constant extension and refinement of justice. I hasten to add that these criteria do not exhaust what is required of the whole society. For it is in and through society—with its voluntary associations, families, friendships, religious and educational institutions, ethnic groups, neighborhoods, recreational organizations—that substantive ends are pursued and partially realized. Moreover, those social contexts are also the generators and communicators of the meaning systems and values upon which the political economy depends. I will return to this issue of substantive ends later in the essay.

While I cannot justify these principles adequately in the space of this essay, permit me a few justifying remarks. Economic efficiency is important for intrinsic reasons. There is something fitting—aesthetically pleasing—about combining the factors of production in an effective way. Excellent economic actors are likened to architects by Whitehead (as cited by Heyne 1968, 119-120). Efficiency is excellence in the economic realm. It is also good stewardship in the biblical sense. Further, an efficient economy lifts the majority of people out of the realm of necessity. This makes democratic politics possible, for people do not have their very existence at stake as they enter the political realm. They can afford to compromise and bargain. Hannah Arendt points this out when she argues that people driven by necessity will destroy the political realm if given direct access to it (Arendt 1982, 83 ff). This is certainly evident in the difficulty developing nations have in establishing democracy when they have a majority living in serious poverty.

When people are free from the pressure of necessity, they can direct energies to higher things, such as education, friendship, good works, aesthetic pursuits, etc. All these good things are curiously dependent upon a productive economy. But a productive economy does not guarantee the pursuit of these higher things; people may also pursue the low and ignoble. Finally, it seems to be the case that governments are able to pursue justice more vigorously in good economic times than in bad. Horrible economic conditions may precipitate radical transformations aimed at justice, but only a few of us wish things to get worse so that they can get better.

The criterion of decentralization is justified on the grounds of both human sin and creativity. First, the argument from sin. Following Niebuhr, I believe that all persons are infected with sin that often issues in will-to-power; the sin of organized groups *always* issues to inordinate will-to-power (Niebuhr 1949, 208ff). Therefore, the tendency toward sin makes democracy necessary. Democratic practices involve checks and balances that prevent tyranny. However, all centers of power need checks and balances so that each center of power and each kind of power is restrained in its exercise of power. An adequate political economy, from a religious point of view, decentralizes power in an orderly way, thereby diminishing the extent of domination in the society.

A decentralized system is also most likely to locate responsibilities at the lowest possible level of social interaction. It brings activities as close to people as possible so that the likelihood of participation is enhanced. Catholic social theory calls this the principle of subsidiarity. When actions are as close to the grass roots level as possible, people are more likely to be creatively involved in them. This is most certainly true of decentralized associational life, and most likely true of economic and political life too. Thus, a decentralized system is likely to be more innovative and dynamic, tapping the creativity of the people.

Finally, a morally defensible political economy pursues justice. Following Rawls, I would propose the following principles of justice in lexical order: (1) equal private and public liberties; (2) fair equality of opportunity; and (3) the difference principle, which justifies inequalities of income and wealth insofar as they enhance the prospects of the least advantaged (Rawls 1971, 83).

The first principle affirms traditional civil liberties as well as the democratic guarantees of consent of the governed, participation in helping to shape the rules that govern us, and rule of constitutional law.

The second principle breaks into two parts. Equality of opportunity means that public positions in the society are genuinely open, that they are filled according to the proper criteria. *Fair* equality of opportunity means that those born into disadvantaged social positions are moved closer to the same starting line as the more advantaged through compensatory strategies.

The third principle commends a floor of dignity for all citizens that rises as the well-being of the whole society rises. Financed by transfer systems from the well-off to the disadvantaged, this floor is limited to the extent that further transfers will disincline the well-off to work further. I depart from Rawls in that I believe that this floor should be set low enough to create incentives for those who are able to work. For those who cannot, I follow Rawls with his principle of *maximizing* the minimum (Rawls 1971, 152-154).

Such principles have clear continuities with the Judeo-Christian religious and moral tradition, regardless of Rawl's claim that they might best arise from bargaining in a hypothetical, ahistorical, "original position". The principles are reverberations of such Judeo-Christian notions as the *imago dei*, the fundamental equality of all humans before God, and compassion for the suffering and oppressed. Though refracted through the Enlightenment categories of liberty, equality and fraternity, their deeper source is in the Judeo-Christian tradition. Now, however, they are a part of the broad cultural heritage of the West and can be appealed to on common, rational human grounds.

II. THE VIRTUES OF CAPITALISM

In this section I shall argue that a market economic system—capitalism if you will—furthers each of these principles as it combines with political democracy in the political economy called democratic capitalism. Capitalism sustains efficiency and growth; it allows a decentralization of centers of power and kinds of power; and it encourages background conditions that support the principles of justice.

Let me elaborate each assertion. The first—that capitalism over the long run sustains efficiency and growth—is difficult to contest. The Western democracies with market systems—joined now by Japan—have experienced just such growth (Shonfield 1969, 61 ff.). This is because competitive market systems stimulate a constant revolution in the means of production. New products and services are created and marketed; new ways of producing old ones are invented. Market economies are characterized by what Schumpeter called "creative destruction", in which older and less efficient production is constantly displaced by something better. The cumulative effect of these revolutions is remarkable.

> Each time they result in an avalanche of consumer's goods that permanently deepens and widens the stream of real income although in the first instance they spell disturbance, losses,

unemployment. And if we look at those avalanches . . . we find that each of them consists in articles of mass consumption and in increases in the purchasing power of the wage dollar more than that of any other dollar—in other words, that the capitalist process, not by coincidence but by virtue of its mechanism, progressively raises the standard of living of the masses (Schumpeter 1975, 68).

Market economies have produced a steadily expanding economic pie from which all segments of society have benefited. Arthur Okun remarks that in the last generation every income group has experienced a doubling of their disposable family income in real terms (Okun 1975, 69). The point is that the conditions of life for the vast majority have improved because of the productivity of capitalist economies. This is of no mean moral significance.

Economic efficiency enables us to achieve other goals. It undergirds the possibilities of civilization in providing occasions upon which we can build artifices of moral, aesthetic, social and religious value. Economic affluence does not guarantee that the right possibilities will be grasped. A profusion of trivial goods will be produced alongside scholarly books, journals, medical supplies, cheap transportation, good design, fine records and human services of great variety. Moreover, the wealth generated supports public pursuits such as education, health, parks, welfare, social security, pensions, and, through higher levels of discretionary income, private non-profit efforts in schools, colleges, voluntary associations, and churches. The highly developed associational life of American society is directly connected to an efficient economy.

These remarks prompt me to indicate where I have some difficulty with Gamwell's argument, which seems to make too sharp a distinction between private-regarding and public-regarding activities. It is hard to imagine many activities which are ends in themselves detached from nurturing and supportive contexts which can and must be supported monetarily. The scholarly conversation of this volume, for instance, cannot go on without a good deal of financial support from activities that would have to be considered private-regarding.

Three more reflections about the "creative destruction" of capitalist mechanisms are in order. First, there is the destructive side to the process, which we are experiencing in many older cities of the midwest and northeast. The government, I believe, must find ways to cushion the effects of the creative destruction on workers and communities without stopping the process itself. Second, I see no reason why the process will come to a halt or why the destructive side should overcome the creative side. The high tech revolution that we are in the midst of will probably increase the living standards of ordinary people and make it possible for them to pursue more of their aspirations. Finally, since the process of creative destruction is a vast experimental system, I expect that our private sector will be coming up with more human contexts for work as we take part in the global competition for higher productivity. Capitalism has created, and will continue to create, more fulfilling work opportunities than any of the planned economies have been able. In the process, we will eliminate the most burdensome, dangerous, and repetitive kinds of work.

A second argument for market economic arrangements that is very convincing to me is that it allows a distinction between economic and political power, i.e., it allows some decentralization of the key centers of power in society. I marvel to think of the economic life of the Chicago metropolitan area of eight million people working out in a reasonably efficient manner. Millions of economic decisions govern the flow of goods and services of the city, all of which go on without a centrally directed intelligence. It works itself out in an unconsciously coordinated way, and it works very well. Because most of the economic decisions of the society can be made in this unconsciously coordinated fashion, the role of the state can be limited. It is not required to know about all of these things, decide about them, and more importantly, enforce those decisions. In short, the state need not be omnicompetent. Further, competition inherent in market economies and encouraged by government anti-monopoly and free trade policies provides needed restraint on private economic power, holding it accountable to other producers and to consumers. Government need intervene only when competition fails.

There is no automatic harmony about the market. Large enterprises can and sometimes do dominate smaller ones. Consumers can be fleeced. Workers can be exploited. Private economic power can gain too much political power. Therefore, democratic polity must intervene to make sure the market works, to redress imbalances, to do things the market cannot or ought not do, and to protect itself from incursions of concentrated economic power. Business can swallow up government; and government can swallow up the market. But neither has happened to a disastrous degree. We must be vigilant in keeping economic and political power distinct and balanced.

This capacity for distinguishing and balancing economic and political power is a mark of democratic capitalism, made possible to no mean extent by the self-coordinating capacities of the market. In this way market economies make it possible to avoid concentrations of political power. It is unclear to me how democratic socialism will ever get economic decision-making under political control without either unduly concentrating political power or becoming terribly inefficient.

A third contribution that capitalism makes to our political economy is that it encourages background conditions that support the principles of justice. The market economy encourages liberty, provides opportunity, and produces a reward-for-contribution system. In other words, the market system helps to shape a rough, partial and flawed system of natural justice upon which more intentional approaches can be constructed. It is important to note that the market does not do this unaided; it is supported in turn by propitious social, political and legal conditions.

First, liberty. There is a certain sense in which the economic liberty encouraged by market economies is constitutive of freedom itself. Individuals are free to enter the market when and where they please, constrained of course by their own abilities and initiative as well as what the market demands at a particular time. We have wide latitude to pursue our own chosen vocations.

And as long as the economy remains innovative and open, choices will continue to be wide. Further, on the consumption side, we are free to choose how our money is spent. Money is simply an exhange item, hardly ever an end in itself. It can buy many important things from primary goods to goods of "higher" value. It can support activities that are familial, social, cultural and even spiritual in character. On the other hand, it cannot buy the most important qualities for fulfilling life, although it can support activities that nurture such qualities.

The freedom to spend our money as we see fit enables us to live according to our chosen values—to choose our sources of information, to live where we want, to support institutions and causes we hold dear, to carry on family life with as much human richness as possible. Market systems, with their considerable autonomy of persons and households, enhance the possibilities of living according to our values. This is part and parcel of freedom in general. The quality of our values is what determines whether these possibilities will be used creatively or nobly; markets reflect what we choose.

It should be noted in passing that much dissent in our society is supported by this very freedom to dispose of discretionary income. Dissenting individuals and groups have access to many private sources of money to finance their organizations and causes. In a large pluralistic society such as the United States, many independent foci of support—from wealthy patrons to poor students—are available to causes in lurid variety.

I hasten to stress that these freedoms are not only individual ones. Much of the above can also be said about the support of social groups. Social pluralism is an important by-product of widely shared economic freedom. Universities and religious organizations, for instance, are privately supported from the voluntary gifts, contributions and tuitions of many persons. Indeed, much of our lives are lived within these private, mediating structures. They are a cherished legacy of economic and political freedom.

If capitalist market arrangements support private and public liberties of individuals and groups, they also distribute economic opportunity widely. In fact, they *proliferate* opportunity and allow millions of agents to pursue those opportunities according to their own interest, abilities, and initiative. A tremendous profusion of economic opportunity has been the hallmark of American society for the majority of individuals and families. And even in the many cases where there was little "fair" equality of opportunity—where people did not enter the race at the same starting line—there was opportunity to better oneself. This widespread opportunity to better oneself has been and continues to be the great drawing card of the United States. It is the kernel of the American Dream. I believe it is *the* most important element that a society—or an economy—can offer. In the eyes of average people it far outweighs strategies of income redistribution. And the lived experience of the great majority of the American people in the past and present is one of greater or lesser social mobility. A large country socially and geographically, a high degree of freedom, an open and fecund market, and millions of enterprising newcomers have produced the dominant American experience.

There has been a powerful "dark side" to the American experience; mobility has exacted its costs, many people have not been able to achieve mobility, there have been serious disruptions in economic life, and sections of the population—various minorities, for instance—have not been allowed to participate freely in the quest for betterment. This "dark side" needs to be made visible to American society, and that need is being answered. The exploration of the "dark side" in historical research, art, media, plays, novels and movies has been so intense that it has led many Americans—and foreigners for that matter—to believe that the "dark side" has been normative. But if that were the truth, there would be many more radical political options. Or, at the very least, people would have quit coming to American shores or, as it happens at present, infiltrating our borders. It is not lax to insist that a good deal of natural justice has been experienced through the proliferation of opportunity. That has been the normative experience. The "dark side" must be attended to with moral and political earnestness; but if strategies of improvement are constructed solely out of interpretations of the dark side, serious distortions are likely.

Market systems—decentralized and unconsciously coordinated as they are—encourage a wide distribution of freedom and opportunity. The third element in our triumvirate of distributed goods is reward. The market rewards those who freely take advantage of opportunities it offers, and it does so without central political direction. The market distributes reward according to contribution, thus providing incentive to those who do the things society needs or wants to have done.

The market is a system of economic mutuality characterized by voluntary exchange. One party supplies a good or service to someone who wants it for the price he or she is willing to pay. Business enterprises do the same thing. There is a competitive context in which suppliers and purchasers make their offers. Like other forms of human mutuality, economic mutuality—if voluntary and informed—betters the situation of those involved. Market arrangements reward the excellence by which one party supplies what someone else wants or needs, and is willing and able to pay for. The greater the want or need dictated by demand in the marketplace, the greater the reward for services delivered well. Thus, in this age able economists seem to be paid highly, as are doctors, lawyers, executives of large companies, skilled craftspersons, professional basketball players, among many others. More of us are more moderately paid. Some contributions to the economy, such as those made by dishwashers, are very modestly rewarded because there is such a large supply of people able to provide those services. Thus, the calculus of economic mutuality works out to reward most those who best supply the wants and needs registered by the market. Income is distributed according to such a system. There are of course distortions introduced by monopoly, by limiting access to the market, by the lack of economic wherewithal to register preferences, by discrimination and other factors. But in a rough sense, economic reward is proportional to economic contribution. Our incomes, for better or for worse, reflect what it is that people value and on which they can put a price tag. (The last qualification is very important because many of the highest valued elements in life are not exchanged in the market-place.)

Reward is therefore unequal. Some commentators are very bothered by this inequality in income distribution. But except for those on the very low end of the income scale, and to a lesser extent for those on the very highest, I do not have a great deal of complaint. And I believe my attitude is similar to most other Americans'. Income inequality in this vast middle ground is much more related to choice about vocation, life-style, and levels of risk, than to systemic injustice. I think the vast majority of Americans do not want to make the kind of commitments it takes to become rich and/or powerful. They have other interests that are not correlated with high income. They are not "marginal utility maximizers." As some wag put it: there is a marginal utility from not bothering about marginal utility. The bulk of us want a comfortable standard of living, but we choose patterns of life and vocations that are consonant with values related to our own definitions of human fulfillment, values not generally consistent with those needed to gain very high incomes.

Hence, in addition to the market economy's contribution to economic efficiency and growth, and to an effective decentralization of power, it also encourages a wide distribution of liberty, opportunity and reward-for-contribution. These three contributions encourage me to say "yes" to the market economy, not least because all three of them have important moral dimensions. But I could not affirm a market economy unqualified by democratic polity. I am willing to make a moral case for the market economy's future only as it is in lively combination with democracy. The reasons for this are only too clear. A government representing all people must tend to the health of the market system itself so that it can be productive. There is no automatic harmony about it. Monopoly must be limited by law; wise macroeconomic policies must be pursued. Imbalances of power must be redressed; economic power must be prevented from subverting political power. Further, public, common goods must be provided for by government. Clean air and water, a beautiful environment, education, domestic and national defense, streets and sanitation, and postal services are all rightful domains of the government.

But, above all, democratic polity must pursue justice for all. This means it must go beyond, and sometimes even counter, to the market in assuring equal justice. We have already celebrated the liberties that are part of our political and economic systems, but those liberties must be given worth for all. In principle, we all have equal rights to legal defense, but those with sufficient income can enjoy the "worth" of their liberty; those with little or no income experience diminished "worth" of liberty. As to opportunity, positions must be made genuinely open so that discrimination is made on the basis of relevant criteria, not irrelevant criteria such as sex or race. Moreover, equality of opportunity must be pressed in the direction of *fair* equality of opportunity so that all are moved closer to the same starting point as they compete for open positions. Fair equality of opportunity will mean compensatory treatment, particularly in education, so that past injustices or neglect can be redressed. As to inequalities in income, in the reward-for-contribution that the market deals out, those inequalities must be used to improve the prospects of the least advantaged among us. Taxes must be levied on those who are highly rewarded so that an adequate and rising floor of decency can be provided for all citizens. Mobility is affirmed, incentives held out, and inequalities allowed insofar as these significantly promote the prospects of the least advantaged. This will mean particularly the promotion of the prospects of the most defenseless in our society—the mentally and physically ill, the retarded, the elderly poor, the children who are orphaned, abused, or neglected. Our record can be much better than it is on these scores; it is the role of the polity to insist that justice be better achieved.

The extension of these entitlements to all by democratic constitutionalism transforms the capitalism we have been talking about into "reformed" capitalism, "redistributive" capitalism, or simply "democratic" capitalism. I could elaborate further an agenda for the future work of government, but this essay is primarily about economies, not polities. It should be clear that I believe that a market economy is an appropriate partner for a democratic polity, and that, in combination, they arguably provide the best arrangement. The partnership will always be full of lively tension, however; we should not expect a completely tranquil marriage. Market arrangements may reflect the imbalances of power in a society; they will not always correct them. On the contrary, they may exacerbate them. The record is mixed. As government intervenes to establish and extend the rights mentioned above, participants in the market place will resist. Redistribution is no easy prospect.

In our efforts in that direction we should allow competitive markets to operate as freely as possible, for they produce the wealth we need to redistribute. They tend to disperse power and decision making, thus encouraging a limited state. They distribute freedom, opportunity, and reward in a roughly equitable way for most of us. As long as they do these things in a way tolerable for the majority, we should not attempt undue manipulations. We ought to correct the distortions and make up for its failures through intentional strategies of justice but should not destroy something that can do so much for us, and do it without centralized control.

III CLOSING REMARKS

I fear that my arguments will place me squarely in Gamwell's "established liberalism" camp. These children of darkness are characterized by the sole concern freely to maximize preferences. This leads them to promote purely formal principles of justice in the public sphere and the dominance of private-regarding activities. In such a liberal society, public-regarding activities languish at the periphery.

With such an evaluation of my argument, one understands why I might feel uncomfortable, bending a bit more toward the light of "reformed liberalism."

Let me conclude by moving slightly in that direction.

The normative political economy I have outlined *allows* freedom in the political, economic and social arenas. It does not commend maximizing freedom as arbitrary preference or freedom *from* social interdependencies. Perhaps a libertarian view of human nature and its role in the market commends such a view, but I certainly do not. A Christian ethicist cannot have that kind of anthropology. My view of human fulfillment is decidedly relational. It is constituted by a dynamic harmony between the self and God, the self and the self, the self and others, and the self and the non-human environment. Freedom viewed from this perspective is definitely freedom *for* at least partial realization of those dynamic harmonies, which, from my particular religious stance, is often occasioned by God's grace rather than human achievement.

I doubt that this general perspective is too far removed from Gamwell's own. Where then, do we part company? Let me suggest two areas. First, I believe the partial realization of those dynamic harmonies can take place in what Gamwell calls private-regarding activities. Can humans not express their gifts and talents in constructive ways, can they not engage in friendship, can they not participate in a calling, and can they not really produce something useful in these so-called private-regarding activities? Can working at IBM be as humanly and socially fulfilling as teaching at a Divinity School? I suspect it can. I catch in Gamwell's outlook an aristocratic-Greek disdain for commerce, a slight tinge of the arrogance of the "theory classes."

The second area regards substantive ends. As I stated above, my normative outlook *allows* freedom, but it does not *commend* an atomized life devoted to arbitrary preferences. I see those substantive ends emerging from the free communal and associational life of the private sector—from families, churches, friends, ethnic groups, neighborhoods, schools and colleges, recreational groups, etc. No doubt some come from the public sphere as well. But the primary carriers of the ends toward which we direct our freedom are the voluntary, private ones—the elementary republics where we learn and transmit those ends through the practice of virtue.

Thus, the substantive ends in my view come from below, not exclusively, but primarily. Gamwell, I fear, has lost patience or confidence in the capacities of these voluntary groups to provide adequate substantive ends. He is ready to have the state be the arbiter of substantive ends. In his view the state should drastically curtail what he has called private-regarding pursuits. This I find to be implicitly authoritarian even if executed through a democratic process. I think the state has enough to do in pursuing the more or less formal principles of justice I outlined earlier. Approximating those principles will itself be a Herculean task. That kind of state-craft is soul-craft enough for me.

CHAPTER V

Neo-Aristotelianism, Liberalism and Socialism: A Christian Perspective

Cornel West

The burden of our civilization is not merely, as many suppose, that the product of industry is ill-distributed, or its conduct tyrannical, or its operation interrupted by embittered disagreements. It is that industry itself has come to hold a position of exclusive predominance among human interests, which no single interest, and least of all the provision of the material means of existence, is fit to occupy. That obsession by economic issues is as local and transitory as it is repulsive and disturbing. To future generations it will appear as pitiable as the obsession of the seventeenth century by religious quarrels appears today; indeed, it is less rational, since the object with which it is concerned is less important.

R.H. Tawney

The purpose of studying economics is not to acquire a set of ready-made answers to economic questions, but to learn how to avoid being deceived by economists.

Joan Robinson

In his provocative book, *After Virtue* (1981), Alasdair MacIntyre argues that moral discourse in the modern West is in a grave state of disorder. The central terms, privileged notions and key expressions in Western moral vocabularies constitute fragments of past conceptual schemes, residues of lost theoretical contexts. According to MacIntyre, we are left with the ruins of the West, mere simulacra of morality with no rational standards to adjudicate between conflicting moral theories and perspectives. The dominant moral fictions of our age—rights, utility and expertise—hide and conceal irrational wills to power, arbitrary expressions of desire.

MacIntyre's creative response to this crisis is to recover and revise Aristotelian ethics. He promotes a virtue-centered moral theory which specifies an essential nature of human beings—a nature that defines their *telos* (or true end understood as a certain kind of life), and a set of moral precepts which enable people to progress toward their *telos*. MacIntyre suggests that only this sophisticated recuperation of an Aristotelian teleological scheme and context can safeguard and sustain us "through the coming ages of barbarism and darkness" (1981, 244).

One reason that MacIntyre's understanding of the present crisis in Western morality, culture and civilization is highly relevant to Christians is because it is rooted in his own personal pilgrimage from Christian to Marxist to neo-Aristotelian. The common denominator of this pilgrimage is the search for the intelligible and rational bases for morality, community, solidarity and praxis.

79

MacIntyre ultimately concludes that the traditions of Protestant Christianity and Marxism cannot provide such bases.

For MacIntyre, Protestant Christianity fails because of its devaluation of reason. Luther's characterization of Aristotle as "that buffoon who has misled the church", along with Calvin's severe circumscription of human capacities, both symbolize the Protestant Christian claim that human reason yields no genuine comprehension of the telos of human beings.

Marxism fails owing to its lack of "a morally distinctive standpoint" (MacIntyre 1981, 243). In situations in which moral responses are required, Marxism tends to resort to Kantianism, as with Eduard Bernstein, Karl Vorlander and Max Adler; to utilitarianism, as with Lenin and Trotsky; or to Hegel and Spinoza, as with Georg Lukács and Louis Althusser, respectively. In addition, Marxism is excessively optimistic regarding human capacities, especially in the face of the vast moral decline and decay in capitalist societies. MacIntyre succinctly states:

> A Marxist who took Trotsky's last writings with great seriousness would be forced into a pessimism quite alien to the Marxist tradition, and in becoming a pessimist he would in an important way have ceased to be a Marxist. For he would now see no tolerable alternative set of political and economic structures which could be brought into place to replace the structures of advanced capitalism. This conclusion agrees of course with my own. For I too not only take it that Marxism is exhausted as a *political* tradition, a claim borne out by the almost indefinitely numerous and conflicting range of political allegiances which now carry Marxist banners—this does not at all imply that Marxism is not still one of the richest sources of ideas about modern society—but I believe that this exhaustion is shared by every other political tradition within our culture (1981, 244).

MacIntyre concludes that present projects of political and economic liberation must be abandoned for the more tempered practice of a revised moral Aristotelianism.

> What matters at this stage is the construction of local forms of community within which civility and the intellectual and moral life can be sustained through the new Dark Ages which are already upon us. And if the tradition of the virtues was able to survive the horrors of the last Dark Ages, we are not entirely without grounds for hope. This time however the barbarians are not waiting beyond the frontiers; they have already been governing us for quite some time. And it is our lack of consciousness of this that constitutes part of our predicament. We are waiting not for a Godot, but for another—doubtless very different— St. Benedict (1981, 244-5).

In what follows I would like to defend Protestant Christianity and the Marxist tradition against MacIntyre's powerful criticisms and against the present challenges of the neoconservative/liberal defenses of "Democratic Capitalism". These two perspectives are the major contenders and alternatives to my own position. My defense shall take the form of putting forward a rudimentary Christian case for democratic socialism. I shall attempt to show that a particular version of Protestant Christianity provides a conception of human nature and morality that requires adopting a social analytical viewpoint deeply influenced by the Marxist tradition. Furthermore, this conception of human nature and morality and this social analytical viewpoint results neither in elitist disengagement from present political and economic struggles and nostalgic yearnings for holistic schema and contexts (as with MacIntyre) nor in ahistorical justifications for the "free enterprise" system. Rather, my view promotes engaged social insurgency—a position tempered by a Christian worldly skepticism, regulated by Christian values of democracy and individuality, and guided by undogmatic Marxist social analysis. I shall begin my defense by critically engaging MacIntyre's argument. I will then try to reveal the empirical vacuity of Robert Benne's liberal defense of capitalist democracies. My own constructive position will emerge in the course of my examination of MacIntyre and Benne.

I find acceptable MacIntyre's claim regarding the interminability of public argument regarding crucial moral issues. This is neither shocking nor surprising in a highly pluralistic culture and heterogeneous society. As MacIntyre notes, the very aim of the secularization of public discourse—the bourgeois liberal effort to establish minimal frameworks of tolerance (a theory of the right) within which differing ways of life (i.e. conceptions of the good) could be aired—presupposed fundamental disagreement regarding the telos, or true end, of human beings. And there is little doubt that any attempt to reestablish a single teleological scheme or context constitutes an authoritarianism rightly abhorred by most moderns, including modern neo-Aristotelians like MacIntyre himself. Aristotelianism, like many other premodern authoritarian moralities, does not take seriously the plurality, heterogeneity, opposition and conflict inherent in human life and society. Yet such matters are the very motivations for the modern political discourse MacIntyre castigates. Hence, his total rejection of modern politics.

> Modern systematic politics, whether liberal, conservative, radical or socialist, simply has to be rejected from a standpoint that owes genuine allegiance to the tradition of the virtues; for modern politics itself expresses in its institutional forms a systematic rejection of that tradition (1981, 237).

But what does such a rejection amount to if one still believes, as MacIntyre does, that conflict is at the heart of modern society? If, as he states, "Modern politics is civil war carried on by other means" (1981, 236), how is such conflict to be dealt with? Is it not preferable over civil war itself? How would a virtue-centered theory of morality come to terms with other conflicting virtue-centered theories of morality? I suggest that MacIntyre's passionate rejection of modern politics is symptomatic of a postmodern weariness of confronting the insoluable problems of social conflict and disorder. He indeed prefers the liberal response to these problems over "the barbarous despotism of the collective Tsardom which reigns in Moscow" (1981, 243)—yet his neo-Aristotelianism which builds local communities on the margins of society presupposes the very liberties and protections provided by the liberalism he rejects.

So, despite his castigation of liberal politics, MacIntyre remains, on a practical plane, a liberal; that is, the *praxis* of his viewoint assumes and affirms liberalism. On a deeper level, MacIntyre's neo-Aristotelianism bears the indelible stamp of the liberal Enlightenment—no matter how persuasive his claim regarding its failure. This stamp can be seen in his discarding of three basic features of past forms of Aristotelianism, namely, the acceptance of fixed inherited social roles, the naturalization of cultural ways of life, and the promotion of exclusivism in societal relations.[1] Once one has been bitten by the Enlightenment bugs of critical consciousness, historical consciousness, and universal consciousness, a wholesome rejection of liberalism is impossible. The only credible alternative is to build upon and go beyond it. What is needed is a thoroughgoing critique of liberalism's own uncritically accepted assumptions. The tradition of Protestant Christianity provides many of the resources needed for just such a critique.

The distinctive strength of Protestant Christianity is neither its worldly skepticism (for this can be found in pagan cynicism or secular poststructuralism) nor its anticipatory triumphalism (for this can be found in non-Christian forms of apocalypticism and millenarianism). Rather, this strength resides in its recognition of the interplay between fallible finitude and the demand for engaged praxis, between acknowledged fallenness and received empowerment. This interplay incorporates worldly skepticism and sustains anticipatory triumphalism thereby precluding ill-founded optimism and paralyzing pessimism. More importantly, it promotes and encourages an unstoppable predilection for alternatives grounded in the present. In other words, Protestant Christianity—at its best—possesses a unique capacity to highlight critical, historical and universal consciousness.

This capacity owes principally to its realistic assessment of human proclivities, its processive view of life and history, and its all-inclusive moral outlook. The Protestant Christian tradition—especially as developed by American thinkers from Jonathan Edwards and William James to Reinhold Niebuhr and Martin Luther King, Jr.—views *history* as a battlefield upon which to fuse with comrades in a struggle against evil, and *nature* as a realm of reality with which one communes and in which one delights. These viewpoints provide resources and riches which aid in the effort to go beyond modern, liberal, bourgeois society. Put simply, these resources are as follows. First, there is a recognition of the indispensable yet inadequate capacities of human beings to solve problems— hence the deep anti-dogmatic thrust of Protestant Christianity which fans and fuels critical consciousness. Second, there is the good news of Jesus Christ which empowers and links human capacities to the coming of the kingdom—hence the spiritual resources necessary for coping with despair, dread, disappointment and death itself. And finally, there is an acceptance of and an insistence upon the moral obligation to view all human beings as having equal status, as warranting the same dignity, respect and love, especially those who are denied such dignity, respect and love by individuals, families, groups, social structures or political regimes—hence the Christian identification and solidarity with the downtrodden and disinherited, with the exploited and oppressed.

The systematic ecclesiastical interpretations of these crucial resources and riches of Protestant Christianity remain the province of Protestant theologians. And this activity should persist. But what is most interesting about our present postmodern moment is that there is a consensus among many contemporary Christians regarding the need to struggle against forms of dogmatism, despair and oppression. Furthermore, there is widespread agreement that the preferable rhetoric of Christian ethics should be that of freedom and democracy, self-determination and control over one's destiny. No longer are Christians seduced by pagan venerations of the power and benevolence of reason nor by secular projections of a "new humanity" or an "unselfish, altruistic species" rising upon the advent of the good society in history. The moral debates in modern society among intellectuals in general and among Christian thinkers in particular are lively and intense—but assumptions against dogmatism, despair and oppression as well as preferences for rhetorics of freedom and democracy are widely shared by most interlocutors.

This situation forces us to amend MacIntyre's characterization of public moral discourse as conceptual fragmentation. This fragmentation surely exists when the situation is viewed diachronically (in relation to the past); but when viewed synchronically (in relation to its internal character and structure) public moral discourse contains a consensus of assumptions and agreement on rhetorics. A genuinely creative response to the present crisis in ethics cannot consist simply in an historical reconstruction that accounts for conceptual fragmentation. Rather, what is needed is a theoretical and methodological reflection on the *social analytical* presuppositions of the varying moral positions which share common assumptions and rhetorics. MacIntyre hints at these crucial strategies when he states that "Philosophical analysis will not help us" and, more importantly, that any moral philosophy "characteristically presupposes a sociology" (1981, 2, 22). Yet he does not pursue the latter strategy in regards to his own neo-Aristotelianism.

I suggest that the major terrain of contestation in moral discourse for Christians and non-Christians alike is no longer over the degree of mutability and plasticity of human nature or philosophical attempts to provide ahistorical grounds for standards and criteria for principles and judgments. Rather the major terrain is that of contesting social analytical understandings of forms of power, wealth, status, oppression, freedom and democracy in modern societies. For these understandings are what deeply shape one's conception of human nature as well as one's formulation of ethical standards and criteria. The starting point of one's ethical reflections is always already sedimented and permeated with presuppositions of social theory, cultural perceptions and personal socialization. This acknowledgement leads neither to a vulgar sociology of knowledge in which persons are locked into social boxes unable to change or be changed nor to a crude amoralism in which morality is rejected owing to its impurity or lack of full-fledged autonomy. *Instead, a proper historicizing of ethics results in a more self-*

conscious theoretical and methodological articulation of the relations between social theory, hermeneutics and ethical reflection, including such crucial variables as the role of tradition, authority, critique and resistance.

For those of us critically aligned with and self-situated in the Christian tradition there ought to be a deep bias against prevailing forms of dogmatism, despair and oppression. Yet this bias should be followed without making criticism, mental health or liberation a fetish or idol; for such reductions of the Christian gospel result in impotent irony, shallow self-indulgence and superficial justice, respectively. Contrary to MacIntyre's interpretation of Protestant Christianity, reason, like life itself, ought to be viewed as a divine gift wrought with contradictions owing to its various forms, styles and uses. We must continually reflect upon the limits of reason, while perennially problematizing the status of our perception of those limits, if we are to remain true to the insights of Protestant Christianity.

I suggest that Christian ethical reflection upon political, cultural and socioeconomic arrangements yields two fundamental norms: individuality within community and democratic participation in the decision-making processes of those major institutions which guide and regulate our lives. We arrive at these norms neither by transcendental reflection on the nature of morality nor by historical mimicking of the liberal tradition but rather by interpreting the Christian faith in light of our present circumstances. This interpretation accents the egalitarian Christian mandate that all human creatures are made in the image of God and are thereby endowed with a certain dignity and respect which warrants a particular treatment, including a chance to fulfill their capacities and potentialities. This mandate acknowledges the social and communal character of self-fulfillment such that the development of individuality occurs within collectivities, groups and societies. Furthermore, this interpretation of the Christian faith recognizes the depravity of persons thereby requiring institutional mechanisms which check and balance various forms of power, wealth, status and influence. These mechanisms seem to work best in our world when regulated by the ideal of democracy. This ideal of democracy highlights not simply participation within a given set of structures, *but also empowerment to change the structures themselves.*

The important contribution of neo-Marixst social analysis to Christian ethical reflection is that it puts forward a social analytical viewpoint from the vantage point of those victimized by existing structures of oppression and promotes a post-liberal conception of democracy. For the Christian, neo-Marxist social analyses and moral visions are to be judged in light of the interpretation of Christian faith in our time, including the norms of individuality and democracy. To the degree to which such social analyses and visions promote these norms, Marxism is indispensable for Christian ethical practice. To the degree to which they violate these norms, neo-Marxist analyses warrant rejection. Like MacIntyre, I suggest that Marxist social analyses remain important sources of insight and illumination regarding the operations of power in modern societies; unlike

MacIntyre, I will argue that Marxism is not *completely* exhausted as a political tradition—though, like Christianity, most of its visible manifestations should be severely criticized and transformed.

This point is best seen in the case of present-day liberal and neo-conservative discourses regarding modern capitalist countries, especially the USA. I have in mind here the writings of such figures as Robert Benne, Michael Novak, Richard Neuhaus and Peter Berger. There is no doubt that the advent of capitalist modes of production—with their distinctive types of markets, opportunities and motivations for technological innovation and efficiency as well as class exploitation, domination of foreign territories and reappropriation of patriarchal and racist structures—diffused feudal forms of centralized power. This occurred principally by undercutting medieval and mercantilist regulations and controls over the market. There also should be little doubt—given the glaring economic failures and political despotisms in the command economies of marketless communist regimes—that market activities of some sort, with price mechanisms that balance supply and demand and reflect cost and use-value, are the only modern alternative to large, powerful, unaccountable bureaucratic hierarchies of full-fledged central planning. On this point, the powerful insights of major conservative thinkers such as Ludwig von Mises (1951), Friedrich Hayek (1961), and Milton Friedman (1962) should not be overlooked—though we must reject their morally repugnant laissez-faire conclusions. The central problems of liberal and neo-conservative thinkers regarding modern capitalist societies is that their claims about prevailing distinctions between economic and political power and the decentralization of power are theoretically naive and empirically weak. It is this naiveté and weakness which leads many of their critics to view their claims are mere vulgar ideology deployed to buttress the status quo.

Robert Benne's recent book, *The Ethic of Democratic Capitalism: A Moral Reassessment* (1981) is an exemplary defense of capitalist democracy. It is informed, urbane, liberal, Christian—yet theoretically naive and empirically weak. Benne brings together a version of Niebuhr's heuristic mythological interpretation of Christianity with Rawls' revisionist liberal conception of justice in a creative way. Yet his Achilles' heel is his third pillar: the refined neo-classical economics of Paul Samuelson.

For example, in defense of his claim regarding the decentralization of economic power in the USA, Benne argues that from 1899 to 1959 the national income gained by monopolistic enterprises has decreased from 17.4 percent to 11.5 percent. Relying heavily on the Warren G. Nutter and Henry Einhorn study (1969), Benne suggests that the clout of monopolies is far less than Marxist thinkers claim it to be. In response to this suggestion, I would note first, and Benne acknowledges this, that any such picture can look quite differently depending on one's definition of monopoly. Second, and more importantly, the crucial index is not earnings but holdings, not income but wealth—especially given escalating income taxes in the period studied. And when we turn to wealth and holdings, empirical studies done from various ideological persuasions concur that 0.5 percent of the population own 22 percent of the wealth, 1.0 percent own 30 percent of the wealth, including 50 percent of all corporate stock and 52 percent of the bonds.[2] These figures have remained roughly unchanged since 1945. Furthermore, as long ago as 1971, Harvard Professor William Hueller reported before the U.S. Senate Select Committee on Small Business that 111 industrial corporations with assets of a billion dollars or more had more than half of all assets employed in manufacturing and received more than half of the earnings on more than half of the sales (Galbraith 1973). So much for the decentralization thesis.

Benne goes on to argue that effective, fair and robust competition exists in the corporate sector of the American economy (no one doubts this is so in the entrepreneurial sector). His aim is to controvert the claim concerning the dominating and price-setting role of oligopolies and monopolies put forward by socialists like John Kenneth Galbraith or Marxists like Paul Sweezy. He defends this claim by invoking the neo-classical fiction—promoted by M. A. Adelman and others—that there is no necessary relation between firm size and market power—as if large corporations are not relatively large in their markets principally owing to the advantages of their size and their capacity to disproportionately influence the market.

The major empirical gap in liberal and neo-conservative analyses of modern capitalist societies is found in the central power dynamics of these societies: *the well-documented realities of corporate influence in the political and governmental processes, especially the intimate behind-the-scenes relations between the public bureaucracies of the government and major corporations.*[3] Such relations can be seen between the Department of Agriculture and agribusiness, the Department of Transportation and the automobile industries, the Federal Communications Commission and television and broadcasting networks, the Interstate Commerce Commission and the trucking industry, the Atomic Energy Commission and its supplying industries and, most notoriously, between the Department of Defense and weapons firms. These relations, often cozy ones, do not simply raise crucial questions regarding the scope and intensity of competition; they also require serious scrutiny of their relative lack of public accountability. This is so because when we closely examine the special-interest process in American government— especially the money committees of Congress such as the Senate Banking, Housing and Urban Affairs Committee, the House Banking, Finance and Urban Affairs Committee as well as the advisory committees to both the Congressional committees and public bureaucracies—we find overwhelming evidence for far-reaching corporate influence (Salamon 1975; Fenno 1973; Green, Fallows, and Zwick 1972; Hall 1969). Examples of the vast impact of oil executives on the National Petroleum Council or that of corporate polluters on the National Industrial Pollution Control Council are well known.

Even a self-proclaimed liberal political scientist such as Grant McConnell (1966) sadly concludes that the decentralization thesis of fellow liberals (and neo-conservatives) is not simply problematic, but more pointedly, faulty. He then tries to show that the collapse of the decentralisation thesis does not entail that there is a ruling class in America. Instead he holds that there is a small corporate elite that influences and controls a substantial part of the U.S. government but that it does not have full control owing to the nature and character of the presidency and Supreme Court. It is no accident that when liberals and neo-conservatives defend the autonomy of American politics from corporate influence they often invoke Presidential elections. Yet rarely do they engage in serious empirical scrutiny of the candidate-selection process (Alexander 1976; Hamilton 1972). Not only does such scrutiny reveal vast corporate influence in both parties (often the same corporation in both parties!) but also surreptitious efforts to discourage sustained policy discussion, serious political education and even sometimes voter registration. Furthermore, similar empirical studies would have to be done regarding the hidden policy-formation process—the institutional mechanisms which develop and implement general policies—that includes such powerful formations as the Council on Foreign Relations, Committee for Economic Development, Business Roundtable, Business Council, the American Assembly and the Conference Board. Attention also should be given to the crucial ideological process, especially the role of mass-media, schools, and churches in the formation and dissemination of beliefs, sentiments and viewpoints throughout the general populace (Domhoff 1970; Shoup and Minter 1977; Hunter 1959).

If the decentralization thesis is false, then liberal and neo-conservative defenses of capitalist societies in the name of democracy rest upon shaky ground. And if this is so, then their arguments must justify anti-democratic capitalist social relations and corporate domination of the economy and government on other grounds—such as efficiency, high productivity and increased standards of living. Such arguments contain a moral dimension yet lack serious moral substance; they remain within the limits of technological rationality, instrumental reason and cost-benefit analysis.

The typical strategy employed by liberals and neo-conservatives against the democratic socialist claim that workers should have some say in the decisions made at the workplace that shape their destinies is that workers' control over the productive process is not required by a substantive ideal of democracy. As Benne notes, " A person can be paid for specific services in a complex process without having a claim to control over the process (1981, 223)."

It is difficult not to view this strategy as a justification not simply for class subordination (or lack of democracy in the workplace), but also, by implication, as an argument against democratic participation per se. My concern here is not that workers should have "full control" over the process of production. Such claims about "full control" are undesirable in a fully democratic order, because non-workers should also have a say in such decisions. Rather, my point here is that the liberal and neo-conservative strategy against democratic mechanisms in the economic sphere can serve as well against democratic mechanisms in the political sphere. Such mechanisms must indeed be coordinated with considerations of efficiency, demographic difficulties and technological innovation; but they surely ought not to be prematurely precluded from the economic sphere on dogmatic ideological ground. If so, this constitutes a blow against the ideal of democracy. Furthermore, it reveals just how deep one's commitment to the ideal of democracy really is.

For the Christian thinker, the basic problem of libral and neo-conservative arguments supporting modern capitalist societies is that *their social analytical presuppositions and economic theoretical assumptions are antithetical to the Christian mandate for peoples' participation and empowerment in regard to fulfilling their unique capacities and potentialities.* This mandate can be best enacted when one adopts social analyses of power, wealth, status and influence and economic theories of production, distribution and consumption that look at the world from the situation of the"least of these"—the victims—in existing societies. Neo-Marxist analyses and theories presently are the most developed perspectives which adopt such a victim's viewpoint.

Just as I believe that the Christian faith in the modern world—given its allegiance to democracy and individuality—requires resistance to race-based and gender-based social hierarchies, so I believe that it demands opposition to class-based social hierarchies. These hierarchies undermine the God-given dignity and violate the respect due to each of God's creatures. Wholesome Christian rejection of such hierarchies must lead to some form of democratic and libertarian socialism—a socio-economic arrangement with markets, price mechanisms, an induced (not directed) labor force, a free press, formal political rights and a constitutionally-based legal order with special protections for the marginalized. Such an arrangement would consist of five major sectors: First, state-owned industries of basic producer goods, e.g., electricity networks, steel, oil, petrochemicals and financial institutions whose macroplans must be approved by an elected democratic assembly. Second, independent self-managed socialized enterprises which operate on a local scale. Third, cooperative enterprises that control their own property. Fourth, small private businesses run by self-employed entrepreneurs. And last, a large number of self-employed individuals, e.g., artists, freelance writers, plumbers, farmers.

This version of democratic and libertarian socialism—similar to those defended by distinguished economists such as Ota Sik (1976), Branko Horvat (1982), Wlodimierz Brus (1972; 1980), John Kenneth Galbraith (1973) and especially Alec Nove (1983)—is well aware of the dangers of the centralization of power and management in multi-leveled, hierarchically organized, plan bureaucracies found in marketless Communist command economies. Yet this view also recognizes existing forms of centralization in capitalist democracies—including vast corporate influence in the economy and government. It attempts to make such centralization publicly accountable, while preserving the separations of powers, countervailing forces, and checks and balances against abuses of publicly controlled centralization. This is why the fusion of limited centralized planning, socialized and private enterprises in the market with democratic political institutions is so important.

Centralization, hierarchy and markets are inescapable economic realities for modern social existence. The crucial question is how various forms of centralization, hierarchy and markets are to be understood, conceived and judged in light of Christian commitments to democracy and individuality. And, given the threat to the biosphere, non-human organisms and the planet itself, it is clear that we must rethink whether industrial modes and expansionist policies are desirable. For Christians, the desirable and feasible society—both here and abroad—should consist of a distinctive version of democratic and libertarian socialism which encourages non-racist, non-homophobic and non-sexist cultural ways of life and which incorporates ecological consciousness in its future outlook. In this way, the riches of Protestant Christianity are conjoined with the best of neo-Marxist, feminist, ecological, anti-homophobic and anti-racist perspectives.

The ideals of democracy and individuality are tenuous in our world. They are associated with risky social experiments that have a short history and heritage. The crucial issue of our time is whether this history and heritage can be extended and strengthened—can the vast human misery and suffering be lessened by democratic empowerment and libertarian constraints within societal institutions? MacIntyre says "no," weeps bitterly and retreats into his intellectual monastery. Liberals and neo-conservatives say "yes," enshrine the limited success of the American experiment and shun additional innovation and transformation, here and abroad. Democratic socialists say "maybe," but only if our understanding of and commitment to democracy and individuality are deepened. And, for Christians, such deepening has much to do with the depths of their Christian faith.

Notes

1. Note MacIntyre's rejection of Aristotle's metaphysical biology which secures and determines human development on the chain of being (1981, 183).
2. For pertinent sources see Turner and Staines (1976, 39, Table 13) and Smith and Franklin (1974).
3. The best treatment of these relations is G. William Domhoff (1978). This paragraph leans heavily on this indispensable text.

CHAPTER VI

Toward a New Social Covenant: From Commodity to Commonwealth

Douglas Sturm

In each age of the world distinguished by high activity there will be found at its culmination, and among the agencies leading to that culmination, some profound cosmological outlook, implicitly accepted, impressing its own type upon the current springs of action (Whitehead 1961, 12).

The essential point to grasp is that in dealing with capitalism we are dealing with an evolutionary process (Joseph A. Schumpeter 1950, 82).

My topic is democratic capitalism. My task is three-fold: (1) to develop a critique of democratic capitalism from an ethical perspective informed by Christianity; (2) to make explicit the grounds on which the critique is developed; and (3) to outline an acceptable alternative.

The task is as important as it is formidable. It is formidable because of the complexities of meaning associated with democracy and capitalism and because of the intricacies entailed in theological method. But it is important if, as some interpreters would have us believe, we are at a critical turning point in human history and the fate of democracy and capitalism both hang in the balance.

Franklin I. Gamwell rightly reminds us that, in considering this task, we must not forget our place in history. We are inheritors of modernity.

On its negative side, modernity began as a rejection of the central principles of medieval civilization. The ideal of Christendom came under severe attack. The age of faith was repudiated as a time of simple credulity and naive faith. Religion, at least in its traditional forms, has thus become a problem for the modern mind.

On its positive side, modernity affirms the principle of autonomy and has given rise to kinds of thought and practice that, it is alleged, honor that principle. In social practice, autonomy as the liberty of individuals to act as they please is the principle customarily invoked to justify capitalism and democracy. In intellectual pursuits, autonomy as the unfettering of the mind to see and to think for itself is the central interest underlying the inductive method in modern science and the development of empirical and rational methods in modern philosophy.

Given that simplified version of modernity, a religious critique of democratic capitalism may seem quaint, possessing the character of a belated counterreformation. But it may not be so quaint after all. It may be that a religious critique is a way of honoring modernity through the projection of the possibility, if not the need, for a new epoch in social and cultural history, a post-modern epoch whose forms of thought and practice will more fully realize the principle of autonomy than those of the past three hundred years. In this respect, we have much to learn from the impetus of liberation theologies, for they have been inspired, out of profoundly religious motivation, to uncover those hypocrisies of modern thought and practice which, claiming the principle of autonomy, perpetuate structures of domination.

Faith as untested belief and sheer confessionalism is at odds with the modern mind's commitment to autonomy and devotion to critical analysis. But faith as appreciative awareness, as openness of the human spirit to the most fundamental realities of experience, even to the life of God, deepens the probings of critique and lends to it the possibility of transformative insight. To paraphrase Bernard Meland, faith as appreciative awareness provides a condition of human response to the world in which something creative can happen to our total nature such that our habits of response can be transformed. Under these circumstances, even the criteria we envisage as being designative of the good may undergo radical change (Meland 1953, 124).

Against that background, I shall advance three theses for consideration: first, that, particularly at this point in the world's history, the common good is the first virtue of social institutions; second, that capitalism and democracy, although long associated historically, are in tension with each other; and third, that social democracy is an alternative institutional form more directly ordained to the common good than what has been traditionally called democratic capitalism. In developing the first thesis, I shall suggest that social interpretation and social ethics are, in their deepest dimension, ontological or cosmological. That is, they at least presuppose and sometimes deliberately articulate a vision of the world and they portray human agency as an expression of that world. In presenting the second thesis, I shall distinguish two interpretations of capitalism, orthodox and heterodox, and two sides of democracy, protective and participative. The tension between capitalism and democracy is evident even in instances where they seem most compatible. In stating the third thesis, I shall urge the need for a new social covenant in which concern for economic growth and distribution, while not ignored, is subordinate to the interests of commonwealth. In Gamwell's language, within this social arrangement, the public regarding association is preeminent.

I

God, desiring not only that the human race might be able by their similarity of nature to associate with one another, but also that they might be bound together in harmony and peace by the ties of relationship, was pleased to derive all persons from one individual (Augustine 1950, XIV, 1).

Franklin I. Gamwell annunciates that "the peculiar task of religious ethics is to defend on humanistic grounds a comprehensive principle of evaluation, where 'comprehensive' is used in the strictest sense to mean a principle in terms of which the worth and importance of all things may be assessed." Two criteria are indicated by this statement and its context in Gamwell's essay. First, comprehensiveness is a criterion specifying the religiousness of an ethics. Second, defense of an ethics on humanistic grounds is a criterion, though perhaps not the only criterion, of the adequacy of an ethics, whether religious or not. On the basis of the second criterion, Gamwell is critical of the economic ethics found in recent studies by Philip Wogaman and Robert Benne. In his determination, they justify their evaluative judgments by a heteronomous, therefore non-humanistic, appeal to typical convictions of Christian faith without concern to show whether or how those convictions might otherwise be valid. Their judgments may be religious (if they are comprehensive) but they are inadequate unless and until they satisfy the criterion of credibility.

While the criteria Gamwell declares are onerous, I intend to suggest that the common good is a principle of religious ethics which, while having roots deeply within the tradition of Christian faith, is justifiable on humanistic grounds. On the one hand, the common good is a principle which, while applying with particular force to social practices, is a measure for assessing "the worth and importance of all things." Moreover, the common good is a humanistic principle because it is expressive of the meaning of being a self within the world.

I begin with an examination of the meaning of "social practice," remembering that our topic, democratic capitalism, is a kind of social practice. In ordinary life, we engage in many social practices ranging from conversations and professional conferences to economic exchange and war. Some social practices are occasional and casual, such as in the greeting of a stranger. Others are periodic and, by intent, transformative, as in religious ritual. Still others are constant in their presence and far-reaching in consequence, as in the political and technological systems of the modern world.

But the idea of a social practice, which may seem obvious on the surface, is a matter of controversy. On one level the issue is methodological. What, the question is asked, constitutes the fundamental unit of social analysis? But the controversy is more than methodological. Methodologies are not divorceable from other aspects of social analysis and interpretation. They bear with them normative implications and ontological presuppositions. Thus, at another level, the controversy bears on the subject of social ethics. How the methodological question is resolved sets the conditions for determining what kinds of principles of social ethics are appropriate. And at still another level, the controversy is cosmological; it is a contention over the character of the kind of world within which practice takes place. To understand the point, one might consider Aristotle, Hobbes and Marx in a round-table discussion over the meaning of social practice. The interplay in social analysis of questions of method, ethics and cosmology would, I suspect, be evident in the discussion.

Among parties to the controversy, three positions are dominant: organic, individualist, and relational. Each position conveys something of importance about the character of experience which explains its persuasiveness, but the third, I suggest, is the most adequate in its comprehension of the conditions as well as the problems of human existence.

Within the framework of the organic position, a social practice has the character of a whole, a totality. The social practice is itself the unit of social analysis. Those who enact the practice are its members. Their identity is a function of the inner world of the practice itself. From this perspective, loyalty as devotion to the group and as willingness to perform one's role in its life is a primary virtue. Within local circumstances, the bonds of kinship and the compulsions of family are evidence of the sense of this position. Class consciousness and the urge to press for class interests manifest the strength of an organic understanding of social practice. So do the strong pull of ethnic and racial ties and the mysterious attractions of nationalism. We do seem, at certain times and under certain circumstances, to give credence to the idea of social totalities.

The opposite to the organic approach is the individualistic. According to methodological individualism, only individuals think, feel, and act. Nations and states, classes and ethnic groups are but collective concepts or metaphorical constructs. Such normative ideas as the public interest, the general welfare, the common good are mystical nonsense. As Murray N. Rothbard remarks,

> All these concepts rest on the implicit premise that there exists, somewhere, a living organic entity known as "society," "the group," "the public," "the community," and that that entity has values and pursues ends. Not only are these terms held up as living entities; they are supposed to exist *more* fundamentally than do mere individuals (Rothbard 1979, 15).

But, insists Rothbard, there are no such entities. The fundamental axiom of social analysis is that only individuals exist, only individuals possess consciousness, only individuals have values and desires. This axiom is not without roots in human experience, for indeed experience is always that of a subject, even if the fact of subjectivity cannot without further argument be transmuted into a theory of subjectivism. Individuals, not classes or groups, suffer and wonder why, have desires and yearn for their satisfaction. But individuals conflict with each other, creating a problem of adjudication. From this perspective, the task of ethics lies in the resolution of conflicts whether through principles of utility maximization or distributive justice.

The third position is more complex, but more complete in its reflection of the relational character of our experience. In social theory, the position is represented in Anthony Giddens' concept of structuration which he intends to articulate the point of creative integration between the agency of individuals and the structures of society (Giddens 1979, 49-96). Agents are individuals, but they are not individuals in total isolation from each other. They inherit and they enact social practices. In their identity, they are constituted out of long traditions of understanding and sensibility. In their actions, they reproduce, in some form, a world of social practices. A social practice is a complicated mixture of several structural features. It is a shared knowledge by means of which agents explain their actions to each other and to outsiders. It is a set of expectations, of principles and purposes, through which agents assess what is desirable and correct and justify their responses when forced to do so. It is a structure of power, which both constrains and facilitates. That is, given an asymmetry in the distribution of power throughout a practice, its organized resources are structures of domination and limitation. But, at the same time, they are structures of transformative possibility. Giddens' concept of structuration thus affirms that agents are individuals, but in their agency they draw together, more or less intentionally and creatively, understandings, norms, and resources of social structure. As they do so, they set the conditions for all future agency. The focus for social analysis, from this perspective, is not the social totality as such. Nor is it the individual as such. It is the manner in which agents can and do bear forward through their action the features of social structure.

On the ontological (and theological) level, this position is represented in Bernard Meland's principle of internal relations according to which there is a depth within our experience that connects all we are as unique individuals with all existent events and, ultimately, God, "that sensitive nature within the vast context of nature, winning the creative passage for qualitative attainment" (Meland 1953, 111-112). It is also represented in Philip Hefner's ontology of belonging which formulates the sense of

(1) our belonging to our fellow human beings, across all barriers—racial, sexual, economic, geographical, national, and age; (2) our belonging to the ecosystem of which we are a part, the natural environment which is the womb of our emergence and the support system for everything human; and (3) our belonging to the matrix of evolutionary development out of which our total ecosystem has unfolded (Hefner 1976, 162).

In moral philosophy, the third position is stated in a limited way in Michael J. Sandel's critique of John Rawls' theory of justice as neglecting, save in so far as Rawls presupposes it unknowingly, an understanding of community as basically constitutive of the meaning of selfhood. We live, Sandel asserts, as encumbered selves. To be a self is to be in relation, to have loyalties and allegiances, responsibilities and associations which, taken altogether, enter into our individuality. This means that at least "to some I owe more than justice requires or even permits, not by reason of agreements I have made but instead in virtue of those more or less enduring attachments and commitments which taken together partly define the person I am" (Sandel 1982, 179). Sandel invokes friendship as an elementary case of what he intends, but he refers as well to family, tribe, city, class, nation, people. If Sandel is correct, the first virtue of social institutions is not, as Rawls contends, distributive justice (Rawls 1971, 3). It is the good of the community. The good of the community is a version of what Alasdair MacIntyre calls an "internal good" (MacIntyre 1981, 175-189), that is, a good that is realized only in a practice but that is for all those who participate in that practice. MacIntyre cites the instance of chessplaying.

Relying on Meland's principle of internal relations, I would violate the strictures MacIntyre has placed on the concept to suggest we consider our entire life a practice in which all entities are engaged. This is the sense of Roberto Unger's theory of the self as consisting in a wide-ranging set of relationships to nature, to other persons, and to one's own work and station (Unger 1975, 191-235). The self is separate from these three worlds, yet engaged in them. The dynamic interplay between separation and engagement is, in effect, the generic practice of being human. The ethical problem is to determine what quality of relationship will redound to the good of all parties in it and therefore to the good of the self.

The traditional language for this ethical concern is the common good. The traditional locus of its responsibility, as Gamwell has reminded us, is the political association, for the function of the political association is to concern itself directly and deliberately with the quality of relationships throughout the community as a whole. What I am proposing therefore is that a relational approach to social analysis conjoined with a principle of internal relations implies that the common good is the first virtue of social institutions and that the public-regarding association has priority over those which are private.

What, then, is the common good? In focus, it is the goodness *of* the community, but it is a goodness *for* all its participants. Thus it is common in a double sense. As Jacques Maritain expresses it,

> The common good of the city is neither the mere collection of private goods, nor the proper good of the whole which like . . . the hive with respect to its bees, relates the parts to itself alone and sacrifices them to itself. It is the good *human* life of the multitude . . .; it is their communion in good living. It is therefore common to both *the whole and the parts* into which it flows back and which, in turn, must benefit from it (Maritain 1947, 40-41; italics in original).

In scope, the common good is local and global. Again, in Maritain's words,

> The common good in our day is certainly not just the common good of the nation and has not yet succeeded in becoming the common good of the civilized world community. It tends, however, unmistakably towards the latter. For this reason, it would seem appropriate to consider the common good of a state or nation as merely an area, among many similar areas, in which the common good of the whole civilized society achieves greater density (Maritain 1947, 45; see also 1951.)

In content, the common good is procedural and substantive. The procedures through which a community sets its policies and conducts its work are not merely instrumental. In a significant manner, they constitute the quality of the community. Procedures are ways of living together through time. As a community endures, but changes, its basic character is manifest in large part in the structure of its public forum. Procedures are marked by varying degrees of openness and exclusion, access and denial, participation and domination. Precisely because a common good is intended as common, its procedural features are those of openness, access, participation. Absent those features, the common good can be but deficiently present.

On its substantive side, the common good is more readily specifiable by negative instance than by affirmative criteria: the rapid deterioration of the environment, the depth and extent of poverty throughout the world, the persistence of discriminatory patterns against whole classes of persons, the escalating threat of nuclear holocaust, the stifling of free expression of the artistic impulse in ways direct and indirect. But negative instances are the reverse side of affirmative principles: in the material dimension, physical well-being; in the economic dimension, meaningful work; in the social dimension, civic friendship; in international relations, peaceful modes of conflict resolution; in the dimension of the human spirit, creative openness. I do not mean this as an exhaustive definition of the substantive content of the common good, but as an indication of its qualitative meaning.

Because of the nature of the self as relational, the common good, so construed, is not only the first virtue of social institutions. It is requisite to the flourishing of the individual and is an expression of the deepest meaning of freedom in what Gamwell has called its material sense.

II

A Great Society has nothing to do with, and is in fact irreconcilable with 'solidarity' in the true sense of unitedness in the pursuit of known common goals (Friedrich A. Hayek 1976, 111).

Democracy is not founded merely on the right or the private interest of the individual. This is only one side of the shield. It is founded equally on the function of the individual as a member of the community. It founds the common good upon the common will, in forming which it bids every grown-up, intelligent person to take a part (L. T. Hobhouse 1964, 115).

The second thesis I would advance is that capitalism and democracy are in tension with each other.

In their modern manifestations, capitalism and democracy have been associated together as part of the emergence of the modern world. As modern science and philosophy broke through the dogmatisms of medieval theology, so modern economic and political systems shattered the strictures of medieval society. All these movements bore the promise of a new age in which freedom—freedom of thought and freedom of action—was the centerpiece. Capitalism and democracy, in particular, even where these exact terms were not employed to refer to the movements, were expressions of a new class of persons, the bourgeoisie, coming into a place of prominence. Thus capitalism and democracy would seem to belong together as social practices promoted by the new class as instruments for the realization of liberty. That association of movements and ideals has long been a fixture, at least in the American mind. Joyce Appleby discerns it as central to the republican vision of the Jeffersonians in the late eighteenth century

(Appleby 1984). In a radically different version, Louis Hartz identifies it as underlying the interests of the New Whigs in the middle of the nineteenth century (Hartz 1955). And it is a position espoused by Michael Novak (1982b) and Robert Benne (1981) at the present time.

But however accurate the historical thesis in some sense or other, it begs an important but extraordinarily difficult question of interpretation. How are capitalism and democracy to be identified? The possibilities in the case of capitalism, for instance, range from the axiomatic approach of Ludwig von Mises (1960) to the massive historical studies of Immanuel Wallerstein (1976; 1980; 1983). The resultant differences are striking.

For purposes of this project, I would contrast two understandings of capitalism, one more orthodox, the other more heterodox. For the former, I rely on Adam Smith and Friedrich Hayek. Adam Smith, to my knowledge, never used the word "capitalism," but his treatise on *The Wealth of Nations* is properly considered a classic statement of its meaning. Smith was impressed by the emergence in the modern world of a new form of organizing human relations, the commercial society, a system, in his judgment, of perfect liberty. The central institution of commercial society is the market, the genius of which is that, if unconstrained, it will produce out of the self-interested actions of a myriad of persons a social order of benefit to all. Moreover, through it, the wealth of the nation, that is, the annual flow of its goods and services, will increase. As Hayek depicts the central idea of the system, "The chief cause of [its] wealth-creating character . . . is that the returns of the efforts of each player act as the signs which enable him to contribute to the satisfaction of needs of which he does not know, and to do so by taking advantage of conditions of which he also learns only indirectly through their being reflected in the prices of the factors of production which they use" (Hayek 1976, 115). Resource allocation, capital investment, consignment and division of labor, distribution of products are all questions to be determined by the concerns and pressures of the marketplace. Political interference is held undesirable as infringing on the liberty of individuals to act as they please and as, most likely, resulting in an inefficient allocation of capital. Government is thus limited to a supportive and supplementary role, e.g., protecting infant industries and providing a national defense.

The idea of a self-regulative social mechanism possessed of an inherent drive toward economic growth and efficiency and oriented toward an equilibrium between supply and demand and between cost and price is an elegant conception, however faulty may be its realization in practice. At its heart, it is an individualistic conception in which questions of moral purpose and the exercise of social power are taken as essentially private. Capitalism is pluralistic or, more bluntly, agnostic about the ends of human life. Hayek states this with characteristic clarity.

> Many people regard it as revolting that the Great Society [i.e., the market society] has no common concrete purposes or, as we may say, that it is merely means-connected and not ends-connected. It is indeed true that the chief common purpose of all its members is

the purely instrumental one of securing the formation of an abstract order which has no specific purposes but will enhance for all the prospects of achieving their respective purposes (Hayek 1976, 110).

From the standpoint of the market, depending on the structure of demands placed upon it at any given time, pushpin is as good as poetry (Jeremy Bentham) and cavier as tasty as carrion (Lionel Robbins). The market is in itself a neutral instrument whose sole governing function is the maximization of utility.

From a more heterodox perspective, however, capitalism, discerned historically and contextually, shows a distinctively different kind of face. It is not simply a benign mechanism for increasing the wealth of nations. To some, capitalism is a total culture—rationalistic, atomistic, ahistorical, quantitative in character—that comprises a threat to traditional societies and, more generally, to those ties of social cohesion that hold human civilization together. So Bruno Hildebrand in the 19th century (1848), and George F. Will (1983) in ours.

From a different angle, Joseph Schumpeter (1950) argues that capitalism is an evolutionary reality, expressive originally of the interests of the commercial and industrial bourgeoisie, but driven by the forces of its own success to its transformation and, ultimately, to its demise. The competitive marketplace has become an oligopolistic system. The entrepreneurial function has given way to the managerial role. Older meanings of property and contract, essential to the market system, have become essentially different kinds of legal relationships. The values and motivational drive of the early bourgeoisie are replaced by a consumer mentality (see Bell 1976).

Within the Marxian tradition, as well, capitalism is viewed historically, but governed in its transmutations by internal tensions and contradictions. All history at least heretofore consists in class struggles. According to Marx, in capitalism as a form of production, the struggle is between those who control the means of production and those whose labor power, secured through contract, produce the results. Marx, particularly in his earlier writings, designated the structure of this relationship as alienation. That is, in Bertell Ollman's compact summary:

> Persons are separated from their work (they play no part in deciding what to do or how to do it)—a break between person and life activity. Persons are separated from their products (they have no control over what they make or what becomes of it)—a break between person and material world. Persons are separated from their fellows (competition and class hostility have rendered most forms of cooperation impossible)—a break between person and person. In each instance, a relation that distinguishes the human species has disappeared and its constituent elements have been reorganized to appear as something else (Ollman 1976, 133-124).

Moreover, according to Immanuel Wallerstein, a contemporary socialist historian, capitalism is a movement driven toward self-expansion, toward the endless accumulation of wealth, resulting in the "commodification of everything"

(1983, 13-43). The movement has become a global system, involving an intricate division of labor functionally and geographically. The consequence is a complex commodity chain in which not all exchanges are equal as between classes or geographical zones. In the struggle among groups for benefits, the state is, as it always has been, despite orthodox capitalist doctrine, a critical factor of control and distribution. Furthermore, capitalism is linked inextricably with a scientific and technological culture which it advances throughout the world.

We must acknowledge that both orthodox and heterodox interpretations purport to be describing the meaning of capitalism. They are both, by intention, concerned to specify its identity. But the differences are appreciable. At some points they are irreconcilable: the character of exchange relations (are parties to exchange in a strictly capitalist system by definition equal or is there an inherent tendency toward patterns of domination?); the status of labor (is labor genuinely free in its contractual relations or forced ineluctably into a condition of alienation?); the role of the state (is the function of the state peripheral or critical?); the quality of capitalist culture (is the market culturally neutral or does it propagate an instrumentalist, technologist morality?)

These variances are not merely empirical. They are rooted in divergent understandings of the world and methods of social analysis. But for purposes of the second thesis, it is sufficient to note that at one important point, orthodox and heterodox perspectives seem to converge, a point at which capitalism is in tension with democracy. According to both, capitalism is a kind of social system in which the principle of private governance is preeminent. Capitalism is not simply a synonym for market. Markets of various sorts and sizes may exist, even be encouraged, in a wide range of social systems (see Lange, 1938). But, from the orthodox perspective, a capitalist society is governed dominantly (in the strictest sense of that term as lordship) by the interplay of private interests and the result, if there are no artificial constraints, is a spontaneous order which Hayek calls the "Great Society." The role of the political association is supportive (it enforces basic laws of the system) and supplementary (it remedies occasional defects and failures), but clearly secondary. From the heterodox perspective as well, capitalism is viewed as a social order governed by private interests, but in the sense that, at its foundation, capitalism rests on private control of the means of production. In a classical formulation out of the socialist tradition by Marx and Engels, "modern bourgeois private property is the final and most complete expression of the system of producing and appropriating products, that is based on class antagonisms, on the exploitation of the many by the few" (1978). Thus from both perspectives, capitalism intends a principle of private governance, which, in turn, means it intends that the political association shall not be supreme. On this issue, the central idea of democracy diverges. At stake is the question of authority. Most simply put, democracy means a people as such shall have authority for the quality of its own life as a people.

Within the history of political thought from ancient times to the present, there is an extensive range of theories of democracy. Even within the modern period, the spectrum runs from the direct congregationalist democracy of those whom A. D. Lindsay calls the "Puritans of the Left" (1943, 117-121) to Joseph Schumpeter's influential theory of democracy as competitive leadership (1950, 269-284) and Robert Dahl's polyarchy (1956). At times the theories are constructed out of special concern. Schumpeter, for instance, ponders whether democracy and socialism are compatible. And Dahl intends a theory susceptible to techniques of empirical research.

For the purpose of pursuing the current project, I suggest that there are two sides to the meaning of democracy and that understandings of democracy differ according to which side is conceived as primary. The two sides are the protective and the participative. In protective democracy, participation is secondary to protection. In participative democracy, protection is secondary to participation. These two versions of democracy parallel Gamwell's distinction between established political liberalism and reformed liberalism.

Modern democracy, it is customarily argued, began with the bourgeois revolutions in England, America, and France. In each instance, tyranny was identified as the enemy and liberty exalted as the cause. The differences among these three revolutions and their resultant forms of democracy are of utmost significance and can be discerned even yet in their respective styles of political life. But in one pertinent respect at least they are alike. In Lindsay's words, "Democratic theory in its modern beginnings reflected a society in which men thought it more important to say what the state should not do than to say what it should do. The main emphasis of this early theory is negative" (1943, 116). Democracy was, in a sense, anti-governmental, but, in this context, government meant, first of all, the monarch and therefore the prospects of trampling on the rights and expectations of the people, or at least the class of people most interested at the time with acquiring the facilities and resources for pursuing their own life in their own way. At this juncture, the bourgeoisie, struggling against the constraints of mercantilism, found common interest with republicanism (which we nowadays, without attention to the niceties of differentiation, tend to call democracy). New forms of political association were thus concocted for protective or defensive purposes.

In the tradition of John Locke, for instance, rights were annunciated, the rights of life, liberty, and property, or, in Jefferson's amended version, life, liberty, and the pursuit of happiness. Rights were understood as claims against a government. Congress shall make no law, it was declared, prohibiting freedom of speech or the right of the people peaceably to assemble. Rights constituted a preserve for the freedom of the citizenry. In the tradition of James Madison, on the other hand, institutional restraints were designed out of the shrewd observation that tyranny is a disease not reserved for monarchs. It may infect popular government as well. The remedy is structural: separation of powers, checks and balances, dispersal of rule throughout the governing system, a multiplicity of factions.

To comprehend the full implications of this version of democracy in principle (granting the miserable character of its historical record in practice), we must distinguish its purpose, procedures, and presupposition. Its purpose is protective, to negate whatever forces threaten the privately determined life activity of the citizenry. Its procedures—its legally defined rights and its institutional arrangements—are designed to promote that purpose. At this point, democracy is individualistic. But the procedures have another, more positive side. They are means for participating in the public forum. Rights enable persons to speak and to act. Institutions, especially where their functions and powers are divided, facilitate access to the formulation of policy. Participation may be for purposes of protection, but at the procedural level it is, as well, a form of cooperation with others in the conduct of public business and, more importantly, it articulates a basic presupposition of the entire system: consent.

Procedures constitute a method of consent (see Gewirth 1962), but consent itself is the primordial act of forming a public. It is the determination to live together, to share in a common destiny, to form a common life. Consent, however difficult it may be to construe what precisely that means theoretically or practically, is the beginning of a people. In that sense, it is the deepest authority of social existence. But what is authorized out of consent may be unauthorized. This is the reason for affirming that, within democracy, even of the protective kind, a people as such has authority for the quality of its own life as a people. What the people form for the sake of their living together, they may, with whatever wisdom they possess, reform or transform. There is thus a tension between democracy, which rests on a principle of consent, and capitalism, which intends a principle of private governance, even though, given the purpose of a protective democracy, a market system may be widely supported and encouraged within the economic realm.

The tension is more evident and more acute between capitalism and the version of democracy in which protection is secondary to participation. Where protective democracy, traditionally called "liberal democracy," serves a negative function, the role of participative democracy is affirmative. Moreover, where protective democracy is predominantly solicitous of the individual, participative democracy, more sensitive to the meaning of its grounding in consent, is concerned with the texture of relationship between personal and community life. This concern is the point of Eduard Heimann's affirmation that "The meaning of democracy lies in the liberty and dignity of the person and the community; or one may say that it lies in their dignity, which includes their liberty" (1961, 283). It is also the intent of Lindsay's statement that, "The function of the state . . . is to serve the community and in that service to make it more of a community" (1943, 245). But it is more amply depicted in John Dewey's formulation of "the nature of the democratic idea in its generic social sense":

> The idea of democracy is a wider and fuller idea than can be exemplified in the state even at its best. To be realized it must affect all modes of human association, the family, the school, industry, religion. From the standpoint of the individual, it consists in having a responsible share according to capacity in forming and directing the activities of the groups

to which one belongs and in participating according to need in the values which the groups sustain. From the standpoint of the groups, it demands liberation of the potentialities of members of a group in harmony with the interests and goods which are common (1954, 143, 147).

Participation, from this perspective, is not merely a procedure for conducting affairs or for protecting one's private interests. It is, more profoundly, expressive of the meaning of being a self within a community of selves. It is a good to be cherished, as exclusionary policies and practices demonstrate by contrast. But, the extension and deepening of democratic processes within a community require that the community through its public forum take deliberate control over its resources in a manner not to be expected in a system controlled by the capitalist principle.

The idea of participative democracy lies behind the complaint of those who insist that the traditional rights associated with democracy—rights of speaking, organizing, voting—are only formal without the economic and cultural conditions for their effective expression. As Joshua Cohen and Joel Rogers remark, "Both an unemployed worker and a millionaire owner of a major television station enjoy the same formal right of free speech, but their power to express and give expression to that right are radically different" (1983, 50-51). The idea of participative democracy also lies behind G. D. H. Cole's complaint that

the answer that most people would give to the question 'what is the fundamental evil in our modern society?' would be the wrong one: 'they would answer POVERTY when they ought to answer SLAVERY', The millions who had been given the franchise, who had formally been given the means to self-government had in fact been 'trained to subservience' and this training had largely taken place during the course of their daily occupation. Cole argued that 'the industrial system . . . is in great measure the key to the paradox of political democracy. Why are the many nominally supreme but actually powerless? Largely because the circumstances of their lives do not accustom or fit them for power or responsibility. A servile system in industry inevitably reflects itself in political servility' (Pateman 1970, 38).

In both its versions, democracy means a people as such has authority for the character of its own life as a people. On that point alone, there is tension between democracy and capitalism, for one is fundamentally a principle of public governance, while the other is a principle of private control. But the tension is exacerbated in participative democracy because, since the basic questions of economic life—the allocation of investment, the organization of production, the distribution of wealth—bear directly on the quality of the life of a people as a whole, such questions are considered matters appropriate for public determination.

III

This interrelation of agents, which makes the freedom of all members of a society depend upon the intentions of each, is the ground of morality . . . If we call the harmonious interrelation of agents their 'community' we may say that a morally right action is an action which intends community. . . . If the world is one action, any particular action determines the future, within its own limits, for all agents. Every individual agent is therefore responsible to all other agents for his actions (John MacMurray 1961, 118-119).

To this point, I have proposed that the common good is the first virtue of social institutions and that capitalism and democracy as basic principles of social order are in tension with each other. The third thesis I would advance is that social democracy (an alternative expression for participative democracy) is more directly ordained to the common good than what has traditionally been called democratic capitalism.

Democracy (of the protective kind) and capitalism (understood in the orthodox way) are born in the modern world as parties of a general movement of liberation. The breakthrough of democracy is the effort of a people, or some classes of people, to gain control over their own lives. Civil liberty is among its primary concerns, the liberty to think, to speak, to act as one pleases. The emergence of capitalism is the effort to remove the limitations of restrictive legislation. Free contract is among its dominant interests, the right to associate, to negotiate, and to bargain as one wishes. Both are expressions in social practice of modernity's turn toward the subject. Sights are shifted from the heavens above to the earth beneath, from ultimate destiny to immediate circumstance, from final causes to what works. The shift is toward a world in which the solitary human agent, the subject, is central. Tradition is abjured as the dead hand of the past. Each of us, born as a *tabula rasa*, must ponder: what do *I* think, what shall *I* do, and what do *I* want? Democracy and capitalism are thus linked, granting the basic tension between them, in their avowed respect for individuality. Democracy promises an institutional context protective of open and free thought and action. Capitalism promises a system through which the wants of individuals, whatever they may be, can be satisfied.

The promises are attractive to anyone sensitive to the dignity of individual life. But for that very reason, the promises are easily transmuted into ideological explanations of practices that belie their stated intent and appropriately provoke a hermeneutics of suspicion. It does not take a Marxist to discern that the language of modernity in general and of democratic capitalism in particular has been persistently used to justify institutions of domination. To cite but one prominent example, racism, in its various versions, has accompanied modernity from its beginnings to the present and has been built into its institutional forms, all of which have been justified in the name of freedom. Significantly, the mitigation of racism, where it has occurred, is attributable neither to capitalism (within which, it has been argued, racism is functional [Wallerstein 1983, ch. 2]) nor to liberal democracy (which treats such matters with benign neglect), but to a political struggle in which democracy is transformed into an agent of and for participation.

While charges of ideological confusion may be dismissed with the maxim, *abusus non tollit usus* (abuse does not eliminate use), they must not be dismissed too quickly for the confusion may be symptomatic of a flaw in the practices themselves, their structure or their theory. Thus, for instance, liberal democracy may be unable to honor its ultimate intention of protecting the liberty of the individual without an affirmative move toward the extension and deepening of the rights it professes to honor, in which case liberal democracy must make a move on the way toward social democracy. On the other hand, capitalism may be unable to support a thoroughgoing market system without an aggressive means of assuring the equality of all parties to all contracts, in which case capitalism must engage in the kind of intervention into the distribution of power and resources it abhors. In sum, to honor its own promises, democratic capitalism, understood as the historical conjunction of liberal democracy and capitalism in its orthodox interpretation, must be prepared to transform itself in the direction of the common good but away from capitalism's principle of private governance and liberal democracy's negative orientation.

Moreover, one must pose, at this point, a question of historical interpretation. The structures of social life change over time. While change may be relatively imperceptible to those engaged in it, there are moments of radical transition, of passage from an old world to a new. It is a matter of settled judgment, for instance, that the forms of life we distinguish as medieval and modern are appreciably unlike each other though the transmutation may have been gradual. Now, during recent decades, some interpreters claim to discern signs of a new epoch, a post-modern age, emerging, not in all cases one they cherish (e.g. Heilbroner 1976, Unger 1975, Habermas 1975, Bell 1976). Granting the methodological problem of determining the point at which an epochal change has been effected, the evidence of structural transformation in the life of peoples over the past two hundred years at least in the Western world is compelling.

The industrial revolution transformed methods of production and the social relations of those engaged in the productive process. The allied movement of urbanization shifted the center of life for most of the population from village to megalopolis. Continuous developments in technology introduced both gigantic alterations in means of production and shifts in the expectations and character of daily life. The automobile, for instance, completely altered residential patterns and cultural sensibilities. Furthermore, it simultaneously enhanced the private life of individuals and increased their dependency in extensive ways on the organized economic and political life of the nation.

The emergence of the large corporation in the 19th century and its developments in the 20th century (the managerial revolution, diversification of holdings, globalization of operations) have, among other things, complicated structures in the division of labor, changed the distribution of organizational power in society, and completely reversed patterns of work from self-employment to employment in a productive process controlled by others. The effects of periodic business cycles, culminating dramatically in the Great Depression, demonstrated convincingly the national, if not the global, scope of economic interconnections. The nation-state system, with its militaristic propensities and its increasing reliance on developments in military technology particularly beginning with World War I, has promoted the formation of a military-industrial complex.

Struggles by the working class during the 19th and 20th centuries to improve working conditions led to organized labor as an important economic and political power in the social order.

In short, the actual structure of economic production and distribution in the Western world, throughout the globe, is a far cry from Jefferson's "vision of a free society of independent men prospering through an expansive commerce in farm commodities" (Appleby 1984, ix) or Adam Smith's pin factory (Smith 1937). We are enmeshed in a complicated "material web of interdependence" (Winter 1970). Even if ours is not yet strictly a new epoch, it would seem an anachronism to equate the prevailing structure of our political economy with either Smith's capitalism or Jefferson's democracy.

More importantly, a range of public policies has been instituted in America over the past century which, taken together, manifest a move away from the capitalist principle of private governance toward social democracy. My concern is less with the detailed administrative arrangements of the policies which may be altered from time to time than with the principles they are intended to effect. Principles of public regulation (the Food and Drug Administration, Federal Trade Commission), workmen's compensation, collective bargaining, public employment, social insurance, national economic accounting and control (e.g. the Unemployment Act of 1946), equal employment opportunity, and environmental protection are all part of a limited but remarkable tradition demonstrating the felt need of a people through its public forum to gain some degree of deliberate control over the quality of its life as a people. They represent an affirmative effort to extend the rights of citizens beyond those of liberal democracy and to expand the participation of citizens in the control of their common life beyond the matter of voting in elections. Their overall concern I would argue is with the quality of the community as a whole, that is, with the common good. They represent the judgment that at least in present social circumstances, democratic capitalism as traditionally understood is less able to secure the common good than social democracy.

However, at its deepest level, the difference between democratic capitalism (in its traditional sense) and social democracy lies in their respective understandings of self and world. That issue is at the heart of all social thought. In the relationships between self and world, there are three possibilities. First, the self exists for the sake of the world, whether the world of nation or race or class. This understanding is characteristic of political romanticism (see Tillich 1977, Part One) and of the historical school of economics (see Hildebrand 1848).

Second, the world exists for the sake of the self. This position, I would contend, underlies liberal democracy, orthodox capitalism, and their historical conjunction. The intent of democratic capitalism is to construct institutional conditions conducive to satisfying the interests and life plans of separate selves. These interests and life plans may have nothing to do with each other, but that does not matter. What matters is to design arrangements enabling persons to get on with their lives, whatever they may be, with as little conflict as possible. Within this broad tradition, diverse ethical principles have been constructed to deal with questions of resolving conflict: from Locke's natural rights theory and Bentham's concept of utility maximization to Rawls's two principles of justice and Nozick's entitlement theory. Differences among these principles should not be ignored, but neither should their convergence. All are anthropocentric; all are individualistic; all are agnostic about ends. Underlying all is a view of the world as resource, but as in itself purposeless and senseless.

In the third possibility, self and world exist for each other. The self is not first of all subject or consumer, but friend, neighbor, citizen. Friendship is, in the relation between persons, a goodness in itself: "It gives us an experiential taste of that wholeness to which as persons we are called" (Johann 1966, 46). Friendship is an analogue for neighborhood, civil society, even cosmopolis (see Moltmann 1977, 114-121, 314-317). The ethical expression of this understanding of self and world is the common good. As we have already noted, the common good is a quality of community life composed of two interpenetrating dimensions. Procedurally, it means participating in the deliberations and decisions of a community by its members. Substantively, it embraces several qualities—in material life, physical well-being; in social life, civic friendship; in group relations, peaceable means of interaction; in cultural life, an open spirit— whatever, that is, conduces to the enhancement of the life of its members. The reverse side of the common good is alienation. This is the sense of G. D. H. Cole's exclamation that the fundamental evil of modern society is not poverty as such, but slavery. It is also the sense of Gustavo Gutierrez's designation of dependency or domination as the primary social problem in the Third World and his projection of liberation as the immediate aim and solidarity as the governing purpose of political and economic action (1973).

The institutional implication of the common good, at least at this point in history, is, I would suggest, social democracy. Social democracy, as I have construed it, means the extension of the democratic principle, the principle of public determination, into all modes of social life, including the economic. It means therefore incorporating public determination into the functions of allocating investment, organizing production, and distributing wealth with the governing intention of enhancing the quality of relationships throughout the community of life. It does not mean that markets are inappropriate mechanisms within the economy or that no forms of administrative control are ever acceptable. But it does require explicit structures of public accountability and control. And it does require explicit attention to the governing intention and specific consequences of programs and policies. Among recent proposals for the transformation of the political economy which, while taking account of historical reality, its limitations and possibilities, at least approximate the idea of social democracy, I would cite Carole Pateman's participatory democracy (1970), Daniel Bell's public household (1976), Roberto Unger's theory of organic groups (1975), Alec Nove's feasible socialism (1983), Michael Harrington's democratic socialism (1980), Martin Carnoy's and Derek Shearer's economic democracy (1980; 1983). Once again, then, I am led to affirm the thesis that social democracy is more directly ordained to the common good, the first virtue of social institutions, than what has traditionally been meant by democratic capitalism.

Given the three theses I have advanced, I propose the need for a new social covenant. The language is intentional. At the beginning of the modern age, we were instructed to acknowledge a social contract as the foundation of our common life. The idea of a social contract bespeaks a world of individuals, a state of nature, out of which persons come to effect a *modus vivendi*, for they must live together even if they do not belong together. Each gains some benefit from the arrangement, else the bargain will not long be kept. The bottom line is commodity.

But the idea of social covenant invokes an alternative tradition of thought and action, religious in its expression but ontological in its claim. The idea of a social covenant bespeaks a world in which we already belong together but are called repeatedly to acknowledge that fact anew and to determine what the forms of our life together shall be. As Bernard Meland reminds us, the idea of covenant is a myth both of identity and of dissonance, for covenants are often broken. But even when broken, they remain covenants and compel us to their reaffirmation (Meland 1976, 97-98). In its theological meaning, the idea of covenant is grounded in that God who intends a universal community of being and to whom each self is related in and through all other relationships (Johann 1966, 49-66; Hartshorne 1953, 29-43). In its meaning for social practice, the idea of covenant implies that what is most to be cherished in our associations is not the commodities that derive therefrom, but the commonwealth that is created therein.

CHAPTER VII

The Socialist/Communitarian Vision: New Dream or Old Nightmare?

W. Widick Schroeder

INTRODUCTION

Many religious social ethicists related to major non-fundamentalist religious communities have not been very charitable in their assessments of American democratic capitalism. In fact, democratic socialism or communitarianism has been advanced by a goodly number of religious social ethicists.[1] Douglas Sturm and Cornel West, for instance, are representative of this line of critical thinking.

These critiques have their cultural roots in the European experience and have been embodied in various facets of the American religious heritage. They began in Germany in the early decades of the nineteenth century among "left-wing Hegelians" who rejected the complex ontology of G. W. F. Hegel and who sought alternative interpretations of the nature of things.[2]

In his Christological monism, Albrecht Ritschl initiated a line of liberal Protestant thinking which emphasized the life of Jesus as an exemplar of full human life. Following his graduate work in Germany, Walter Rauschenbusch, the greatest figure of the Social Gospel movement in the United States, helped interject socialist thinking into American religious social ethics.[3] F. D. Maurice and the English Fabians emerging in the latter part of the nineteenth century also gave impetus to socialist thinking among American social ethicists (see Hopkins 1940).

The socialism and/or communitarianism evoked from these modes of thinking was gradualistic. Protagonists envisaged the economic transformation through peaceful democratic processes.

Although not a major factor in these late nineteenth and early twentieth century developments, Marxist categories of analysis became more fashionable among religious social ethicists in the days of the Great Depression and have again emerged in the latter part of the twentieth century.[4] Latin American liberation theologians use Marxist categories of social analysis and interpretation very frequently in their constructive work (see, e.g., Gutierrez 1973; Gutierrez and Shaull 1977; Segundo 1976).

This movement is complemented by various theologies of hope emerging out of the German experience following World War II. Some of these protagonists envisage more gradualist moves to democratic socialism; others promote a more revolutionary move. In the latter case, the dialectic of negation becomes a sociocultural as well as a theological methodological tool.[5]

All of these strands have interplayed with both indigenous American values and also the American appropriation of the Enlightenment notions of liberty, equality and community to produce Liberation Theology. Most proponents of this style of theological thinking are critical of capitalism for its alleged promotion of inordinate individualism, materialism, elitism, hedonism, racism, sexism, classism, nationalism, militarism, colonialism, and exploitation of non-industrialized countries or some combination of these evils.

It is beyond the scope of this essay to deal with all the facets of this complex social and intellectual movement. This essay's more limited focus is on some of the problems raised by the promotion of the public ownership of the means of production—a key notion in most socialist/communitarian schemes such as Douglas Sturm's—and the factors that need to be considered in a moral appraisal of such a proposal.

In our constructive work, both Sturm and I are deeply indebted to Alfred North Whitehead and that movement of thought which has subsequently come to be called process philosophy and its correlates, process theology and process social ethics.[6] In spite of this common legacy, we come to different conclusions about the most fitting relations between institutions in the economic and political spheres of the American social order.[7]

Sturm envisages the emergence of a new social covenant in this nation, resulting in a shift from humans being treated as commodities in the present situation to humans being treated as willing, self-determining persons in the new commonwealth.[8] In this shift to social democracy, the modes of production will become public property, and participatory democracy will be greatly expanded in both the economic and political spheres. By effecting this shift, the harmony of life with life will be enhanced, and human life will be enriched and deepened. Conflict and strife will be reduced, and, in the new commonwealth, the common good will once again take precedence over individual good. The transformed relations between economic and political institutions will contribute to greater social justice, for community and equality—key components in Sturm's understanding of justice—will be enhanced by this projected transformation of economic and political institutions.

In contrast to Sturm's views, I hold that in the current historical epoch and in the foreseeable future (certainly for the next two or three generations and probably much, much longer) economic and political institutions should be separated. A society combining an enterprise economic system based on private ownership (including widely diffused private ownership through personal shareholders and private pension plans) of the modes of production and appropriate government intervention in the economic sphere is more likely to attain both social justice and also growth and efficiency in the economic sphere than is a society coalescing economic and political power in the state. At the same time, the democratic polity should intervene in the economic order in fitting ways to promote some common community interests, to limit some economic practices (monopoly, for example), to promote economic stability and growth through appropriate macro-economic policy (both fiscal and monetary) and to effect some income redistribution through taxation and welfare policies. I am generally wary of the counsel offered by many of the self-proclaimed proponents of the common good, for often their own self-interests and theories of social, economic, and political organization shape their policy proposals inordinately. Of course, properly defined self-interest, including due recognition of the neighborhood effect, does contribute to public policy deliberations in an ambiguously positive manner.

In sum, I affirm the creative possibilities and the normative desirability of the emerging relations between economic and political institutions in the United States currently termed democratic or social market capitalism.[9] The body of the essay seeks to establish the bases for this positive affirmation.

In this essay, the persistence of inordinate self-interest, the primacy of liberty as the constitutive principle of justice, and the values of pluralism and the multiplication-of-factions will be emphasized more forcefully than they are in Sturm's essay. (In this regard, Sturm's emphases may be taken as representative of many persons promoting democratic socialism.) These emphases lead me to a contrasting view of the common good, a more sympathetic reading of past American social, economic, and political history, and an alternative understanding of desirable future relations between economic and political institutions in the United States.

I

> God, desiring not only that the human race might be able by their similarity of nature to associate with one another, but also that they might be bound together in harmony and peace by the ties of relationship, was pleased to derive all persons from one individual (Augustine 1950, XIV, 1).

> And hence we enjoy some gratification when our good friends die; for though their death leaves us in sorrow, we have the consolatory assurance that they are beyond the ills by which in this life even the best of men are broken down or corrupted, or are in danger of both results (Augustine 1950, XIV, 8).

In his discussion of the common good, Sturm cites Augustine to illumine the vision of a perfect harmony of life with life, in which all creatures are lured by the Divine will to coordinate and to harmonize their activities for the good of all. I have cited an Augustinian description of human life after the fall to call attention to the persistence of disharmonious and discordant experiences among humankind. Taken conjointly, the two Augustinian epigrams attest to the pervasive and persistent interplay of harmonious and discordant dimensions of experience in our personal and corporate life.

Two critical issues emerge from human reflection about these aspects of human experience. The first has to do with bases for the experience; the second has to do with the possibility of the diminution or elimination of discord in the future through appropriate human action.

Karl Marx related the alienation he discerned in the world to the objectification and thingification of the products of human labor. His salvific proposal centered on the elimination of private property to overcome the estrangement humans now experience. Non-Marxist socialists such as Sturm are not that sanguine, but most affirm that some or most of the discord can be eliminated through the reorganization of the economic order and the public ownership of the means of production.[10]

In my view, the bases of disharmony in human life are finitude, ignorance, sloth, lethargy and inordinate self-interest. Finitude demands exclusion and, from the human point of view, entails loss. The vivid immediacy of the present fades into the past and is only partially appropriated by the successors of the present experiencing subject. Because of finitude, the evocation of harmony and intensity of feeling is shaped by the sustaining environment. In some instances, discordant experiences are necessary to evoke higher harmonies; in other instances, discordant experiences may evoke anesthesia.[11] Ignorance limits an experiencing subject's capacity to avoid all actions whose consequences may be deleterious, for emerging subjects do not know in detail what their contemporaries will decide to do. Consequently, some actualizations will evoke more discord than an emerging subject has any reason to suspect. Sloth and lethargy are too widespread among humankind to be ignored. Indeed, an efficient economic system must minimize these human tendencies through both suasion and coercion. Finally, human beings all too frequently pursue their self-interests inordinately. The concern for others and for the broader human community is always present in human life, but self-interest qualifies and modifies the concern. Some self-interest is necessary for an emerging subject to become, but this metaphysical necessity all too often leads to excessive self-interest. For all these reasons, I cannot envisage any form of human social organization that will eliminate the foundational experience of discord which fosters various theories of estrangement or alienation. Any scheme of social reorganization that proposes such an outcome is rightly viewed as utopian. The naive optimism often associated with such schemes all too often yields bitter fruits; for in the context of efforts to actualize such schemes, a powerful dictator or oligarchy frequently seizes power and claims the spoils of the reorganization for the benefit of the leadership and its families.[12]

The plasticity of human nature and the possibility (which does not seem very probable in the current historical epoch) of the alleviation of the persistent shortages of food, fiber, and shelter prevent me from rejecting social democracy unequivocally and forever. However, as noted earlier, I see nothing emerging that would suggest the dramatic decline of inordinate self-interest among humankind in the foreseeable future and that would occasion the establishment of a socialist/communitarian society able to sustain both liberty and also economic efficiency and growth.

The system of checks and balances embodied in the American system of government represents a fortuitous blending of Calvinistic and Enlightenment values. James Madison, the author of many of *The Federalist Papers* elaborating the theory informing the structure of the proposed Constitution, was a very astute lay theologian. He took the doctrine of original sin very seriously; and, along with his colleagues, he sought to develop a structure of government which would blunt inordinate self-interest through a system of checks and balances and through the multiplication-of-factions. Both a vision of the harmony of the whole and also the discord embodied in the whole are incorporated in the Constitution.[13]

The inevitability of some discord in human life and the persistence of inordinate self-interest are two of the reasons I resist democratic socialism and prefer democratic capitalism. I am very wary of the increased concentration of power in the hands of the politicians which would occur if the means of production were owned by the state. The state through its monopoly of the legitimate use of force, its capacity to make laws, and its administration of the judicial system already has great power to coerce humans, to suppress individual liberty and self-initiation, and to bestow political favors. To give politicians—even those allegedly chosen through participatory democracy—vastly greater power over economic institutions would be to concentrate power inordinately.

II

A Great Society has nothing to do with and is in fact irreconcilable with 'solidarity' in the true sense of unitedness in the pursuit of known common goals (Friedrich A. Hayek 1976, 111).

Democracy is not founded merely on the right of the private interest of the individual. This is only one side of the shield. It is founded equally on the function of the individual as a member of the community. It founds the common good on the common will, in forming which it bids every grown-up intelligent person to take a part (L. T. Hobhouse 1964, 115).

Our claim for freedom is rooted in our relationship with our contemporary environment. Nature does provide a field for independent activities (Alfred North Whitehead 1961, 251).

The epigrams of Hayek and Hobhouse which Sturm cited in the second section of his essay have been supplemented by one drawn from the writings of Alfred North Whitehead. Taken conjointly, they pose the central issues of this section: the nature of liberty and its relation to equality and to community and the implications of these principles and the persistence of inordinate self-interest for forms of economic and political organization.

In promoting the vision of social democracy as a normative form of economic-political organization, Sturm appeals to a doctrine of internal relations to legitimate the communitarianism he thinks democratic socialism will promote more effectively than democratic capitalism.

This doctrine of internal relations is integral to process thinking. An explication of it and other foundational notions will illumine part of the basis for my view of normative relations between economic and political institutions. It will also illumine the role of contingent empirical data in the elaboration of human social theory.[14]

Metaphysical propositions (if they be such) apply to all actual entities in all cosmic epochs. A metaphysical system seeks to coordinate and to integrate metaphysical propositions into a coherent whole. If a proposition is a metaphysical one, it will not discriminate one entity from another, for it will apply to all. The only way to develop metaphysical propositions is through the use of negative judgments. One must imagine the absence of that which in fact is always present. More specialized propositions apply to some but not to all actual entities. Consequently, a method of difference must be used to develop propositions applicable to a particular subject matter. These propositions must not violate the more general metaphysical propositions, but they will necessarily be more specific to characterize particular subject matters.

As noted earlier, Sturm and I are both deeply influenced by process modes of thought. However, we order the primal notions informing Whitehead's version of process philosophy somewhat differently, and we differ about contingent matters pertaining to human beings in the current historical epoch. Both factors contribute to our contrasting interpretations of the American past and our contrasting visions of the American future.

The doctrine of internal relations, which is a corollary of Whitehead's principle of relativity, is a very important notion for Sturm.[15] It permits him to reject the individualism which characterized much seventeenth century social philosophy and which was salient in nineteenth century English liberalism. The relations of the human organizing center with its body, with nature, and with other humans are fundamental in human experience. This doctrine of internal relations leads Sturm to affirm both participatory democracy and also communitarianism. The primacy of the notion of community and a rather strong egalitarian bias are implicit in this affirmation. The merit of human self-determination is acknowledged, but human freedom is limited very substantially by the appeal to equality and community.

In my view, Sturm underplays the importance of the category of creativity (which is another primal notion in Whitehead's metaphysics). Creativity is the category of categories, the ultimate notion which can be characterized only by its manifestation in the creatures of the world. It stands behind the forms and is inexplicable by the forms. The sole appeal is to intuition. The freedom of the creatures of the world to respond with novelty to the influence of the causal past is an exemplification of the category of creativity. A given creature's capacity for novelty of response to its data cannot be determined *a priori*; this capacity must be assessed through comparative empirical observations of various types of creatures.

Nature appears to be organized hierarchically and, on this planet, humans are the creatures possessing the greatest capacity for novelty of response to circumstances. Human purposiveness and self-determination are too pervasive and too salient to be dismissed as epiphenomenal.

Both community and freedom are important, but, in my understanding, freedom is constitutive of human life, and community is regulative. Freedom of self-determination informed by excellence is the constitutive principle of justice, and the idea of order implicit in the notion of community is one of the regulative principles of justice.

The other regulative principle of justice, rather more implicit than explicit in Sturm's formulations, is the principle of equality. Equality is an idealized mathematical notion, and no two actual entities are exactly equal. In fact, equality as a regulative principle of justice is a vague notion, for equality can be applied only to creatures who are roughly equals. The way in which "form" ought to qualify equality is subject to disagreement. No one would argue, for example, that the same rules and regulations of justice should apply to children as to adults. Yet the nature of the qualifications and the age at which a child becomes an adult is subject to debate.

In human life, the qualifications which form ought to give to equality are even more problematic when sex is the form qualifying equality. Social function is another form qualifying equality; but again people differ substantially in their judgments about the extent to which one's social function should qualify equality.

In addition to these problems about the limits which forms should place on equality, there is a tension between freedom, equality, and order. Freedom evokes inequality, and the community limits human freedom for the sake of order and equality.

Consequently, no perfect harmonization of the principles of justice is possible under the conditions of existence. A rough approximation or a tolerable balance is the most to be expected, and this balance will shift with changing circumstances.[16]

Because I hold that freedom is the constitutive principle of justice, I am wary about the overextension of equality and order, the regulative principles of justice. Sturm's socialist/communitarian views do that, for, even in a relatively "ideal" condition in which inordinate self-interest was contained, the pressure for equality and community would make life very difficult for a non-conformist minority. There would be strong pressures for the state to suppress deviancy excessively. In fact, freedom would be redefined so that the person who was truly free would be the one who conformed to the expectations of the dominant group which claimed to speak for the community.[17] Given the widespread propensity toward inordinate self-interest, persons in charge of socialist political-economic systems could (and have) imposed excessive limitations on the self-initiative of persons in minority groups.

Democratic capitalism, which sustains multiple centers of initiative and power, fosters the development of voluntary associations, offers economic inducements without government sanction or approval, and promotes checks and balances within and between economic and political groups, can sustain the quest for liberty and equality while minimizing the dangers inherent in an omni-component government.

This view does not entail a laissez-faire economic policy. The polity in principle has the right to intervene in the economic order for the sake of justice; because social necessity, the basis for the political sphere of human life is superior to biological necessity, the basis for the economic order. Some income redistribution, unemployment compensation to sustain victims of technological change and/or the business cycle, appropriate measures to protect the environment and to redress the neighborhood effect, and appropriate regulation of business illustrate some of the ways in which the polity may seek to attain economic justice for its citizens. In engaging in these activities, however, public policy should seek to sustain the private sector rather than impede it. Further, various forms of welfare should be designed to enhance the self-determination of recipients rather than to evoke continued dependence.[18]

III

> This interrelation of agents, which makes the freedom of all members of a society depend upon the intentions of each, is the ground of morality . . . If we call the harmonious interrelation of agents their 'community,' we may say that a morally right action is an action which intends community . . . If the world is one action, any particular action determines the future, within its own limits, for all agents. Every individual agent is therefore responsible to all other agents for his actions (John MacMurray 1961, 118-119).

> As a nation we have become increasingly concerned, especially since 1929, about effecting a fair and equitable balance between the conflicting goals of efficiency in production and the preservation of human values. The invisible hand of the market place did not provide compensation for men injured on the job, wages as a matter of right for men out of work, pensions for retired workers, or freedom from unjustified discharges. Much of the strength of this country, I believe, has derived from a strong drive for efficiency in competition, moderated, however, by an inherent compassion in the utilization of one factor of production—labor. Here is the really revolutionary idea of the past century (George W. Taylor, "The Role of Labor Unions," in Samuelson 1973, 67).

> The conception [of socialism] actually lies in the realm of prophecy as well as in that of vague ideals or wishes well designated as 'cloud-cuckoo land.' . . . it is easy to imagine and to believe (as shown by the fact that intelligent people regularly do so imagine and believe) that the (supposed) evils in the world or any particular society (a) are economic in basis (b) more specifically are consequences of the form of economic organization and (c) can without serious difficulty be corrected by replacing the economic organization with a system of control by politicians (Frank H. Knight 1947, 133).

One's retrieval of past American history is shaped by the interplay between one's basic presuppositions and the "facts." Sturm's reading of American political and economic history is an ambiguously negative one; he envisages the emergence of a new social covenant which will facilitate a shift from commodity to commonwealth.

In my view, though, Sturm overstates the negative aspects of the American experience, understates the positive accomplishments of that experience, and offers a highly dubious prescription for the future direction of American life.

My own reading of this history is an ambiguously positive one. Democratic capitalism as it has evolved in the context of the American experience has promoted the legitimate concerns of the citizens of the republic to protect the humanity of persons in the work force, to reduce inordinate inequality in incomes, and to promote economic growth and efficiency.

Obviously, much remains to be done to facilitate more humane relations in the workplace, but much has been done. Because formal factors guided by technical rationalism must always be considered in any reasonably efficient economic system, an economic enterprise will always thwart communitarian dreams to a greater or lesser degree.

The epigram from Taylor is a balanced assessment of the fitting transformation of labor in the American experience, and the epigram from Knight is a trenchant statement of the problems inherent in socialism/communitarianism.

There has been a general drift toward the increased freedom of the individual over the past three thousand years or so. Slavery was presupposed in the ancient world, and it was not until the time of the Industrial Revolution in the eighteenth century that technological innovations made possible the freeing of more than a small segment of humankind from the necessity to spend almost all of their time in pursuit of food, fiber and shelter.[19] The Industrial Revolution, the popular appropriation of democratic and Enlightenment values, and the increasing differentiation of the spheres of the social order all contributed to the extension of some aspects of human freedom in some parts of the planet. The United States shared in and contributed to this development. The heightened individuation that began in the West in the latter part of the middle ages was marked by the increasing differentiation of the spheres of the social order. Institutions in the social, economic, political, and religious spheres became more autonomous, and increasingly the individual came to offer his labor for wages in the marketplace.[20]

As noted in Section II, Enlightenment and left-wing Calvinist values both contributed to the shape of the Constitution and the development of the American experiment. The next two centuries saw both the extension of voting rights to larger segments of the population and increased involvement of the government in economic matters.[21] During most of the nineteenth century the dual values, growth and efficiency, shaped American attitudes toward economic enterprises. By the latter part of the century, the inequities of laissez-faire capitalism led Congress to enact various measures to limit those inequities. The Interstate Commerce Act (1887) and the Sherman Anti-Trust Act (1890) gave the government the authority to limit monopoly practices.

In the twentieth century, equality became a more salient value.[22] Consequently, these limitations on corporate power in the latter part of the nineteenth century were followed by various schemes to promote income redistribution in the twentieth century. Fiscal policy became an increasingly popular way to seek to effect income redistribution.[23]

The capitalist system and its sustaining ethos have harnessed human self-interest and have motivated people to work diligently and to work efficiently. People affirmed the value of technical rationalism, a mind set which seeks to develop the most efficient means to attain a given end. As a result very impressive economic growth has taken place in the past two centuries. Indeed, schemes of income redistribution developed in the twentieth century have been greatly facilitated by economic growth. Food, shelter, and clothing—the primary creaturely necessities—have been available in very substantial quantities.

During the period of the Great Depression in the 1930s, government involvement in the economic sphere increased dramatically. Faced with monumental economic problems, the government sought to foster economic recovery and to aid those whom the Depression had left destitute. (In fact, much of its fiscal and monetary policy were contradictory.) Keynesian economic theory began to come to American in the mid- to late 1930s, and it provided a legitimation for more active government intervention through monetary and fiscal policy to moderate the fluctuations in the business cycle. The Depression saw both the vast expansion of the welfare system and also the extension of labor's rights. This epoch gave shape to the direction of the welfare efforts of the state and promoted the growth of a welfare establishment which has come to oversee and to administer welfare funds.[24]

Overall, therefore, George Taylor's assessment quoted at the beginning of this section is a balanced one. Substantial progress has been made in the United States in the past century to promote a more humane treatment of labor.

This broad interpretation needs to be supplemented by a consideration of two interrelated issues implicit in Sturm's discussion of socialism/communitarianism/participatory democracy. The first centers on the problem of growth and efficiency in the economic sphere; the second centers on the problem of the nature of the changes in the management of production which would actually occur in a socialist economy.

The quest for efficiency, the primacy of consumer reference in determining consumption, and the reliance on pricing mechanisms to guide the production and distribution of goods and services combine to produce "creative destruction," the term coined by Joseph Schumpeter to describe the dynamic capitalist enterprise system, a system which fosters technological innovation and rapid social change and evokes some human insecurity. With technological changes and shifts in consumer preferences, whole industries can be displaced, and new industries can emerge at a rapid pace. Workers caught in these transformations through no fault of their own are subject to both psychological and economic insecurity.

The problems associated with creative destruction would, I think, persist in a socialist economic system. They would likely be compounded by the preferential treatment politicians would extend to their friends and to members of their families to protect them from the impact of these changes. These actions would reduce growth and reduce efficiency.[25]

The second issue centers on the reliance on consumer preferences to guide the production of goods and services. Pricing mechanisms are a very effective and efficient way to guide the production and distribution of goods and services. The price of goods or services is set by the marketplace at a price at which supply and demand are in equilibrium. Price declines will clear the market of surplus goods and services through decreased production and increased demand, and price increases will induce the availability of under-supplied goods and services through increased production and reduced demand. The alternatives to the use of pricing mechanisms to guide production and consumption of goods and services would be rationing by coupon and/or some form of allocation of goods by governmental fiat. (Sturm does not propose to substitute those mechanisms for consumer preference and the pricing mechanisms.)

A socialist/communitarian democratic society utilizing pricing mechanisms and consumer preferences to determine the availability and distribution of goods and services and seeking to attain some growth and some efficiency will confront the same economic problems as a democratic capitalist society. They will most likely be exacerbated because the government will be deeply involved in economic activity.

Unless the pricing mechanisms are permitted to continue to determine production and consumption patterns, the following scenario is very plausible. Great inefficiency, a diminution of human choices in allocation of economic resources, and an expanded government bureaucracy will develop. The government may embrace complex long-range planning operations, and many errors in projections will occur. If goods and services are rationed by coupon rather than by price, black markets will evolve. If goods are dispensed on a per capita basis, complex barter and swapping arrangements among consumers will emerge.[26] The risk and uncertainty inherent in the marketplace will not be eliminated, but political solutions will be much more tempting. Managers will likely be timid and unwilling to innovate, for socialist governments will likely reward managers attaining economic success less fully than they will punish managers encountering difficulties. Faced with the possibility of censure if they go wrong, most plant managers and workers will be tempted to play it safe and try to maintain the status quo.

The likely political consequences of an increasingly inefficient and stagnant economic system will be increasing unrest among members of the society. Because the government would be directly responsible both for managing the economy and also for producing goods and services, key government officials would be the targets of public unrest. Under these circumstances, the maintenance of democracy would become increasingly difficult. Politicians would seek to suppress unrest by appealing to the principle of order, and some entrepreneurs would seek to establish political hegemony so they could run the economy more efficiently and more profitably than the politicians.[27] Consequently, in this scenario a socialist/communitarian democratic society would run the risk of either a totalitarian socialism or a totalitarian fascism.

Sturm advances the ideal of participatory democracy in both the economic and political spheres of the American social order. His relatively egalitarian emphasis and his strong desire for community lead him to this ideal. Participatory democracy conveys a multiplicity of meanings, ranging from *equal* participation in all affairs of government to selective participation in all affairs of government. Because of his egalitarian emphases, Sturm wants to apply the principle of equal participation very broadly in both the economic and political spheres. In fact, the interpenetration of the two spheres he proposes blurs very greatly the distinction between decisions in economic and in political institutions.

In light of the above considerations, I argue that the principles of liberty and equality, along with the persistence of finitude, ignorance, sloth, lethargy and inordinate self-interest among humankind, make democracy the most desirable form of political organization. These factors, though, do not legitimate participatory democracy. In the political sphere, a republican form of democracy is preferable to a participatory form because complex and interrelated decisions cannot be made by the mass electorate. Specialized knowledge and a backlog of concrete political experience are required, for a series of specific *ad hoc* decisions do not constitute a coherent public policy.

As noted earlier, the extension of voting rights to more groups in the United States over the past two centuries has promoted the principle of equality, for many voters have expected the government to countervail inordinate disparities in income and other inequities through various income redistribution plans and legal redress. This pattern has also facilitated increased government intervention in the economic sphere, for voters increasingly expected the government to promote economic growth. These governmental activities have contributed to the emergence of democratic capitalism.

Evaluated by the principles of liberty, equality and order, these developments deserve a generally sympathetic interpretation.[28] However, the process should not be extrapolated to condone the state appropriation of the modes of production in the name of communitarianism or the stifling of individual liberty in the name of equality and/or community. Nor should it suggest the promotion of participatory democracy in lieu of representative democracy.

The appropriate degree of worker participation in management decisions is very difficult to discern. Growth and efficiency are important economic objectives, and no one knows precisely what impact alternative styles of decision making will have on an enterprise. The adversarial labor-management relations so widespread in contemporary America leave much to be desired, and experimentation with alternative forms has much to commend it.

Worker rights certainly need to be protected, and legal restraints on arbitrary management decisions are entirely appropriate. However, the proposals Sturm offers for participatory democracy in the economic sphere ignore the need for specialized and professional guidance in economic enterprises. The government would have inordinate power if it could *mandate* such a decision making process.

These critical observations about democratic socialism/communitarianism should not blind one to the negative aspects of democratic capitalism. Capitalism does appeal to self-interest very strongly, presses the quest for growth and efficiency with great vigor, and leads to significant inequalities in income distribution. It has undoubtedly contributed to a materialistic bent in American life. Market hedonism is a powerful force, and pursuit of material goods and instant gratification of wants are part of the American experience (see Bell 1976). However, if consumers choose to allocate their resources through investment and through the support of alternative goods and services, market hedonism can be minimized.

Unless one is prepared to empower the state with authority to direct human moral activity in substantial detail, one must rely on suasion and on fortitude in the current circumstances. Families and various voluntary associations (including religious communities) may be able to cultivate persons who resist some of the debasing aspects of contemporary life, but people should not be coerced to conform to inordinately high or arbitrary moral standards. The extent to which the state should coerce minimally acceptable societal standards of social behavior is subject to constant redefinition, but some such minimal standards are essential for the sustenance of human communities.[29]

In any reasonably efficient economic enterprise human beings must be remunerated on the basis of their marketable competences. Such a system cannot avoid the displacement of workers due to technological change and/or changes in consumer preferences. Nevertheless, humans are more than mere cogs in an economic engine, and they demand to be treated as such. They seek inclusive, holistic relations in which they are seen in their richness and complexity. Technical rationalism—the understanding of reasoning informing role segmentation and the quest for efficiency and growth—is a truncated view of reason which needs to be supplemented by a broader view of reason grounded in the lure for beauty, truth and goodness.

The communitarian appeal is rooted in these longings for holistic and inclusive relations, but these longings cannot be fulfilled in any reasonably efficient economic enterprise. The longings have the greatest hope of some fulfillment in the family, in small friendship groups, and in some types of voluntary associations, including some religious groups.

IV

As long as a religion rests only upon those sentiments which are the consolation of all affliction, it may attract the affections of all mankind. But if it be mixed up with the bitter passions of the world, it may be constrained to defend allies whom its interests, and not the principle of love, have given to it; or to repel as antagonists men who are still attached to it, however opposed they may be to the powers with which it is allied. The church cannot share the temporal power of the state without being the object of a portion of that animosity which the latter excites . . . The American clergy were the first to perceive this truth and to act in conformity with it. They saw they must renounce their religious influence if they were to strive for political power, and they chose to give up the support of the state rather than to share its vicissitudes (Alexis de Tocqueville 1954, 321-323).

In his essay, Sturm neither discusses religious communities directly nor indicates what role religious communities should play in facilitating the transition "from commodity to commonwealth." One can only speculate about the reasons for this omission. Sturm may think that the new "commonwealth" will so embody the substance of religion that religious communities are no longer necessary.

Whatever Sturm's reasons for ignoring religious communities, it is necessary for me to consider them, for I think that human awareness of the Divine Presence will evoke religious communities in all historical epochs.

Religious communities emerge from human responses to their awareness of Divine immanence in human life. A religious community's constitutive act is worship. Religious communities provide some of the contexts in which humans may become aware of the Divine Reality, and the communities are the bearers of feelings and meanings embodied in religious traditions. They are both institutions and fellowships. As social fellowships they may counteract the hedonistic pressures of the broader culture by contributing to wholesome character formation of their members.

The separation of church and state and the concomitant values of religious freedom, religious tolerance and religious pluralism are deeply embodied in the American experience. While no absolute separation is intended, substantial religious freedom exists. Communities of faith and communities of politics have rarely coalesced in the United States. Most religious communities have members of more than one political party and have members who differ substantially on political and economic issues. In the American context, one does not usually expect to find one's religious association requiring a specific political association.

The inevitable contrast between the vision of the potential harmony of life with life and the actual intertwining of harmonious and discordant dimensions in the life of an actual living community legitimates a separation between religious and political communities.

These contrasts, a consequence of finitude and ignorance, are not the only reason for resisting the coalescence of political and religious communities. The persistence of inordinate self-interest is a second reason. The deification of a government is one of the crudest forms of idolatry, and the temptation is likely to be increased without independent religious communities. Conversely, a given faith community may be sorely tempted to equate its truth with the truth, seeking to impose its teachings on all members of the civil community. A plurality of religious communities and the separation of religious communities and the civil community blunt this temptation.

In political communities, power—both linear and reciprocal—is the leading component, and political life embodies both suasive and coercive elements. While justice and love are important in the political sphere, they are secondary and tertiary components. Without the form of justice and the lure of love, political power is naked. Such a realpolitik cannot endure.

In religious communities, suasive love is the leading component, a love only partially actualizable in the world. Consequently, religious communities should not identify directly with any political community. They should seek to provide a direction for society, but they should be very wary about providing specific directives to a society. Religious communities furthermore should explore the bases for the principles of justice and consider their implications for forms of social organization and for the rules and regulations of justice. In addition, they should encourage their members to participate in other voluntary associations directly promoting particular public policies. In this way, they may promote the quest for justice and the enhancement of the harmony of life with life in a living community without becoming directly involved in the ambiguity of almost all economic and political activity.

Political and economic groups are important in human life, but they are not sufficient for human fulfillment. Humans need more inclusive holistic relations in the family, in small primary groups, and in some types of voluntary associations, including religious communities, for a rich and full life. Ultimate fulfillment is found in the Divine Life, and it is to this reality one must turn for a more encompassing fulfillment than is possible in the world. The sense of peace such fulfillment evokes is more a gift than an achievement. This awareness of the reception and the transmutation in the Divine Life of the contributions of the creatures of the world can help us understand both the lure for the embodiment of love and justice in the world and also the inevitability of some evil and injustice in the world.

V

The art of progress is to preserve order amid change, and to preserve change amid order (Alfred North Whitehead 1978, 339).

In light of both the positive and negative reasons discussed in this essay, I conclude that the relative autonomy of economic, political and religious institutions in the United States should be supported. When these institutions are separated, this large, complex, heterogeneous, post-modern society can best order the principles of freedom informed by excellence and equality appropriate to form in the life of the living community. In this historical epoch and in the foreseeable future, socialist/communitarian proposals to re-order these fundamental relations should be approached with the utmost skepticism. Their re-ordering would most probably entail a reduction of human freedom, initiative, and self-determination in the several spheres of the American social order, the placing of additional burdens on the government, and a reduction in the centers of power and independent initiative which promote checks and balances in American social, economic, political, cultural and religious life. Innovation in the context of the conservation of the basic structure of relations among economic, political, and religious institutions is the most appropriate way to pursue the quest for justice in the context of the American experience.

Notes

1. The following are some religious social ethicists who affirm some form of socialism as normatively desirable, sharply criticize capitalism, or both: Hugo Assmann (1975); John Bennett (1975); Robert McAffee Brown (1981); Dom Helder Camara (1971); Gustavo Gutierrez (1973); Gustavo Gutierrez and Richard Shaull (1977); Jose Miguez Bonino (1975; 1983); Juan

Segundo (1976; 1984); Paul Tillich (1977); and Philip Wogaman (1977).

In *Liberating Creation* Gibson Winter offers a cultural critique of both socialism and capitalism. Following Heidegger, Winter is very critical of the technical rationalism which he sees at the base of both capitalism and socialism. ·

Following his lead, many of the contributors to *Liberation and Ethics: Essays in Religious Social Ethics in Honor of Gibson Winter* explore variations of this theme (Charles Amjad Ali and W. Alvin Pitcher editors, 1984).

Among those seeking to defend democratic capitalism are: Robert Benne (1981); Paul Heyne (1968; 1977); and Michael Novak (1982b; 1984).

2. Karl Marx is, of course, the best known figure in this movement. It is beyond the scope of this essay to trace these developments in detail. The following thinkers explore various facets of this complex development: G. D. H. Cole (1953); Louis Dupre (1983); Sidney Hook (1936); Bertell Ollman (1976); Robert C. Tucker (1972).

3. See especially, Walter Rauschenbusch (1912; 1917). The early writings of Reinhold Niebuhr (1932) reflected this line of thinking.

4. For a detailed history of socialist thought in America, see Donald Drew Egbert and Stow Persons (1952).

5. See, for example, the following representative texts: Ernst Bloch (1970); Jürgen Moltmann (1974); and Dorothee Sölle (1977; 1983).

6. See John B. Cobb, Jr., and W. Widick Schroeder, (1981) for a collection of essays dealing with issues in religious social ethics from a process perspective. In that volume, Sturm also promotes communitarianism in his essay "Process Thought and Political Theory: Implications of a Principle of Internal Relations" (pp. 81-102). In the subsequent essay, Max Stackhouse offers a perceptive critique in his "The Perils of Process: A Response to Sturm" (pp. 103-112). Whitehead's own social theory is developed in various places. *Science and the Modern World* (1925), *Religion in the Making* (1926), *Adventures of Ideas* (1961) and *Modes of Thought* (1938) are the most important resources for this aspect of his thinking.

7. The present paper is focused on the American experience. It does not address the complex problems of appropriate forms of social organization in countries with different historical destinies. It may be observed in passing, however, that socialist/communitarian visions in such countries have consistently been thwarted.

8. In Douglas Sturm's essay in this volume, he uses the typologies "orthodox capitalism" and "heterodox capitalism" to contrast forms of economic organization in the United States and "protective democracy" and "participatory democracy" to contrast forms of political organization in the United States. The unique configuration of relations between economic and political institutions that has emerged in American democratic capitalism is distorted by these typological devices.

9. The term "democratic capitalism" has been made popular by Michael Novak (1982b) and Robert Benne (1981).

10. Socialists differ on the kinds and amounts of property persons may own for their own use and consumption. These family quarrels are not directly germane to the issues being considered in this essay.

11. It is beyond the scope of this essay to explore this issue further. For an extended discussion, see Schroeder (1982, 267-291).

12. For a perceptive analysis of these problems in the contemporary epoch, see Peter Berger (1974). For a perceptive critique of patterns of foreign aid, see P. T. Bauer (1984).

13. It is beyond the scope of this essay to trace in detail the complex socio-cultural movement leading to the breakdown of the medieval social order and the emergence of the new forms of economic and political organization. For detailed and contrasting discussions of these matters, the following texts are illustrative: Joyce Oldham Appleby (1978); Albert O. Hirschman (1977); Leo Strauss (1953); R. H. Tawney (1920; 1926); Ernst Troeltsch (1931); Jacob Viner (1972); Michael Walzer (1968); Max Weber (1958).

14. For extended bibliographical references, see John B. Cobb, Jr., and W. Widick Schroeder, editors (1981).

15. In its most general form, Whitehead's principle of relativity states that every being is a potential for every becoming. It is the basis for the understanding of existence as inextricably social. Life involves both individuation and relationships.

16. While this religious social ethic seeks guidance from principles, it is ultimately a contextual ethic, for changing circumstances require changing responses to enhance the harmony of life with life under the conditions of existence.

17. Aquinas, Calvin, Lenin and Mao all sought uniformity of beliefs in a society.

18. For an interesting discussion of public policy proposals informed by this point of view, see Milton Friedman (1962). For studies exploring the impact of current forms of welfare on their recipients see George F. Gilder (1978; 1981).

   It is beyond the scope of this essay to deal with specific issues of public policy, for it is concerned with generic issues informing one's vision about normative forms of economic and political organization.

19. The pursuit of self-interest and the conditioning effects of one's sustaining environment are always a part of the human condition. One need not adopt a Marxist perspective to affirm the importance of these factors in human life.

   The quest for laws which determine human life and the use of the dialectic of negation to interpret social change distort social analysis. The capacity of humans to surpass the past in the emerging present precludes the development of "laws" of human social change. One can indeed discern tendencies and configurations, but human freedom thwarts all efforts to write a deterministic history.

   Marxist categorization of humans into the groupings "oppressor" and "oppressed" based on their location in the social structure of a given society is fallacious, for human beings surpass the nexus of relations in which they are embedded. Classes are abstractions. Their reification is an example of what Whitehead calls the fallacy of misplaced concreteness.

   This Marxist bipolar categorization of human beings based on their position in the social structure is reminiscent of Augustine's "saved" and "damned" bipolar categorization of human beings at the end of history based on Divine determination. For Marx, the bipolarity can be overcome *within* history, but only for those humans who are extant at the time the public ownership of the modes of production occurs. Prior to that time, the "elect" will be those who are on the right side in the dialectic of the historical process. The tortuous issues about human freedom and an inexorable historical process which Marx and his followers address are analogous to those about human freedom and Divine predestination which Augustine and his followers address.

   For a similar reason, humans are more than a factor in the production processes. They are that, but as human beings they are more than that. These issues are addressed briefly at the close of this section and in section IV.

   Socialists such as Sturm do not employ a full-blown Marxist analysis, but they selectively appropriate facets of the Marxist tradition. Their frequent references to "oppressors" and the "oppressed," their widespread disdain of capitalist achievements, their frequent uncritical acceptance of the theory of dependent capitalism, their almost dogmatic views about the omnipresence of capitalist monopolies and excessive profits, their acceptance of Marxist critiques of advertising, and their convictions of the great benefits to accrue to humankind following the public ownership of many or most modes of production illustrate the complex influence Marxist modes of thought have had on advocates of democratic socialism.

   Notions drawn from this tradition appear frequently in the social analyses of advocates of one or another form of liberation theology.

20. For a suggestive discussion on this process see Robert Bellah (1970, 20-45).

21. In the present context, the author is interested in very broad tendencies and movements. More specialized monographs have amply documented these broad trends.

22. Insofar as economists were preachers they emphasized growth and efficiency in the late eighteenth and in much of the nineteenth century. In the later part of the nineteenth century in and much of the twentieth century they emphasized equality. Freedom is more closely related to growth and efficiency; equality is more closely related to community. For a perceptive discussion of these patterns, see George Stigler (1982, 3-37).

23. For a discussion of the tensions inherent between efficiency and equality, see Arthur M. Okun (1975).

   How successful these schemes have been is an empirical question about which there has been some debate.

24. It is beyond the scope of this essay to address specific public policy proposals, but freedom as

the constitutive principle of justice provides a basis for judging public policy issues. Government income redistribution policies should seek to enhance the self-determination of the recipients. Therefore, government grants to the poor should be in the form of direct grants whenever possible. Further, the schemes should seek to avoid continued dependence.

25.   The notion that politicians would suddenly be transformed into utterly altruistic beings devoted to the pursuit of the common good in a socialistic/communitarian society is belied by human experience generally and by the experiences in many countries where the modes of production are owned by the state.

26.   Socialist economies in Communist countries have increasingly come to rely on free market pricing mechanisms to allocate resources. Such arrangements are compatible with government ownership of the modes of production. However, as noted in the body of the text, if they are used, the "creative destruction" and displacement of workers that occur in capitalist economies will also plague socialist economies. The negative impact on growth and efficiency is most likely to be much greater, for government "subsidies" to sustain declining industries will probably be easier to come by.

27.   In a socialist economy, some accounting mechanisms to assess relative costs and returns on investment analogous to "profits" in a capitalist economy must be used to assess the efficiency of a particular enterprise.

28.   Friedrich A. Hayek presents an extremely staunch opposition to government intervention in the economic sphere, holding that economic reform is the road to serfdom. Sidney and Beatrice Webb press for an extremely strong support of communitarianism, holding that without the economic democracy coming from collectively equal ownership of the means of production political democracy is nothing. Sturm comes close to this latter view.

29.   For a suggestive exploration of some of the issues involved in this problem, see Richard John Neuhaus (1984).

It is beyond the scope of this essay to consider the public faith of America and the relation of the religions of America to the religion of America.

Part Three

Christianity and Capitalism: Perspectives from Economics, Social Theory and Anthropology

CHAPTER VIII

Contributions of Orthodox Economics to Ethical Reflection

Daniel Rush Finn

In this essay I will consider the contributions to ethical reflection of "orthodox" economics, that majority opinion within economics that includes conservative monetarists and liberal Keynesians. The essay begins with a short consideration of some methodological problems in mainstream economics, noting that the discipline officially employs a broadly empiricist method which rules out of the science any substantive assertions about the human psyche, in spite of the fact that most of the discipline's practitioners really do *believe* that people are rational maximizers. I then outline the three basic presumptions of orthodox economics: scarcity, self-interest, and rationality. The bulk of the paper develops the five theses which I believe economists would most want to contribute to ethicists: prices matter; most change is marginal; optimality is not perfection; even altruistic behavior is responsive to prices; and public policy should employ narrowly self-interested incentives.

Both within economics and within the broader intellectual community it is presumed that the economist contributes a description of the workings of the economy prior to a moral evaluation of it. (Given the scope of this essay, I will employ the short-hand term "economist" to refer to orthodox economists, without intending to imply that other economists have a weaker claim to that name.) There are without doubt problems with this construal, and many have been the critics who have articulated the implicit biases and proclivities of the orthodox position (see Heyne 1978). Nevertheless, the economist is generally understood to be providing to others accurate empirical claims about economic reality.

These "empirical claims", of course, range widely from quite concrete ones (e.g., estimates of the dollar amount of currency and coin in circulation) to others in which definitions of concepts are admittedly arbitrary (e.g., estimates of the size of "M1", one of the measures of the money supply) to yet others in which causal relationships are entailed (e.g., the claim that a high rate of increase in the money supply will cause inflation) to still others where a long series of causal relationships is presumed (e.g., the claim that erratic changes in the rate of growth of the money supply will lead to lower economic growth than will a steady rate of growth of money at even an inflationary level). These claims, then, range from simple empirical measurement to arbitrarily defined concepts and "facts" to more controversial "explanations" of phenomena.

In summary, the sentiment within economics asserts that individuals such as ethicists who might want to change the world should first understand how it works. This conviction is an old one. Taking morality and public policy as subsets of "art," John Stuart Mill put it this way:

> The art proposes to itself an end to be attained, defines the end, and hands it over to the science. The science receives it, considers it as a phenomenon or effect to be studied, and having investigated its causes and conditions, sends it back to art with a theorem of the combination of circumstances by which it could be produced. . . . Science then lends to art the proposition (obtained by a series of inductions or of deductions) that the performance of certain actions will attain the end (Mill 1875, bk. VI, chap XII, sect. 2).

We should note that Mill's conception of the relation between values and economic science has remained largely unaltered within mainstream economics. Economists continue to see their discipline as one in service to wider societal goals, goals which are set in the usual democratic process and with which the majority of economists might well disagree. Some people find surprising the economist's sense of making a worthwhile contribution even if the ultimate values served may not be wholeheartedly endorsed.[1]

If understanding how the economy operates is the primary thing ethicists should learn from economists, this single goal leads to two admonitions that most economists would share with ethicists, as they do regularly with students in their introductory courses. The first is that an *intention* to cause good outcomes is not sufficient to effect them. The second is that even if you *can* cause to occur something you wish to happen, the process will almost always have important secondary effects, some of which are contrary to the intended outcomes.[2]

However, if asked what ethicists could learn from economics, almost all economists from Milton Friedman to Paul Samuelson would not be satisfied merely to report their empirical findings and state their explanations. Rather, they would likely judge it even more important to articulate the general principles and concepts which economists depend on (and which they would judge ethicists to be well-advised to employ).

This is sufficient reason for attending to the broader system of economic analysis. Such an effort is, in addition, necessary because contemporary insight into epistemology and the sociology of knowledge has already convinced most of us that it is naive to assimilate discrete "facts" or even "explanations" without assessing the broader conceptual scheme out of which those facts and explanations arise. All of our knowledge is perspectival and incomplete. While there are no easy rules of thumb for adjudicating disputes among alternative perspectives, achieving clarity about the "sense" inherent in each approach is a first step.

Thus social ethicists need to grasp the broader "economic approach" to human action. This remains true despite the fact that most mainstream economists show little interest in the subtleties of ethics and would, if the tables were turned, rather nonchalantly adjudge Immanuel Kant to be inadvertantly a consequentialist, since his refusal to tell a lie arises out of the same maximizing logic as the felon's canard. This asymmetry between the two disciplines of ethics and economics illumines an unfortunate psychic posture on the part of the latter which can variously be interpreted as naive, small, over-confident, or imperialistic. While this tends to make our inquiry less enjoyable and renders the prospects for progress slightly less encouraging, the effort remains a crucial one and deserves our attention.

Economists, then, would argue that their most significant contribution to ethicists is not the analysis of the *particular* primary and secondary effects of a proposed action, though this is critical in any particular situation. Rather, the most significant contribution is a *procedure* of analysis of such effects, a way to uncover and forsee them.

Given the importance which economists attribute to their analytical system, it is crucial that we examine this structure in some detail. No analytic procedure is without its presuppositions, and the question of a proper method for economics has long been a disputed issue. I would argue that orthodox economists at the present time are in the anomolous position of officially holding an empiricist methodological position while thoroughly believing in psychological foundations for the discipline which empiricism requires them to reject. The second portion of this essay will address in some detail the system of analysis which economists employ. First, however, we need to outline the historical context within which these developments have occurred.

A VERY SHORT HISTORY OF METHODOLOGY IN MAINSTREAM ECONOMICS

In an earlier era the debate over the status of economic claims about reality centered on the distinction between inductive and deductive reasoning. Classical political economy, especially after Ricardo, was severely criticized within England and in Germany for being *a priori*, abstract, and unrealistic (e.g., Jones 1831, xx; Cliffe Leslie 1888, chap. xv; and Sidgwick 1962, 74). John Stuart Mill was the dominant influence on methodology (the theory about good scientific procedures), though not on method (the procedures themselves), within classical economics. It was he who combined a deductive *a priori* method with an empiricist foundation within economics.

Mill was convinced that the best and most mature sciences, such as physics, operated in accord with a deductive procedure. Each science applied well-established laws to particular situations. The laws themselves, of course, were originally inductive generalizations, but they had since been proven worthy by subsequent testing (Mill 1875, bk. II chap. iv. & vi.). In his definition of the discipline, Mill defines political economy as

the science which traces the laws of such of the phenomena of society as arise from the combined operations of mankind for the production of wealth, in so far as those phenomena are not modified by the pursuit of any other object (Mill 1874, 140).

Economics, then, is a "hypothetical, deductive science" in that the economist begins with mental laws (in particular, those related to the production and distribution of wealth) which "it borrows from the pure science of mind" (Mill 1874, 133). It then deduces therefrom the effects caused in some concrete situation, say where a particular tax or technological change takes place.

For Mill, the economist knows that people have motives other than wealth-seeking, and these may interfere with or even supercede the one upon which economics focuses. Yet this only relativizes the accomplishments of economics; it does not deny them. Later economists generalized this "wealth seeking" to include all possible human motives. With the use of the calculus in economics, marginal utility theory and marginal productivity theory rounded out the model of economic action as "maximization".[3] Nevertheless, Mill's basic methodology dominated mainstream economics into the twentieth century (see, e.g., Keynes 1917).

As is usually the case in most disciplines, methodology followed method in mainstream economics in this century. A strong empirical orientation had appeared sporadically in earlier eras (see, e.g., Jevons 1865). It was, however, only over the first fifty years of this century that discussions of method began to incorporate a stronger and eventually dominant role for empirical study, while so-called "a priori" methods came to be considered "unscientific." This was not yet a complete rejection of Mill's methodology, as economists were to reason from general principles (e.g., a rise in the price of a good will reduce the amount demanded). But general principles would now have to be validated *within* economics itself. Thus, there would be no more "borrowing" of laws about the workings of the mind from other disciplines.

This basic move was exemplified by the development of the revealed preference theory (which began with consumers' choices in the marketplace) which replaced the utility theory (which began with a model of human choice).[4] Economics was, at least officially, to be purged of theories about the human psyche, and such concepts as "diminishing marginal utility" were to be replaced by other strictly empirical ones like "increasing marginal rates of substitution." Predictably, the methodology of the discipline developed into a clearly empiricist one (e.g., Hutchison 1965).

The single most controversial issue in economic method over the past three or four decades has been the status of "unrealistic" beliefs about human behavior in economics. Simply put, if the economist as economist has no way to observe directly or test empirically assertions about the rationality or self-interest of economic actors, how can such presumptions continue to function respectably within the discipline? Central to the discussion of this issue has been the dispute between Milton Friedman and Paul Samuelson concerning the *realism* of premises employed in economics.

Friedman argues that the only true test of any theory is its ability to predict outcomes. Thus it is of no matter that economists begin with unrealistic assumptions; the real question is whether these assumptions will provide accurate predictions.[5] The economist is right, he argues, to assert that economic agents act *as if* they are maximizing returns to themselves—not because we can prove that individuals actually *intend* to do this but because this presumption leads to accurate predictions.

Paul Samuelson views a theory as a set of empirically refutable statements about the world. Both the "minimal set of assumptions" that gives rise to the theory and the complete set of consequences entailed by it possess the same degree of realism as the theory itself (Samuelson 1963, 233-34).

Much has been said about this dispute (for an overview, see Wong 1973). For our purposes, though, this debate in the philosophy of social science is of secondary importance, since economists on both sides of this issue would likely include assertions about self-interest, rationality and maximizing behavior in the package which economists have to contribute to ethicists. Even among the strict constraints that Samuelson imposes for the realism of the economist's assumptions, he too on some occasions employs "unrealistic" conceptions. He refers to this as dealing with systems by resorting to ". . . the natural anthropomorphic habit of imputing 'will' and 'volition' to them. This is perhaps only a figure of speech; but often it is a useful one, for the maximum systems react to certain disturbances *as if* they were reasoning beings (Samuelson 1965, 140)." Thus, the olive "tries" to reach the bottom as it slides down the side of the martini glass, and the farm sector in America "tries" to maximize its profits by a general increase in fertilizer use when the price of fertilizer falls. In this way, both Friedman and Samuelson are convinced that self-interest and rational maximizing are appropriate presumptions for economists to entertain even if these cannot be scientifically corroborated within economics.

In fact, I would argue, self-interest and rational maximizing are so thoroughly a part of the mindset of mainstream economists that they are *actually* taken as realistic in spite of methodological misgivings. This occurs, I believe, because of a deeper conviction that explanations of phenomena must be based not just on statistical correlations but on some sort of intuitive plausibility, and that, in addition, in the social sciences, no such plausibility can be had without an appeal to human intentions—even if there is no easy empirical access to them. As Philip Wicksteed argued at the end of the last century, supply and demand analysis without the psychological element lacks "demonstrative cogency" (Wicksteed 1899, vol. 3, 141-42).

Much has been said in debates within the philosophy of social science about reliance on an empiricist method.[6] Nevertheless, my purpose in considering these issues is not to adjudicate such disputes but rather to provide some background to the ambiguity surrounding some of the most crucial convictions the economist holds about the world. A thorough treatment of these debates is beyond the scope of this essay. Methodologically self-conscious economists will, when pressed, provide strictly empiricist explanations. It seems clear, though, that the vast majority of mainstream economists actually do believe that people are *in the aggregate* self-interested and rational (properly defined, we should be careful to note) and that most of the tools of economic analysis can really be traced to this basic fact.

I believe economists are largely correct here. And it is because they are right that they have had so hard a time rejecting such assertions about the human psyche out of empiricist scruple. I would argue that most economists actually follow Carl Hempel's deductive-nomological form of explanation as they approach economic phenomena. As Hempel sees it, a phenomenon is explained if it was to be expected from one or more general "covering laws" and the particular facts describing the situation in which the phenomenon occurred (Hempel 1965, 336). The "covering law" economists begin with is a non-empirical one: that economic actors respond to changes rationally with a mind to interests they hold and act upon.[7]

What sort of status would we give to this universally held covering law or conviction about the world? I would propose that in our context we might understand it as an example of what Ralph Potter has called "the 'facts' of the non-empirical theological or quasi-theological realm," one of the four elements he identifies in social ethical argumentation (Potter 1972, 108). The term "empirical interpretation" might be used in place of "non-empirical fact," but the meaning is clear. The economist's assessment of his or her contribution to ethicists will almost certainly incorporate this presumption. The ethicist's assessment of that same contribution will necessitate an evaluation of its descriptive accuracy and its subsequent fruitfulness for ethical analysis.

The former lies primarily, by the economist's own claim, in predicting aggregate responses to changes in systems, whether those changes are due to market shocks or government policy. The latter is more problematic because orthodox economics is clearly a child, though a precocious one, of a culture the ethicist must critique. Still, as Walter Muelder put it, "Even when it is recognized that the methods and models of the social sciences tend to correlate with what is popular intellectual style in a given era, greater openness by theology is indicated, despite the danger (Muelder 1983, 205)." With this, we turn to the substance of the economist's vision.

THE PERSPECTIVE OF ORTHODOX ECONOMICS

Orthodox economists begin with three fundamental presumptions about the world, and these are implicit in the definition of the field. The predominant definition within mainstream economics is nearly universal. Economics is the study of the use of scarce resources to attain competing ends. As we have already seen, this has not always been the definition. Mill and others saw their discipline as studying the production of wealth or material welfare. This older approach to economics as the study of a *particular arena or department* of human life has given way to a conception of the field as the study of a crucial *dimension of all* of human life, namely, the tension of scarcity in every decision everyone makes. Lionel Robbins' work in the 1930's is widely recognized as a watershed in the sentiment within the discipline on this matter.[8]

Thus, *scarcity* is the first fundamental presumption of the discipline. Scarcity names the condition which exists when our goals (or wants or felt needs or hopes) lie unachieved because of the limited resources we have at our disposal. It is a first presumption of economics that this condition obtains in all societies and for all (or almost all) people.

In an effort to achieve their goals, people engage in two sorts of economic activities. The first is production. Both neolithic woman, who plants seeds for a later harvest, and silicon valley man, who designs smaller computer chips, are engaged in production as a means to achieve their goals. The second activity is exchange. A grower of grain *may* exchange some for other products instead of consuming it all directly; the producer of microchip designs will certainly do so. Production is the ultimate basis for fulfilling goals; exchange enables us to achieve our own goals by producing goods or services which others value.

We have already seen much of the debate within orthodox economics over the status of claims about the consciousness of economic agents. The predominant conception of that consciousness was provided, though not invented, by Adam Smith. Smith's primary concern was understanding the causes of wealth, but this pushed him to consider human intentionality. The three-phased argument he made in the first two chapters of *The Wealth of Nations* remains as the single most famous rendition of the modern economist's view of things.

In very broad strokes, Smith's argument was, first, that wealth increases as the division of labor increases, i.e., as people become more and more specialized in the production process. Second, this greater division of labor slowly develops out of "a certain propensity in human nature . . . the propensity to truck, barter, and exchange one thing for another."[9] The third phase of the argument entails the self-interest motive. Smith observed that when, in order to attain some goal, one individual proposes to another an exchange, the most *prevalent* and the most *effective* approach is to make an offer which is in the interest of the other (as well as the self, of course). As Smith's classic passage has it,

> It is not from the benevolence of the butcher, the brewer, or the baker, that we expect our dinner, but from their regard to their own interest. We address ourselves, not to their humanity but to their self-love, and never talk to them of our own necessities but of their advantages. (Smith 1937, 14)

Self-interest is the second fundamental presumption of economists and has long been a controversial topic within and around the discipline. No sorting out of the issues will allay the controversy completely. Technically speaking, mainstream economics holds to a psychological egoism and not an ethical one. Technically, no normative claim is made about self-interest. Rather, the claim is that all action in fact does arise out of "self-interest." The self need not be the immediate *or* the consciously intended beneficiary of action. While some people are egoistic, others act on altruistic motivations. The model presumes only that all actions aim to achieve the goals held by the self. All action is "self-interested" in what I will call the broad sense of that word in that it is the self that holds those interests and acts out of them.

With the application of the calculus to the self-interest framework about 1870, the approach to human decision-making came to be called "the marginal utility theory." Each individual is presumed to have a "utility function" within which each value or interest the person holds appears as a parameter in the equation, with each contributing a certain amount of "utility" (or satisfaction or fulfillment or whatever) to the individual's overall well-being. (The conceptual baggage that comes along with the term "utility" has usually been considered a liability, and this has led a few economists to propose less objectionable terms. Vilfredo Pareto proposed the neologism "ophilimité" in its place (Pareto 1896, 3). Irving Fisher offered "wantability" (Fisher 1918, 335-37). Both L'Academie Francaise and the Modern Language Association can rest relieved that neither of these suggestions caught on.)

It is quite clear that with this conception of human decision, no form of ethics other than consequentialism makes much sense. If all one's values are commensurable, then the trade-offs between values are made implicitly and intuitively, if not explicitly and systematically, in decision-making. This is a significant liability (at least in the view of non-utilitarians) and the ethicist will do well to remain vigilant here. For example, a consequentialist analysis of a public policy (say, to dam up a river for recreational purposes) is a weighing of the costs and benefits according to current preferences of the populace. Yet, as Laurence Tribe has argued, more than these payoffs and penalties are effected. In addition, the experiences open to the community afterward are irrevocably altered, and thus the future development of preferences and consciousness will take an as-yet uncharted course (Tribe 1973, 655-56).

The vast majority of economic actions taken by people appear to be adequately described as choices based on the advantages and disadvantages of the available options. Even rather complicated decisions such as the student's choice between offers of admission from two graduate schools do somehow get made, with apparently incommensurable pros and cons being aggregated intuitively. Obviously, many of the arguments within ethics concerning the reliability of a utilitarian conception of decision are at stake here as well.

Implicit in the presumption that people aim to achieve their goals is that, in doing so, they would prefer to and actually strive to achieve them to the greatest extent possible. *Rationality* is the third fundamental presumption of orthodox economics. It is presumed that all the goals of any one person are measurable against one another, and in deciding how to allocate money, time, energy, etc., each person strives to use those resources as efficiently as possible. Since the economist's primary goal is understanding what will occur in the aggregate, he or she does not need to presume that each and every person is rational in each and every decision. In fact, even many forms of explicitly irrational behavior will correspond to the outcomes predicted by the presumption of rationality. For example, changes in prices not only make it rational to change behavior in certain directions, but they change the configuration of what is possible with any given income so that even irrational choice, if it occurs, must take place within a different and predictable set of possible alternatives (Becker 1976, 167).

Thus we have the three fundamental presumptions of orthodox economics: scarcity, self-interest, and rationality. Out of these emerge a myriad of further assertions about the way the world operates and any choice from among these will be arbitrary to some degree. For our interest in describing the contributions of economists to ethicists, five particular theses are most important. The first concerns the function of prices.

If there is a single assertion that mainstream economists would want to contribute to the reflection of ethicists it is most likely the assertion that prices matter. On the face of it, of course, few would object. It is worth our investigating the idea of price and people's responses to changing prices more closely, for implicit in this discussion are most of the notions already treated.

In common parlance, price and cost are roughly equivalent, and I will use them so (even though for most economic purposes a distinction is made, as when a firm charges a price for a commodity which is different from its cost of production). We usually think of price or cost in terms of money, but there are two important ways in which this is incomplete. Both are shortcomings which should be well understood by ethicists.

The first is that, as economists put it, the "true" cost of anything is its "opportunity cost," namely, what has to be forgone because of it. Since realizing any goal will require the expenditure of resources, the true cost of a goal is best measured by the value of what would otherwise be the next best use of those resources. In practice, it is the easily measured resources that get most of the attention (commodities, labor time, even human "energy"), but in principle, *all* other "resources" should be included (and even a slight diminution of broad cultural standards of values should be counted in as a cost). The true cost of the defense department budget is measured not in dollars but in mass transit systems that didn't get built and in the human suffering and alienation that could have been prevented if our national priorities had been different. The similarity to utilitarian ethical analysis is clear.

Once opportunity cost is seen as the best measure of the cost of a thing, it becomes clearer how economic welfare can increase over time. In the economist's scheme of things life is made better as each of us takes up opportunities where the resources we expend in accomplishing something are thereby put to a higher valued use than any other. Let me temporarily summarize this by referring to goods or services whose "value" to consumers is higher than their cost.

In many cases the difference between value and cost can only be enjoyed by the individual directly benefiting from the opportunity. Spending Sunday afternoon on a picnic may be of greater value for a particular graduate student than spending that time studying in the library, but only the student may be able to gain from that difference between the value of the picnic and the cost in lost study time. In many other cases, opportunities exist for people to enjoy an excess of value over cost, but those very people may not be aware of them. Thus, for example, in trying to sell a house, many people will rely on a realtor and, in return for being presented with a buyer, will be willing to give up some of that excess of value over cost in the form of a realtor's fee.

Viewed from the other side of such a relationship, an "entrepreneur" is someone who sees such opportunities and takes the steps necessary to offer these opportunities to individuals (who choose to buy a good or service whose value to them is greater than its opportunity cost even after they must pay an additional cost, the entrepreneur's "profit"). The economist views the advance in any nation's standard of living as consisting in changes where the value of that change exceeds the cost of achieving it. For this reason mainstream economists appreciate the role of the oft-despised "middle-man," who buys goods or services from some people, gathers those resources up and produces a product or service in order to sell it to someone else.

Thus, it is a basic principle of economics that the essence of economic development is the production of goods and services whose value is greater than their cost.

A corollary of this principle is that allowing the market to reward entrepreneurial initiative is a key to greater economic welfare. If such a reward is allowed and even encouraged, entrepreneurs will work hard to provide (at a price) new opportunities whose cost to consumers will be judged by those consumers to be less than their value to them. (I will return presently to the problems caused when entrepreneurs, out of narrow self-interest, do not pay for or charge consumers for the full costs of goods or services, the case of such "negative externalities" as pollution.)

When economists advise ethicists and others that "prices matter," there are several other implicit elements that need attention. The first and most important is the principle that has enjoyed the most widely recognized empirical corroboration of any in economics. Putting it in a somewhat crude manner, if the price of a good rises, people will buy less of it; if the price falls, they will buy more. In the usual graphic image, the demand curve slopes downward to the right. Similarly, a rise in the market price of a commodity leads producers to supply more: the supply curve slopes upward to the right.

Prices themselves are often paid in dollars and cents, but they need not be. An increase in non-pecuniary costs such as a rise in psychological discomfort attached to a certain behavior will reduce the occurrence of that behavior. Much would need to be said for the full story, but a good bit of it is probably familiar, and a few anecdotal references make the range of relevant phenomena clear. A cut in student aid dollars with no cut in tuition will lower the number of students in school. An increase in welfare payments to unwed mothers will lead to more children born out of wedlock. Public challenges to sexist terminology will lead to a wider use of non-sexist language. In each case forces other than those mentioned are, of course, at work. The point here is to trace through the effects of these particular changes on the behavior of the people affected.

We should be clear that although prices matter, it is "relative prices" that matter most. When tuition at a school rises by six percent, the effect of that price change depends on the relation of the new price to *other* prices. If all prices rose by six percent (a six percent inflation rate), the rise in tuition rate would have no effect on admissions if the incomes of prospective students and their families also rose by six percent. If the only price to rise at all were the tuition of a single school, a significant drop in admissions might be safely predicted as students will go instead to comparable schools. If the only price rise were a six percent tuition increase at all comparable schools, admissions at any one school would be a bit lower, but only as some students chose other options in place of school altogether (since education is now more expensive relative to *other* activities such as employment). It is relative prices that matter, and, in fact, when the economist speaks of a change in price, it is presumed that a change in relative prices is meant.

If the assertion that "prices matter" is the first thesis that the economist would offer to the ethicist, *the second would likely be that "changes are almost always marginal changes."* Consumers only rarely decide whether they are going to stop consuming a particular kind of product altogether. Whether it is electricity, bread, leisure, gasoline or books, nearly all our important decisions about consumption are concerned with consuming more or less than we now consume and not whether we will stop completely. Producers, as well, alter their behavior in the face of changed conditions by marginal adjustments. Legislators, bishops, and even university faculties rarely make all-or-nothing changes. In economic jargon, the question is one of *changes at the margin.*

In consumption, the marginal utility theory posits a diminishing utility to each additional unit of a good consumed in any time period. Thus, the rational consumer will see to it that the last dollar spent on each good will effect as much utility (or satisfaction or happiness, etc.) as the last dollar spent on any other good. Technically, the ratio of their marginal utilities will equal the ratio of their prices when the consumer is "in equilibrium," that is, when the consumer can gain no more by buying less of one good and using the money saved to buy more of another.

Implicit here is the economist's presumption that the questions most in need of attention (or at least most tractable under the economist's hand) concern the effects of changes in our current economic environment. The basic concern is not to explain the underlying reasons why our environment is different from that of other societies and cultures.[10]

This circumscribes a particular arena wherein the economist may fruitfully ask questions, but the idea of marginal adjustments is also a reminder to the ethicist that there is a difference between the overall value of a good or activity and marginal decisions concerning it. Economists lived through most of the nineteenth century without resolving the famous "diamonds and water paradox." Diamonds were doubtlessly less important to every human being than water, but they commanded a far higher price. Does one's willingness to pay a high price for a diamond contradict the common-sense notion that water is more valuable? The solution that marginal utility theory brought was that while a few ounces of water per day would be of tremendous value to someone who had no other liquids available, at the level of consumption which is common for most of us, the last ounce of water we drink each day, the marginal ounce, is of relatively little value to us, far less value than that of even a small diamond.

The moral relevance of this thesis that nearly all change is marginal is that although any particular decision of ours may be in favor of one value rather than another, this says nearly nothing about our "ultimate" assessment of the two. For example, in the moral life of someone heavily committed to a career, strains at home with one's spouse over the amount of time absorbed by one's professional life may be open to similar insight. A decision, infuriating to one's spouse, to spend yet another evening at work does not prove that career is "more important than" marriage. At stake is a marginal decision, not an absolute one. Proposals, for instance, to cut the defense budget do not imply that defense against the threat of external tyranny is "less important than" social welfare or some other goal, though it might be for some who advocate such cuts. (The analogous assertion is true for cuts in welfare spending.)

Alfred Marshall included on the title page of his vastly influential economics text the statement: *Natura non facit saltum.* (Nature does not make leaps.) Of course, this is not literally true in nature (mutations, for example, do occur spontaneously), but it is true most of the time. Similarly in social ethics, most public policy decisions are concerned with marginal changes, not the overall approbation or condemnation of forms of activities. All change (or nearly all) is marginal change.

The third major thesis that economists would offer to ethicists is that optimality is not perfection. Putting it the other way round, perfection is not optimal, at least not under conditions of scarcity. To some extent this is a semantic issue, since by "optimal" the economist means not the best that might be (not the perfect) but the best that can prudently be (given our various goals and the resources at our disposal). More importantly, the central role that scarcity and opportunity cost play in economics tends to ensure that we are aware of the costs and trade-offs that are attendant upon our most sincerely held goals. Whether the issue is the NASA budget or a re-construal of the core requirements for a masters degree in ethics, the optimal plan is not generally the one we would most like to have.

This view of what is "best" leads economists to such testy but true dicta as the assertion that "the optimal amount of air pollution is not zero." We *have* the technology to clean up the smokestack emissions in Gary, Indiana, in the sense that it can be purchased and installed. While those downwind who are not employed by the mills have it in their interest to legislate a complete clean-up of the air, the unemployment that would be caused by a complete ban on toxic emissions renders the ban unwise, and in the estimate of most citizens, immoral. Harkening back to marginal changes, the first forty percent reduction in pollution does far more good for public health and costs far less than does the second forty percent reduction from current levels. As one wag has put it, "not everything worth doing is worth doing well." Everything is, however, worth doing optimally.

One of the most pervasively underestimated scarcities is that summed up by the term "ignorance." Even the well-educated, who have paid a high price to get to that condition, often do not think of knowledge as an economic good. Yet the economics of information presumes that knowledge, like any scarce good, will be sought after rationally. The economic logic of choice leads us to expect that people will expend resources to gain more information (note that this is a marginal decision) up to the point that the cost of gaining more information would outweigh the gain expected from that additional knowledge. Thus, one would expect people to compare prices and qualities carefully when buying automobiles, only casually when buying a pocket calculator and perhaps not at all when buying a carton of milk. There are, of course, markets for information; they range from free flyers at political rallies to the evening newspapers to expensive brokerage services to the CIA. The optimal amount of information to purchase (with our time and other resources) is almost always less than all the information that can be had.

The decision to end a search and make a choice without perfect information requires some estimate of just what it is we *expect* we would find with more effort. This the economist formalizes with a probabilistic model. If we presume that people are rational, we will consider them to estimate the value of an uncertain outcome as the value of the outcome if it were certain to occur multiplied by the probability of that outcome occurring. This may sound severely abstract, but consider how the really difficult decisions are made when they entail a strong element of uncertainty. Often we hear ourselves saying something like: Well, such-and-such would be really bad, but it's very unlikely to happen.

This approach to uncertainty and risk leads to some iconoclastic rejections of claims like "human life is infinitely worthwhile." If this claim were true, even the slightest risk or loss of life would be an unacceptable likelihood. Because it is false, the optimal expected annual number of highway deaths is not zero. We could, after all, set the speed limit at 40 instead of 55, but, while it would undoubtedly save lives, the losses we would impose on ourselves would be substantial. The moral difficulty arises even more acutely when the logic is extended from plane hijackings and murders to core meltdowns and limited nuclear exchanges. At each point where there is a decision to be made, the question is: what are the costs of a slight reduction of the probability of each of these tragedies and what are the expected benefits of such a marginal change? We might rationally decide to do away with nuclear power plants (or some other risky ventures) altogether, but, in general, the moral relevance of this third thesis is that the complete elimination of all risk of the occurrence of evil is not morally optimal under conditions of scarcity. Optimality is not perfection.

The fourth and fifth theses that economists might present to ethicists concern self-interest and the degree to which even altruistic behavior (which I will define as behavior where others are the primary intended beneficiaries) is similar to narrowly self-interested action (where the actor or the actor's family is the primary intended beneficiary). In a crass form, many economists assert that people are, by and large, *narrowly self-interested.* While few economists would assert that people seek out *only* their own narrow interests, they tend to presume that most actions are narrowly self-interested in the sense above. This comes as a depressing idea to most virtuous people, who work hard to contain their own self-interest in their daily lives. In addition, I would argue, it is not as descriptively accurate as a slightly different formulation which I would phrase in two separable assertions.

The fourth thesis is that even altruistic behavior is responsive to prices, or in an economist's jargon, the demand curve for even altruistic activity is downward sloping. Altruism is by no means identical to narrowly self-interested action, but in some economically crucial ways it is the same. Economists presume that at any particular time, based on personal goals and preferences, people already have allocated their time, money and other resources to some combination of narrowly self-interested and more broadly altruistic causes. In the economist's terminology, the person is in equilibrium. Let us take charitable contributions as an example of altruistic behavior. If there is a marginal change like the elimination of the income tax deduction for such contributions, it is clear that the now-higher price of altruism will lead to some reduction in this one kind of altruistic behavior. Similarly, we would expect that a change in the tax code that would allow *an increase* in the deduction (say to double or triple the size of any charitable contribution) would lead to an increase in such contributions, though by a smaller amount than the reduction in taxes. Changes in the law probably do not affect the individual's assessment of the worthiness of good causes, but raising or lowering the cost of giving will affect this activity in basically the same way as raising or lowering the cost of any good or service one holds as a narrowly self-interested goal. Even altruistic behavior is responsive to a change in its price.

The fifth thesis is that public policy should depend on narrowly self-interested incentives and not on altruistic ones. This, I believe, is the more fruitful form of the belief that people are, by and large, narrowly self-interested. It does not deny that altruism exists or that public leaders can effectively appeal to it. President Nixon did just that when he asked all of us to turn down our thermostats to 68 degrees. It claims, though, that if the goal is a reduction of oil consumption, it will be far more effective to allow a rise in the price of oil, in response to which a far greater number of people will cut their consumption. (The inequitable distribution effects of this policy will then need to be dealt with by subsidies to the poor.)[11]

Neither of these formulations asserts that selfishness is better than altruism. But they do say that it was no surprise that blacks led the civil rights movement.

They do say that waiting for men to give equal rights to women is like leaving the runway lights on for Amelia Earhart's return. They do say that only the naive will set up a government agency to accomplish a social goal and then just presume that the right things will occur.

In addition, if we appreciate the extent to which people tend to act in their own narrow interest, we will be attentive to what the economist calls the "free rider" problem and the special interest effect. Since most beneficial collective decisions will benefit everyone in some particular group, there will be a predictable tendency for many group members not to work to achieve the result, since they'll benefit anyway. In very large groups, where the average individual can rationally expect to have at most a negligible effect on the outcome, it might be rational not to participate. As a normative suggestion this is clearly objectionable. As a descriptive generalization, it leads the economist Mancur Olson both to expect under-participation of large and unorganized groups in the political process and to beware of predictable over-participation of small and well organized groups (see Olson 1971).

This latter phenomenon is referred to as the special interest effect. Individuals in a small group (such as a trade association) have an incentive to push for legislation favoring themselves, since their portion of any legislated rewards for the group will still be substantial, while their portion of the cost will be small. Individuals in a large group (like taxpayers or consumers) have little or no incentive to try to prevent such subsidies, since any effort to stop the scheme may itself be costlier than the benefit to the individual of preventing it, and even then most efforts by individual citizens will predictably have little effect. In fact, it may even be rational for an individual to remain *ignorant* of such pork barrel projects, since the very cost of information about them will often exceed the costs the projects will impose on that individual.

If ethicists are inclined to accept and act upon this contribution from economists, some operationally significant implications will appear. One is that special attention must be paid to appointed and elected officials, and that the smaller the constituency, the greater the danger that the official will be subject to strong special interest pressures. Thus, public funding of campaigns and registration of lobbyists is actually more important for the members of Congress (where a pork-barrel project is paid for by all taxpayers but may benefit only a single district) than for the President (who is accountable to all the voters).

A second important implication is that even within groups with very large constituencies, every individual and every leader will have personal interests which may or may not correspond with the overall general interest of the group. As a result, the economist would raise an important objection to the analysis of private-regarding and public-regarding associations outlined by Franklin I. Gamwell in this volume.

While there may be an important normative difference between the sorts of activities legitimated in different types of groups, the economist would consider it naive to expect that the internal dynamics of the two will be radically different.

Gamwell lists universities as an example of a public-regarding institution and cites education among the relevant purposes of public-regarding associations more generally (Gamwell, p. 53). Yet it is questionable whether any institution created for scholarship and education sheds the mantle of private-regarding interests simply because its hopes are high. Students applying to graduate school feel all-too-similar to applicants for a scarce number of jobs at the local factory (though the ones who get in probably do not feel this as clearly as those who do not, and they're usually not around to tell us about it.) Junior faculty at "publish-or-perish" schools rarely feel the camaraderie accessible at the small town hardware store or the worker-owned cooperative. It may be that scholarship is judged inherently more social a phenomenon than the production of goods (though this is questionable), but it hardly seems accurate to assert that association is its primary or controlling end.

The economist's insight into relational dynamics would lead Gamwell's re-formed liberal not, I judge, to "maximize" public-regarding associations and to limit "economic" ones. Rather, it presses them to attend to and reconfigure the incentive structures within *both* sorts of institutions to channel private-regarding interests so they flow in the same direction as public-regarding ones. A classic example from the field of comparative economic systems is relevant here. Soviet agriculture has been consistently inefficient not primarily because of centralized planning but because (except for small private plots) local farm income is in-variant to changes in the productivity of the farm. Chinese agriculture—just as avowedly socialist—is far more productive, because the economy is structured so that the annual income of the communal farm is higher in years when production is up and lower when it falls. A multitude of other examples closer to home make the same point. Economists may harp too long on the importance of incentives in human decision, but there are very few graduate faculties which have such confidence in their students' motivations that they are inclined to drop their degree requirements as a means to improve their students' education.

One final implication of the economist's presumption that people are pre-dictably self-interested in the narrow sense is that because of their interest in promoting their goals, people will have a tendency to ignore what the economist terms "the externalities" which they effect. Whether it is pipe smoke at the faculty meeting or smog in Los Angeles, whether it is a decision to divorce one's spouse or to close down a plant, most people are willing to accept the fact that they impose costs on others. To some degree, this is morally unobjec-tionable: few would find campfires in the Grand Tetons morally wrong because of the smoke they create. The problem is one of agreeing on the point where the rights of some outweigh the efficiency of autonomous action by others. Society is in the position of the man who sits in a luke-warm bath and turns on the hot water at full volume. It's hard to know when to let out the first yell.

Economists are generally willing to allow society's values to determine which activities will be subsidized by the community. Yet the general rule which ethicists might develop from the economist's contribution is that the presumption should be in favor of economic actors' paying the full "social" cost of their activities. For example, firms planning to build a new plant make concerted efforts to capture (or "internalize") the social benefit the project will cause for a geographic area by bargaining with competing municipalities for tax concessions and preferential financing. This is possible because market pressures are currently working in their favor and against that of the city seeking their presence.

The economist's insight will lead the ethicist to insist that the firm also pay (i.e., "internalize") the social costs when the firm moves out. Yet those same market pressures work against their having to pay the full cost of a plant shutdown, since states and cities risk creating "a bad business climate" if more restrictive laws are implemented. Social costs will be internalized only if an umbrella political structure mandates this. A recent rise in the forces of international competition have put pressures on hard-won national laws aimed at humanizing the economy. The insight into the prevalence of self-interest often pushes economists to press for less government intervention in the economy, yet it should also push them and all ethically concerned citizens to press for stronger and not weaker international organizations.

CONCLUSION

I have outlined the three basic presumptions of economics: scarcity, self-interest and rationality. In addition I have cited five theses which I believe most mainstream economists would want to "contribute" to ethicists: prices matter; most change is marginal; optimality isn't perfection; even altruistic behavior is responsive to prices; and public policy should employ narrowly self-interested incentives.

In a very important sense, these topics might be inappropriate because they are so basic. There are many more concrete economic insights and tools with which ethicists would do well to become acquainted. I have ignored price and income elasticities and the causes for shifts in demand and supply, at any one time or over time. I did not examine the economics of the firm or marginal cost pricing. I overlooked measures of the distribution of income and the fact that for all of our efforts to help the poor, distribution of wealth in the United States is quite similar to that of Bangladesh. I have ignored macroeconomic analysis and the disputes between Keynesians and monetarists. I have not examined index numbers or defined inflation or shown how inflation differs from changes in the cost of living. I have overlooked the distinction between income and substitution effects, and have not investigated the meaning of "the strength of the dollar" abroad and how that is related to employment at home. The list could go on.

In another sense, the general approach may be objectionable because it has stressed the cogency of the economist's view and has largely left unattended critical evaluations by ethicists and heterodox economists. The orthodox perspective clearly misreads the dynamics of the human psyche. As a result it misunderstands the texture of individual moral action and overlooks possible public efforts to mold individuals' attitudes. Although every introductory text-book in the field includes the admission that the market will *not* achieve the morally best outcomes if the initial distribution of income is not morally correct, this warning is a sort of "hedgeless hedge," since most orthodox economists go on to act as if the admission were not true after all. The problem, for example, is that, working as it "should," the market allocates the best land in the Third World to the production of cash crops for the wealthy citizens of the North and not for food for poor people locally. Most economists continue to "believe in" the market as the best solution to world poverty and tend to oppose efforts at substantial redistribution of income. I believe that many hold to· at most a vitiated notion of social justice and that, without admitting this non-scientific moral judgment even to themselves, they believe they support the market on the basis of scientific analysis alone.

In addition, orthodox economists have historically tended to be inattentive to the institutional structures (e.g., legal systems, social patterns, cultural values) within which individuals carry on economic activity. Whether this is the cause or the effect of their interest in marginal change is debatable. In any case, beginning with a skewed vision of both individual human activity and human institutions, economists tend to be oblivious to crucial issues such as cultural change (e.g., Max Weber's or Thorstein Veblen's assertions that rationality or "the business system" slowly undermines the cultural values on which the suc-cesses of modern industrial society are founded). A particular but critical example of this shortsightedness is an incomplete interpretation of various forms of power active in the economy, due largely to the economist's conviction that compet-itive market transactions are the norm.

To deal well with these problems, much more would need to be said about them, and this is impossible here. Still the question arises: if orthodox economics has these shortcomings, why should ethicists even bother with the discipline? It is my presumption that *any* single perspective on the world will be incomplete and skewed. And there are no rules for the adjudication of differences between different perspectives that are not themselves based in still another perspective. The vision of the world that orthodox economists offer is not ethically important simply because it exists. It is important because it is quite helpful, I judge, in understanding and even interpreting economic activity. Several presumptions that ethicists often make are balanced or broadened by the sort of insight contained in the five theses articulated in this essay.

The advantage to conversations such as the one this volume enables is that each author and reader gains a fuller sense of how other thoughtful people understand reality and can afterwards carry on more appropriately, though not always less ambiguously. Engaging in this conversation is an act of faith, but I take it to be one that is essential to the public-regarding life of the university.

Notes

I am indebted to Joseph M. Friedrich for many helpful suggestions.

1. One need only think of the expectations concerning George Stigler's policy positions at the time of his Nobel prize award. Taking him to be a conservative, pro-markets and pro-business, many in the press and in the Reagan administration were surprised to hear him describe the anti-pollution laws as a matter of the public's discretion based on the tastes of the American citizenry. (Though to be sure, he holds strong opinions about the *kind* of anti-pollution laws that are appropriate).

2. A classic example here is the effort to save domestic jobs through protectionist barriers to imports (which inevitably induces other nations to do likewise, with the aggregate effect being the reduction of world trade, the loss of opportunities for specialization of production and a lower GNP for both nations.) The state of Minnesota recently passed a law requiring that an out-of-state firm must underbid all in-state firms by more than ten percent before it is awarded any official state contracts in competitive bidding. Minnesota-based contractors would obviously gain from this, but only as long as the surrounding states choose not to reciprocate. Predictably, Iowa now has a similar law. A majority of state legislators in Minnesota now seem willing to put an end to the law, but there's no telling what the Iowans will do then. The most clearly predictable outcome is that much time and energy will be spent trying to undo the mess.

3. Emboldened by the dominance of the utilitarianism of the day, Francis Edgeworth went so far in his book *Mathematical Psychics* as to construct triple integrals representing the aggregate happiness of society over time.

4. Vilfredo Pareto argued early in this century that the utility theory was not necessary as the foundation for economic analysis, and that revealed preference theory (which presumed only that consumers are able to state their preference or indifference between any two bundles of commodities) was actually superior (Pareto 1971, 133). Later developments (see, e.g., Hicks and Allen 1934, Samuelson 1938, Houthakker 1950) showed in great detail the general equivalence of the utility and revealed preference analysis as analytic bases for demand theory.

5. In doing so, according to Friedman, the economist operates like the physicist who predicts the path of a falling stone on the presumption that it occurs in a vacuum and predicts the path of a falling sheet of paper on the presumption that it does not. The issue is not whether there is or is not a vacuum (of course there isn't!). The issue is which presumption will give an accurate prediction.

6. The provision of economic "explanations" which rely on the rationality presumption, for example, might at times be traced to what Michael Scriven has termed considerations of "type-justifying grounds" for explanations, where "the practical requirements of the person or public to whom we address our explanation" push the social scientist to do so (Scriven 1959, 96).

7. Thus, if we ask "Why have U. S. oil imports over the last fifteen years not risen in proportion to the rise in GNP?", the strictly empiricist answer is that the price of oil has risen dramatically relative to other prices. The answer that most economists believe (because it is by far the better one) is that due to the higher price of oil, consumers, out of a rational concern for the many different goals they hold, have reduced their consumption of oil-related products and services and have directly or indirectly substituted other goods in place of oil (e.g., coal, home insulation and more efficient cars). The fact that most orthodox economists would also *describe* the latter explanation as "better" illustrates the basic point.

8. We should also note that this definition centering on scarcity is not universally preferred among mainstream economists today. For example, Gary Becker has argued that this usual definition articulates the scope of inquiry broadly enough but is all too silent on the *tools* which "the economic approach" to human behavior employs (Becker 1976, 4; see also, e.g., McKenzie and Tullock 1981). He would prefer to make more explicit that the economic approach explains behavior not by appeal to tradition or to sudden shifts in the individual's values, but by appeal to maximizing behavior and stable tastes (see, e.g., Stigler and Becker 1977). Still, this is essentially an extension of, rather than a challenge to, the prevailing definition. Becker is also perhaps the primary force in extending the economic approach to areas of life not traditionally considered "economic": politics, crime, drug addiction, and even

marriage and the decision to have children. This is, however, an issue separate from the definition of the field.

9. His erroneous examples of primitive hunters trading beaver for deer say as much about his philosophical and religious convictions as they do about the state of cultural anthropology in the eighteenth century, and those convictions largely endure today, though in a more nuanced form.

10. Some Marxist economists have argued that for all its failure to understand the more important long-term questions about the transition of economic structures, orthodox economics does, at least, deal better than Marxian economics with short-run changes caused by tax policy and price shocks and the like (e.g., Lange 1945). On the other hand, some orthodox economists have striven to explain broad political and cultural differences in terms of the maximizing logic in the face of the constraints of such variables as climate and topography. Mancur Olson argues that the logic of collective choice based on individual maximizing decisions goes far to explain the long-term cycle of prosperity and eventual decline of national economies (Olson 1982).

11. A *very* important additional effect of this use of self-interested incentives in national energy policy is that it will also induce suppliers to produce more energy. The appeal to an altruistic frugality will, if effective, do just the opposite.

CHAPTER IX

Christianity and Capitalism: Perspectives from Social Theory[1]

Bruce Grelle

The several founders of modern social theory—including Marx, Weber, and Durkheim—shared, in Anthony Giddens' words, "an overwhelming interest . . . in the delineation of the characteristic structure of 'capitalism' as contrasted with prior forms of society" (1971, xvi). The fact that these "prior forms of society" are generally considered to have been *religious,* as compared to the more thoroughly secular forms of society characteristic of modernity, nicely underscores the significance of perspectives from social theory for religious studies.

This significance has nowhere been more apparent than in the various typologies of society that inform so much writing in both social theory and religious studies. One thinks here of the different ideal-typical constructs devised by social theorists in order to account for what many have perceived as an historical transition from one kind of society to another. Thus, we have accounts of the transitions from status to contract societies (Maine), from *gemeinschaft* to *gesellschaft* (Tönnies), from mechanical to organic solidarity (Durkheim), from traditional to legal-rational authority (Weber), from feudalism to capitalism (Marx). Taken together, such themes as these constitute the more generic notion of a transition from tradition to modernity—a notion that informs a number of the papers collected in the present volume.[2]

In addition to this widely shared theoretical framework, there are also a variety of more particular intellectual and historical connections between social theory and religious studies. One thinks here of the extensive appropriation of the evolutionary sociology of Herbert Spencer by William Graham Sumner and other turn-of-the-century American religious thinkers (see Winter 1966, 5-14). The influence that the Durkheimian tradition of social thought has exercised over the anthropological study of religion and over contemporary discussions of civil religion is widely recognized. And finally, many contemporary political, liberation, black, and feminist theologians have been explicit in their adoption of selected aspects of the Marxian tradition.

However, the most influential perspective from social theory with respect to the specific issue at hand—the relationship between capitalism and Christianity—has been the one developed by Max Weber in *The Protestant Ethic and the Spirit of Capitalism.* Moreover, many of the concerns first articulated in that work continue to set much of the agenda for contemporary discussions of the historical and normative relations between capitalism and Christianity.

In order to understand Weber's thesis about the relationship between capitalism and Protestant Christianity and to understand the controversy that has surrounded this thesis since its appearance in 1904-1905, two contexts must be borne in mind. One is a *theoretical-methodological context* which involves disparate ways of understanding the relation between ideas and social change—in this case the relation between certain theological ideas and changing forms of economic activity. Another is a *political-ideological context* which involves disparate evaluations of both the economic and moral dimensions of capitalist civilization.

THE THEORETICAL-METHODOLOGICAL CONTEXT OF THE WEBER THESIS

The immediate theoretical-methodological context of Weber's work was characterized by the widespread belief that modern capitalism was the outcome of a natural growth that could be explained by purely economic factors such as increased trade, technological advances, and increased demand created by population growth.[3] This economic interpretation was prominent among Marxist and non-Marxist historians alike. What was of interest to Weber, however, and what was neglected by thoroughgoing materialist perspectives, was the extent to which the economic changes characteristic of modern capitalism were bound up with changes in the religious ethos of Western culture. This shift in ethos was nowhere more evident than in changing attitudes toward money and money-making.

It is frequently noted that in the middle ages both the church and society frowned upon trade and despised the money lender. Though its necessity was admitted, Thomas Aquinas designated the making of money as "turpitude" and roundly castigated the sin of avarice (Fullerton 1959, 6). The notion that the shopkeeper could only with difficulty please God even found its way into canon law. Several church councils condemned usury, by which was meant not only extortionate interest but interest of any kind, and a usurer was often denied the sacraments. While there were always numerous practical qualifications on these judgments, it is fair to say that money-making was regarded as "socially degrading and morally and religiously dangerous" (Fullerton 1959, 6; see also Noonan 1957; and Nelson 1969).

Yet if there was such a gap historically between many forms of economic activity and Christian ethics, if the pursuit of riches for their own sake and other forms of market behavior characteristic of capitalism had once been condemned as sin and concupiscence, how had it come to pass that such activities came to be morally acceptable and, in some instances, positively sanctioned by theological beliefs? Weber's thesis in *The Protestant Ethic* was an attempt to answer this question. This thesis has two dimensions. The first involves a claim regarding the "spirit" that distinguishes modern capitalism from previous forms of capitalism. The second involves a claim regarding the unintended economic consequences of certain Protestant theological convictions.

To the extent that capitalism is simply equated with "an acquisitive instinct" or with "pecuniary society", then it is clear that capitalism has existed in one form or another in every age. Weber however was concerned to designate the uniqueness of modern industrial capitalism as distinct from other types (Gerth and Mills 1946, 65-70). Distinctive to modern capitalism were such concrete economic factors as the emergence of a specific production establishment based on formally free labor, a fixed plant, and so on (Gerth and Mills 1946, 68). But in addition to these material factors, Weber recognized the significance of developments at the levels of psychology and ethos. These factors are collected under his notion of the "spirit" of capitalism.

The concept of the "spirit" of capitalism was employed by Weber in order to help account for the fact that transformations of traditional economic forms frequently occurred without any technological change taking place within the enterprise and without any sudden influx of capital into the industry in question. Rather, the rational reorganization of production and the maximization of efficiency in such enterprises were the result of the introduction of a new spirit of entrepreneurial enterprise (Giddens 1971, 127). It is this spirit of enterprise—this peculiar ethos defined as a sense of obligation in money-making (Fullerton 1959, 8)—that constituted the crucial difference between modern capitalism and other forms of capitalism. For while many other forms of capitalism are founded on the amoral pursuit of personal gain, modern capitalism, at least in its initial stages, seemed to rest upon the disciplined obligation of work as duty (Giddens 1971, 126; Weber 1958, 53).

It would be a mistake, however, according to Weber, to think that the spirit of capitalism could simply be inferred from the growth of rationalism as a whole in Western society. This would assume a progressive unilinear development of rationalism, when, in fact, the rationalization of different institutions in Western societies shows uneven development. It takes many concrete forms and it develops variably in different areas of social life (Giddens 1971, 127; Weber 1958, 76-78). Rather, the concern of The Protestant Ethic is limited to discovering "whose intellectual child that particular concrete form of rational thought was, from which the idea of a calling and devotion to labor in the calling, has derived . . ." (Weber in Giddens 1971, 127). This brings us to the second dimension of Weber's thesis—the one concerned with the unintended economic consequences of certain Protestant teachings.

Weber began The Protestant Ethic with the preliminary observation that the most economically advanced nations of his day were primarily Protestant. Moreover, Protestants made up a greater proportion of business leaders, technically and commercially trained personnel, and highly skilled labor than did Catholics (Weber 1958, 35). This notion of an affinity between modern capitalism and the Reformation was not unique to Weber. What was at issue was the nature of this apparent link. The characteristic Marxist interpretation of the day, for example, had argued that Protestantism was the ideological mantle of a newly ascendant bourgeoisie. Protestant theology reflected the economic changes brought on by the early development of capitalism. Others suggested that the break with economic traditionalism that occurred in the new commercial centers encouraged autonomy from tradition in general and from older forms of religious institutions in particular (Giddens 1971, 125). Yet Weber was struck by the fact that the relation between Protestant religious ideas and the economic values of capitalism was not what one might expect it to be if the ideas were simply the reflection of an underlying economic reality or the religious expression of a more general break with tradition (Weber 1958, 75). For far from reducing the areas of life under control of the church, the Reformation had injected a religious factor into all spheres of the life of the believer. Rather than relaxing the control of the church over everyday activities, Protestantism demanded of its adherents a more vigorous discipline than had Catholicism (Giddens 1971, 125; Weber 1958, 80-89, 212). In view of this, Weber turned his attention to the character of Protestant beliefs themselves. Foremost among these were the concept of the calling and the doctrine of predestination.

The most obvious link between the spirit of modern capitalism and Protestant theological doctrines was the concept of the calling. This concept served to bring the mundane affairs of everyday life under an all-embracing religious influence. Each individual is called to fulfill his duty to God through the proper conduct of his daily life. In Lutheranism, though, this notion remained quite traditionalistic in many respects, particularly with regard to the moral limitations placed upon acquisition (Weber 1958, 85). It was rather in the Calvinist forms of Protestantism, where the notion of the calling was combined with the doctrine of predestination, that Weber ultimately identified the affinity between the Protestant ethic and the spirit of capitalism.

The doctrine of predestination—the teaching that from the first moment of creation only certain individuals were chosen to achieve eternal grace—provoked a great deal of anxiety among believers. This anxiety was met by a variety of pastoral responses. One such response was to assure believers that even though good works could in no way promote salvation, success in one's calling could nevertheless be regarded as a token of God's grace. Too much concern over one's destiny was taken to be due to a lack of faith and thus evidenced a lack of grace. The best way to avoid this concern and at the same time to indicate one's membership in the community of the faithful was to fulfill one's obligations to society. These obligations could be met by performing the tasks of everyday life with the utmost degree of seriousness, effort, and discipline. All distractions and temptations were to be thrust aside in favor of a life of continuous service. Wealth continued to be regarded as a temptation but now only insofar as it could be used to support an idle or luxurious way of life. Significantly, the accumulation of wealth as such was no longer condemned. Weber's interpretation of the economic consequences of this constellation of ideas and code of behavior are well-known. In the words of one commentator, "consumption was limited, production was encouraged, and surplus capital which could not be spent on vain luxuries was reinjected into the business, thus providing a plentiful flow of capital, the lubricating oil of economic advance" (Kitch 1967, xvi).

Thus, a religious worldview that was geared toward other-worldly and non-material concerns unintentionally served to stimulate a valorization of economic activity—activity traditionally viewed as antithetical to typically religious concerns—to an extent previously unknown in history. Weber, however, rejected the suggestion that the Calvinist ethos is a necessary component to the functioning of modern capitalism once it is established on a broad scale (Giddens 1971, 131; Weber 1958, 70). On the contrary, what was for the Puritan compliance with divine guidance increasingly becomes, for the world of contemporary capitalism, a mechanical conformity to the economic and organizational exigencies of industrial production at all levels of the division of labor. "The specific conclusion of The Protestant Ethic is that, while the Puritan, because of his religious faith, deliberately chose to work in a calling, the specialized character of the capitalist division of labor forces modern man to do so" (Giddens 1971, 131).

As mentioned above, Weber's thesis generated a great deal of controversy. A host of scholars took up the issue of the historical relations between capitalism and Christianity, frequently criticizing various aspects of Weber's scholarship and methodology along the way. One such figure was Werner Sombart from whom Weber had borrowed the concept of a distinctive "spirit" of modern capitalism and who had actually published on the subject before the appearance of The Protestant Ethic. [4] In the 1902 edition of Der Moderne Kapitalismus, Sombart had argued that there was such a thing as the spirit of modern capitalism and, in keeping with Weber's subsequent work, stressed that its role had been crucial in the development of the modern capitalist economy. Weber had gone on from here to explore more explicitly the possible origins of this spirit.

In the revised 1916 edition of the same work, however, Sombart concluded that the evolution of modern capitalism had begun earlier than he had previously believed, thereby lending support to some of the historical criticisms of Weber's position that were beginning to be made. In addition, Sombart published his reflections on the extent to which religious factors other than Protestantism might have affected the development of the capitalist spirit. In Juden und das Wirtschaftsleben (1911) (translated as The Jews and Modern Capitalism), he argued for the importance of the social attitudes and economic practices of Judaism as a source of the spirit of capitalism. And in 1915 in Der Bourgeois (translated as The Quintessence of Capitalism), he continued to stress the thesis regarding the contribution of religion to the spirit of capitalism but applied it to Catholicism rather than to Protestantism.

One of the chief supporters of Weber's position and one of the most influential participants in the controversy so far as religious social ethics has been concerned was Ernst Troeltsch. In The Social Teaching of the Christian Churches, Troeltsch basically supported the Weberian theory regarding the relationship of Protestantism to capitalism and sought to use Weber's methodological perspective to illuminate the entire history of Christian social thought. Troeltsch's work continues to provide one of the most direct links between social theory and religious ethics.

In addition to Sombart and Troeltsch, a number of other well-known scholars including R. H. Tawney, Lujo Brentano, H. M. Robertson, and Henri Sée have contributed to the controversy surrounding Weber's analysis of capitalism and Christianity. There are at least three themes that have characterized this critical literature. One is that, to the extent that there was something that could be identified as the "spirit" of capitalism at all, it either had earlier historical origins or different geographical locations than those concentrated upon by Weber and his supporters.[5] A second theme was developed by scholars who disputed the manner in which Weber drew a causal connection between Protestantism and capitalism. Even if the existence of a "spirit" of capitalism was granted, these critics argued that a close inspection of either the textual sources or the relevant economic data simply did not support the specific manner in which Weber's thesis was elaborated.[6] A third theme in the critical literature has been developed by those who reject the manner in which Weber characterized the differences between the economic teachings of Catholicism and Protestantism. Like Sombart, some have emphasized tendencies in Catholicism that may be viewed as having fostered a capitalistic spirit. Others have accepted Weber's emphasis on Protestantism but have questioned his relatively narrow focus on various aspects of Calvinism.[7]

THE POLITICAL-IDEOLOGICAL CONTEXT OF THE WEBER THESIS

With an awareness of the controversy that has surrounded The Protestant Ethic, we begin to move from the theoretical-methodological to the political-ideological context of the Weber thesis. While many of the participants in the controversy have focused primarily on the descriptive adequacy of Weber's work—upon his selection and interpretation of the "facts"—it is nonetheless possible to detect ideological overtones in some of their conclusions. Implicit in many of the discussions of the methods best suited to the study and analysis of the relations between capitalism and Christianity are concerns not only about what these relations have been historically, but also about what they should be. This shading of one context into another helps account for the manifestations of both the religious and political partisanship that are frequently apparent in scholarly discussions of capitalism and Christianity. Thus, there have been predictable differences between some Catholic and Protestant controversialists. The former seek to discredit various Protestant beliefs by associating them with some of the more mercenary practices of capitalism while the latter congratulate themselves for allegedly having fostered economic progress (Kitch 1967, xix). But even more striking than occasional differences between certain Protestant and Catholic positions—and certainly more characteristic of the essays in the present volume—are differences between political-ideological opponents and allies of capitalism.

The overlap of these descriptive and evaluative contexts is nowhere more apparent than in the work of Weber himself. Both his activities as a German politician and the ambivalent judgments of capitalist civilization that are scattered throughout his scholarly work attest to this.[8] The political-ideological dimension of Weber's thought has often been drawn out by focusing on his commitment to the values of classical European liberalism. Thus, Anthony Giddens has demonstrated the extent to which the writings of both Weber and Durkheim originated in an attempt to reinterpret and defend the claims of political liberalism within "the twin pressures of Romantic hypernationalistic conservatism on the one side, and revolutionary socialism on the other" (Giddens 1971, 244). Likewise, Gerth and Mills have presented Weber as a representative of "the humanist tradition of liberalism, which is concerned with the freedom of the individual to create free institutions" (1946, 73). Yet it is precisely this commitment to the classical liberal values of freedom, creativity, and spontaneity that accounts for the oft noted pathos of much of Weber's writing (see Giddens 1971, 190, 242; and Löwith 1982). Weber's analysis of capitalism had led him to the conclusion that the field of responsible freedom was shrinking (Gerth and Mills 1946, 70). As an historically developed phenomenon, freedom was now on the defensive against the rational impersonality of both capitalism and bureaucracy.

Weber's concern was with the decline of the well-rounded human personality in favor of the technical expert, who, from the human point of view, is crippled (Gerth and Mills 1946, 73). Moreover, as an adherent of "humanist and cultural liberalism rather than economic liberalism," Weber saw the economic system as "a compulsive apparatus rather than as the locus of freedom" (Gerth and Mills 1946, 73). Thus, *The Protestant Ethic* has not only set much of the agenda for various socio-historical analyses of capitalism and Christianity. Weber may also be viewed as having posed in 1906 an ethical question that the authors in the present volume continue to wrestle with.

> It is utterly ridiculous to see any connection between the high capitalism of today . . . with democracy or with freedom in any sense of these words. Yet this capitalism is an unavoidable result of our economic development. The question is: how are freedom and democracy in the long run at all possible under the domination of highly developed capitalism? (Weber in Gerth and Mills 1946, 71)

It is this "defensive pessimism" regarding the present and future prospects of freedom in Western civilization that a number of writers have found most objectionable about Weber's evaluation of capitalism.

Apart from those who continue to assert the positivist dictum that evaluative or normative judgments are altogether out of place in social science,[9] there is a distinguished group of scholars who have taken issue with Weber's critique of capitalism and, even more, with the influence this negative assessment of capitalism has enjoyed in social theory. Thus, such writers as Hayek, Nisbet, Shils, and Bell—all of whom themselves represent distinctive political-ideological perspectives within social theory—have separately challenged what they see as a sort of romantic anti-capitalism that they feel has been all too prevalent in social theory generally.[10] Like Benne and Schroeder in the present volume, these writers have emphasized what they see as the progressive, democratic and pluralistic aspects of capitalism.[11] This contrasts sharply with the sorts of social theory that have been developed by members of the Frankfurt School and by the theorists of mass society who have appropriated such themes as rationalization, alienation, and domination from both Weber's and Marx's critiques of capitalism.

This concern with the human condition under capitalism that is evidenced by allies and opponents of capitalism alike underscores the evaluative dimension of social theory and provides an important point of contact between those working in the fields of social theory and religious social ethics.

RELIGIOUS ETHICS AND SOCIAL THEORY

In recent years, there has been increasing interest on the part of many religious ethicists in the ideological underpinnings and normative implications of various social theoretical perspectives (see Winter 1966; Wogaman 1977; and Stackhouse 1972). At the same time there has been a great deal of discussion about the status of social theoretical knowledge, methods, and models within the field of religious ethics itself. Thus, in discussions of the relation between religious ethics and social theory we are confronted once again with both theoretical-methodological and political-ideological questions.

At the more specifically methodological level, many religious ethicists have underscored the importance of social theory as a constitutive aspect of ethical reflection on economic, political, and social issues. Walter Muelder, for example, has long emphasized the interdisciplinary nature of religious social ethics and has himself made outstanding contributions to the field of economic ethics (Muelder 1953; 1959; 1972). Likewise, James Gustafson (1974, 197-286) has given serious attention to the relationship of empirical science to moral thought and has been especially interested in the nature of the interplay in ethics between theological and scientific interpretations of human existence. While sensitive to the presence of normative assumptions that are often embedded in the claims of both the social and life sciences (see, e.g., Gustafson 1974, 229-244), both of these writers have been primarily concerned with delineating the methodological difficulties and possibilities entailed by the use of empirical research in normative ethics.

Other writers, however, have focused on the ideological dimensions of one's choice of social theory. José Míguez Bonino, for example, has, like Muelder and Gustafson, insisted on the methodological significance of social theory for religious ethics (1983, 38, 54). But Míguez Bonino has also made a great deal of the fact that there are a number of competing social theories—a number of competing versions of empirical reality. Thus, he has emphasized the extent to which one's choice of social theory is influenced by one's social location and basic value commitments. Míguez Bonino elucidates this point by appealing to Juan Luis Segundo's understanding of the relation between faith and ideology.

According to Segundo, the source of human motivations is faith, which involves the non-empirical choice of an ideal. In our concrete situations, however, this choice issues in an "ideology," which, in Segundo's usage, refers to a "system of goals and means that serve as the necessary backdrop for any human option or line of action" (1976, 102). Míguez Bonino has sought to come to terms with this relationship between faith and ideology by arguing that the Christian is not without orientation for the choice of social theory that must be made. When faced with what he sees as the two mainstreams of social theory—the functionalist stream with its vision "from the top" of existing society and the dialectical stream with its vision "from below"—Míguez Bonino opts for a dialectical social theory which he claims corresponds more adequately to the "perspective, the understanding, and the concerns that emerge in an option for solidarity with the poor" (1983, 44-47).

This particular manner of relating faith and ideology has, of course, been the subject of much controversy. This is especially evident in criticisms of the widespread adoption by Míguez Bonino and other liberation and political theologians of various sorts of Marxian social theory. Again, what is at issue here is not only the existence of competing moral claims, but the existence of competing claims about empirical reality.[12] Yet despite fundamental differences on this issue, few deny the importance of some form of social theoretical knowledge for religious social ethics.[13]

Questions about the grounds of one's choice of social theory raise issues of intellectual honesty and objectivity and of the relationship between scholarship and partisanship. These issues cry out for serious attention. For now, however, it is enough to have noted that the topic of Christianity and capitalism is a particularly fruitful site for an exploration of the relation between social theory and religious ethics. Not only do they converge around an interest in the sociohistorical relations of Christianity and capitalism but frequently in their normative interests as well. From Rauschenbusch, Ryan, and Henry George to Gutierrez, Novak, and Míguez Bonino, from Marx and Weber to Giddens and Habermas, religious ethicists and social theorists have shared a preoccupation with analyzing and evaluating the human condition under capitalism. Whether this condition is something to be praised and defended or is something to be condemned and overcome remains a matter of dispute within both religious ethics and social theory. But the similarity of interests and the importance of the issues suggest that both fields might profit from a more direct and sustained conversation with each other.

Notes

1. For present purposes, I follow Anthony Giddens in viewing "social theory" as "a body of theory shared in common by all the disciplines concerned with the behavior of human beings. It concerns not only sociology, therefore, but anthropology, economics, political science, human geography, psychology—the whole range of the social sciences" (1982, 5).
2. Peter Glasner (1977) provides a thoroughgoing critique of this notion of a historical transition from tradition to modernity and of the theory of secularization generally. See also Mary Douglas (1983), and Kay Warren's essay in this volume.

3. This discussion of Weber is adopted from Fullerton (1959), Gerth and Mills (1946), Giddens (1971), Green (1959), Kitch (1967), and Samuelsson (1961), in addition to *The Protestant Ethic* itself.

4. This summary of Sombart is adapted from Green (1959, xii-viii).

5. R. H. Tawney (1926) and Lujo Brentano (1916), for example, disputed the usefulness of the concept of a "spirit" of capitalism. In addition, Tawney, Brentano, Felix Rachfahl (1909) and H. M. Robertson (1933) all argued that the historical origins of capitalism were to be found much earlier than in the period of the Reformation. With regard to Weber's account of the geographical setting of early capitalism, Brentano offered an alternative explanation for the shift of the economic center of gravity from southern to northern Europe; Tawney and Rachfahl disputed Weber's account of the relation between Protestantism and capitalism in Britain and the Netherlands respectively. Tawney and Robertson emphasized the antecedents of capitalism that could be traced to medieval Italy, Flanders, Spain, and Portugal.

6. Albert Hyma (1955), for example, attacked Weber's thesis on historical grounds, adducing extensive documentary evidence to support an interpretation of the economic views of the leading reformers that is at odds with Weber's. Contrary to Weber's characterization of Calvinism, Hyma maintained that Protestantism was in no way progressive in its teachings on economic behavior and could not have had the decisive effect on the development of modern capitalism that Weber had attributed to it. The notion that the rise of capitalism was due primarily to political and economic factors rather than to religious ones was advanced two years before the appearance of Weber's work by W. Cunningham (1904) although his later views on the matter (1914) reflect the considerable influence of both Weber and Troeltsch. Likewise, H. M. Robertson (1933) emphasized material rather than spiritual factors as the crucial elements in the rise of capitalism. Amintore Fanfani, a prominent Catholic economist who later became premier of Italy, also emphasized the importance of such economic factors as the reorientation of trade and geographical expansion. In *Catholicism, Protestantism, and Capitalism* (1955), he both disputed what he felt were common misunderstandings of Catholic teachings on economic matters and maintained that, ultimately, religion was of subordinate importance for explaining the rise of capitalism. Finally, Kurt Samuelsson (1961) has denied that a clear correlation between Protestantism and economic progress exists at all and has suggested that the many inquiries into possible causal connections between the two phenomena may be entirely misplaced.

7. Thus Robertson (1933) has pointed to the energy and discipline of the Jesuits and the thrift of the Franciscans in this connection, though his position on this question has been vigorously challenged by James Brodrick (1934), himself a Jesuit. Tawney has insisted that Weber's emphasis on the unique role of Calvinism was inadequate to explain the broad overall relationship between Protestantism and capitalism. Rather, Tawney has sought to place more causal emphasis on the role of the whole Protestant movement. In addition, both Tawney and Kraus (1930) have questioned the manner in which Weber drew such sharp distinctions between Calvinism and Lutheranism, particularly with regard to each tradition's views of usury. Winthrop Hudson (1949), on the other hand, while critical of what he sees as Weber's oversimplified understanding of Calvinism, is also opposed to what he feels is a distorted characterization of Puritanism on Tawney's part—particularly as regards Tawney's use of the writings of seventeenth century Puritan preachers. Henri Sée (1927) has argued that this charge of oversimplification is just as applicable to the economic portion of Weber's argument as to the theological portion.

Along these same lines, more specific criticisms have been levelled against Weber's claim about the distinctiveness of the Protestant concept of the calling. Brentano argued that *vocatio*, the term applied to labor in the Latin translations of the Bible, has the same sense as Luther's *Beruf*. This suggests that work and duty were thought to constitute a "calling" in the sight of God even before the Reformation. Robertson makes the same point by noting that in the Latin language the word "office" (Latin and Italian *officio*, French *office*, Spanish *oficio*) denoted not only "vocation" in the everyday sense of "employment" but also in the sense of the religious calling of worship. He cites a number of writings by Jesuit writers which support his contention that the idea of a connection between everyday worldly duties and service to God was one that had long been present in Catholicism (see Samuelsson 1961, 13, 17).

This summary of the controversy in notes 5 to 7 is drawn from Green (1959, vii-x); Kitch (1967, xiv-xx); and Samuelsson (1961, 4-26). The volumes edited by Green and Kitch contain excerpts from the primary sources. For what is widely recognized as the classic treatment of the controversy up to 1944, the interested reader may consult Fischoff (1944). See also David Little's overview of the literature critical of *The Protestant Ethic* (1969, 226-237).

8. There is no question that Weber himself desired to maintain a clear distinction between his political and scientific vocations and judgments. The extent to which he was successful in this attempt has itself been the object of a great deal of controversy. For a good introduction to the alternative perspectives that have been brought to bear on this issue, the interested reader may consult Bendix and Roth (1971) and Stammer (ed.) (1971). For a discussion of the normative dimensions of Weber's thought by a contributor to the present volume see Douglas Sturm (1974).

9. Although Weber's methodological essays on such issues as value-neutrality and objectivity are frequently enlisted on the side of positivist arguments regarding the separation of fact and value, there remains a great deal of debate over just how this aspect of Weber's work is to be understood (see note 8 above). Within social theory itself, there has been increasingly wide-spread criticism of the positivist model of social science. Giddens (1982, 1-18) discusses this in terms of a dissolution of the "orthodox consensus" in favor of a hermeneutical turn in social theory. This same topic has been taken up by a number of writers including H. Stuart Hughes (1977) and, more recently, Richard Bernstein (1978; 1983).

10. For an interesting treatment of the widespread influence of romantic anti-capitalism over the modern European intelligentsia see Michael Löwy (1976).

11. Any number of writings by Hayek, Nisbet, Shils, and Bell illustrate this point. See for example Hayek, "History and Politics" in Hayek (1954); Nisbet (1966); Shils (1972, especially the Introduction); and Bell (1976). On Shils' and Bell's interpretation of mass society as pluralistic democracy see Alan Swingewood (1977, 18-23). On the general issue of the political-ideological dimensions of social theory see Leon Bramson (1961).

12. Thus, Peter Berger makes much the same point as Míguez Bonino but to a different end.

> Since the late 1960's there has been a widespread identification of Christian morality, if not Christianity as such, with the political agenda of the left. The concept of "liberation" has come to serve as the *idée-clef* of this identification. . . . There may be all sorts of *normative* assumptions underlying the new Christian leftism—about the moral imperatives of the Gospel, about human rights, about egalitarianism, and so on—but the application of these norms to concrete socio-political situations depends on a *cognitive* grid: "This is what the world is like."
>
> Thus we are told that capitalism is intrinsically exploitative and oppressive, that socialism by contrast is intrinsically "liberating", that America is the most violent nation on earth, that racism is endemic to Western culture, and so on. These and comparable statements are not primarily normative; rather, they purport to be statements of facts. . . . And the most important criticism to be made of the new Christian leftism is *not* that it promulgates false norms, *nor* that it is theologically mistaken, *but that it is based on demonstrable misconceptions of empirical reality.* Put differently: What is most wrong about "liberation theology" is neither its biblical exegesis nor its ethics but its sociology (Berger cited in George Will's "Foreword" to Ernest Lefever (1979, viii-ix).

13. The status of social theory in religious social ethics has been central to recent discussions of the nature and scope of the field. Two articles are particularly interesting in this connection. In response to the work of Ralph Potter, Glen Stassen has argued for the methodological significance of social theory in "A Social Theory Model for Religious Social Ethics". William Everett has attended to the ideological dimensions of one's choice of social theory in "Vocation and Location: An Exploration in the Ethics of Ethics". These and other relevant articles appear in *The Journal of Religious Ethics*, 5/1, 1977.

CHAPTER X

Capitalist Expansion and the Moral Order: Anthropological Perspectives[1]

Kay B. Warren

Anthropology and other comparative social sciences are committed to the precept that through examinations of "the other" we will learn something about the processes that encompass both their realities and our own. It is in such a spirit that this analysis—which focuses on *peasant* moral orders and economics—is offered as a contribution to the examination of cultural values and economics in general and to this volume's discussions of Christian social ethics and Western liberal capitalism more specifically.

From the anthropological perspective, the question of Western liberalism and capitalism requires a *global* approach because international divisions of labor that transcend our boundaries have been an important part of Western economic development, and, as will be clear throughout this essay, the West has been a fundamental part of other nations' development.[2] Thus, while this volume focuses largely on the industrialized West, I would suggest that there are important benefits to far-reaching phrasings of the issues so that they focus on international—not singularly on Western—patterns of economics and change.

In studying the tensions in the social philosophy of liberal capitalism, one can compare the logics of its established-liberal and reformist variants, as Gamwell does, or one can pursue its conflicting political and economic principles and contrast them with those of other systems, as Sturm does with social democracy (see this volume).[3] To these approaches anthropologists would add an examination of cultural systems in action, asking, for example, how societies have been transformed as they have been incorporated into modern capitalist orders. In this case we are seeking to understand social ideologies and worldviews, rather than social philosophies abstracted from the lives of their practitioners. What are the ethical tensions that people actually experience as their societies move in the direction of liberal capitalism? What are the major debates that become central to communities in transition? Do societies with growing involvements in capitalist economics construct their own notions of "individual autonomy," "the common good," and "public-regarding" versus "private-regarding" institutional priorities? This distinctive multi-cultural approach has several advantages, not the least of which is to open to empirical questioning many of the coventional contrasts between "modern" capitalist and "traditional" precapitalist societies drawn by political philosophers and religious ethicists. Anthropology, then, converts questions about the logics of liberalism and capitalism into questions about social change and the interplay of cultural ideologies in their wider economic and political contexts.

The comparative social sciences have succeeded in producing a detailed picture of the currents of change created by Western colonial expansion, the integration of distant societies into international markets, and the development of national political systems and policies in response to these processes. One noteworthy area of conceptual complexity, however, is the diversity of approaches formulated to study the interplay of changing economic, political, and moral orders. Comparing recent perspectives on change enables us to evaluate alternative approaches to the study of economics and belief, to ask important questions about variations in cultural responses to capitalist economic expansion, and to discuss the extent to which the origin of these analyses in the modern liberal tradition of social science shapes their modes of analysis and conclusions.

I

Despite the very large proportion of the world's population that falls into this category "peasant," there is increasing uneasiness in fields like anthropology when the term is used to refer to rural subsistence producers embedded in the wider state. For some analysts the term falsely homogenizes rural societies' great *cultural* differences. For the peasants of Indonesia and the Andes, for example, the meanings of gender, class, ethnicity, and social change are worlds apart (cf. Geertz 1965; Peacock 1968; Bastien 1978; Isbell 1978). As a consequence of such variations, comprehending distinctiveness rather than finding generic uniformities might appear to be the most logical role for anthropology. For other social sciences, however, the term peasant, even if somewhat imprecise in the particulars of socio-economic class positions, is cross-culturally useful in a *structural* sense: peasants are subsistence and small surplus producers living in face-to-face communities. They are taxed and otherwise politically controlled by the state; they are mobilized as a labor reserve by various land tenure and plantation systems.

Cultural and structural views push the questioning of economics and moral understandings in different directions. The first is part of anthropology's current revitalization of the role of culture and extension of the symbolic systems notion to history and economics (cf. Todorov 1984; Sahlins 1976; 1981; Bricker 1981). Until recently, when anthropologists wanted to study change, they worked to reconstruct the factual past through a synthesis of oral histories, mythologies, genealogies and archival materials. Of course the anthropological tradition determined what was "factual," and so, as it is presently argued, repackaged culturally distinctive notions of the past into Western notions of history. What was actually experienced and the cultural frameworks for apprehending change may be obscured by such quests for the truth as we know it. These critiques of historical reconstructions warn us about the cost of exclusively relying on external standards—be they notions of what pertains to myth versus history, our sense of the distinctive domains of economics and politics, or our belief that the material world is more real than the symbolic—to frame our descriptions of other societies.

The second perspective stresses the common economic and political positionings of rural populations in distinctive settings, producing similar experiences and parallel trajectories for change. Culture, as distinctive understandings of the world, plays a secondary role in these explanations. Instead, differences in class systems, land tenure, and the strength and political designs of the state are seen as shaping peasant lives and their responses to change. There is an historical dimension to this inquiry as well—the international transformation of peasants to proletarianized workers with industrial production and the movement from rural to urban centers of economic production throughout the Third World in the nineteenth and twentieth centuries.

Can we reconcile these contrasting approaches to understanding change? Both are necessary to comprehend *experience* which is relational and not uniquely tied to the moment or the individual, as well as *economics* which rarely presents itself as a neatly bounded system of production and exchange. More concretely both would be useful, for instance, to deconstruct rather than to dismiss peasant references to embracing or rejecting "the traditions that our first ancestors created," traditions which may date less than a century in Western reckoning. Such statements pose intriguing anthropological problems, for clearly change has occurred and has been culturally repackaged to hide its temporal roots.[4] We need to know about other cultures' frameworks for understanding, as well as about the nature of culture contact and the state over time, in order to make more than functionalist statements about people's commitments to and perceptions of belief.

To pursue the interconnections of belief and economics in peasant society is to raise important questions about how we conceptualize social change for those who appear so often as its victims. In the course of this analysis, I examine a range of models of changing economic and moral orders in peasant society: those of Joel Migdal (1974), James Scott (1976), Michael Taussig (1980), and my own work (1978; 1985). This comparison asks the following questions: What role does peasant culture—specifically their moral and social understandings of the world and their concepts of community—play in peasant responses to change? How are peasant worldviews and value systems transformed by economic change? Do our theoretical lenses discover a counterpart to the Western liberal debates with the expansion of capitalist markets into peasant communities? Or do their concerns take a very different form?

What is striking about these major approaches to peasant society is their distinctive answers to these questions and the images of peasantries that they create as a result.

Migdal's Defeat of the Community as a Moral Force—Perhaps the most appropriate place to start our analysis is with the work of the political scientist Joel Migdal (1974), because it represents what has become a dominant comparative view of the economic and political forces that influence peasant life. Much less often do readers see this work as a statement about peasant moral orders. For Migdal, a formative crisis occurred in the eighteenth and nineteenth centuries when direct colonial rule and indirect imperial domination transformed societies throughout Asia and Latin America. State control was strengthened, administrative bureaucracies expanded, and urban and rural linkages were created through new roads and communication systems. Most importantly, these changes greatly enhanced the role of national and international markets in rural life.

On the one hand, state expansion restricted banditry and regional warfare, improved public health through epidemic control, limited the arbitrary power of local lords, and increased non-agricultural urban employment. On the other hand, change meant that increasing aspects of local politics and economics were determined by extra-local policies and crises. Taxes and rents increased, forcing peasants to participate in the national market whether or not it was profitable in terms of labor inputs and financial security. Craft production, formerly an additional source of income, often proved uncompetitive as mass-produced goods were introduced into rural markets. What used to be produced and exchanged locally was soon to be purchased externally for cash.

Peasants responded to political and economic changes—which were often accompanied by population increases—by intensifying agricultural production, seeking temporary work outside the community, switching from subsistence to cash crops, and migrating to less populated regions or to the cities. From Migdal's point of view the net effect of mounting change was the erosion of peasants' capacity to maintain a traditional "inward orientation" focusing on their own community, because change favored those who desired greater external involvements.[5]

Explicitly, Migdal sees peasant worldviews and value systems as secondary in importance, as embedded in the dominant story of changing politics and economics. Implicitly, however, his model rests on a conception of the inward-oriented peasant community as a powerful moral force which resolved tensions between individual self-interest and the general welfare. Historically, freeholding communities developed mechanisms to minimize if at all possible external intervention, exploitation, and dependency. In practice this meant avoiding unnecessary external involvements and developing local responses to the needs of its members—all accomplished where life-threatening shortfalls in agricultural production were continually possible. Significantly, some individuals, particularly those who managed to accumulate more than others, found that their aspirations for greater status and wealth called for stronger ties with the broader society.

From Migdal's point of view, inward-oriented peasant social institutions accomplished two goals simultaneously. First, they provided for the general welfare and protected individual families from starvation in the face of illness or crop failures. This they did by providing a security net of social relations, reciprocal labor exchanges, and communal resources such as access to land for subsistence production and to forests for the gathering of fuels. Second, they restricted ambitious individuals, denying them the opportunity to accumulate sufficient resources to dominate others in the community or to breach its protective boundaries. This they accomplished by organizing institutions with alternative forms of prestige and by requiring the wealthy to "redistribute" surpluses in sponsoring communal festivals and religious celebrations.[6]

The political and economic crisis of "imperialism" became a moral crisis for peasants because, with the weakening of village autonomy, individuals with surpluses and the motivation to engage the broader world were able to consolidate power and privilege. The worst community fears became reality as increased inequality destroyed the distributive, safety-net characteristics of the communal order. In Migdal's terms, change freed wealthier villagers who "saw the village social and political organization as oppressive and stifling" (1974, 138). Now, as they pursued new opportunities for work and political participation, new elites could resist local disapproval and censure. As the innovators consolidated their new positions, the traditional egalitarian, self-regulating community gave way to one that was stratified, divided in loyalties, dependent on national politics and the courts for settling internal problems, and externally-oriented for access to resources. In some cases, the economic benefits were great, in others new poverty was created as subsistence farmers became marginal, landless laborers.

One of the casualties of these transformations was the freeholding peasant community as a moral force. It simply lost the power to control wealthy members in the face of growing individualism, the erosion of primary identification with the community, and the loss of communal resources to the market. In the face of competing inward and external orientations, the community found it difficult to maintain collectively-held values that were distinctive from those of the wider society. Older, localized solutions to economic problems and injustice were no longer viable in the face of change which brought wide-spread bureaucratic corruption and the need for personal connections to gain access to national political and economic resources.

Scott's Moral Economy of the Peasant—James Scott's political analysis of nineteenth and early twentieth century Southeast Asia (1976) centers on the effects of the same currents of change that are important for Migdal: the commercialization of agriculture, the growing power of colonial militaries and courts, and the development of new landholding classes which were not tied to local politics and cultural practices. However, his findings differ in important ways from Migdal's, because he concentrates on communities where landowner-tenant roles were differentiated and because he sees important moral issues in these paternalistic relationships. Rather than eroding and destroying the moral order by unleashing nascent individualism, change, in Scott's eyes, caused peasants to struggle to recapture earlier moral understandings that defined and regulated hierarchical relationships.

Scott presents an interesting combination of structural and cultural arguments in his concept of "the moral economy." Peasant economics was at once a relation of exchange and a derived set of cultural values that governed what counted as fair and just reciprocity. The development of similar, transcultural moral expectations was an important result of their structural position as subsistence producers in an atmosphere of uncertainty and potential famine. First, peasants believed they had the right to subsistence, despite fluctuations in yields. Second, their work for landowners was thought to bring them into a broader set of reciprocities obligating patrons to their clients. In exchange for work, rent, and political loyalty, clients expected such reciprocities as food loans before the harvest, assistance with production costs, variable shares of the yield, financial help in the event of family illness, and long-term access to rented lands. Reciprocity became a moral obligation for the welfare of the client and a defining characteristic of patron-client relationships.

Scott stresses the fact that peasants' moral understandings flowed from the severity of their economic situation. Peasants continuously faced crop failures, famines, and market fluctuations which jeopardized their survival at unpredictable intervals. As a result their economic strategy was to look for continuous *minimum* subsistence guarantees rather than attempting to maximize average returns at any one moment. Since their needs as consumers were primary, peasants preferred rents that varied proportionately with their capacity to pay and always left a basic subsistence, rather than paying a fixed charge which might represent a smaller average proportion of their production but in the event of crop failures would not leave enough for subsistence. The ideal landlord cut rents and even subsidized the peasant in bad years while taking larger shares of the harvest in good years. Scott concludes that, from the worker's moral perspective, the form of exploitation was more important than its objective amount. This, he argues, was a rational and realistic posture where starvation was a possibility and land shortages and employment opportunities a chronic problem. Patron-client relations, kinship networks, forms of community redistribution, and communal lands were all forms of insurance for survival.

Like Migdal, Scott notes the redistributive egalitarian ethic of the semi-autonomous peasant village. He argues, however, that the safety-net features of these communities—including their moral basis in concepts of equity and justice—were not designed to inhibit differences in wealth but rather to guarantee a basic livelihood for all members. The poorest could, in semi-autonomous cohesive villages, make major claims against local landowners for protection in the event of a crop failure. Scott adds that peasants extended their moral vision not only to landlords and wealthy peasants but also to the state and its reciprocal duties with respect to agrarian populations.

Change, as one would now expect, eroded the moral claims of the poor. With the rise of absentee landlords, who were not as strongly connected to the community or to individual families, the moral force of earlier understandings and reciprocities was weakened. Increasingly, landowners and the state favored fixed rents and taxes, rejecting the entanglements of traditional reciprocities and "socially regulated generosities." New landlords successfully used the state to enforce contracts which violated traditional terms of tenancy and the peasant moral economy.

For Migdal, the growing fragmentation of peasantries through vertical patron-client ties weakened peasants' moral community, joint political action, and class consciousness. In contrast, Scott argues that despite the fragmenting social nature of plantation life, common moral understandings could successfully unite peasants, especially those who shared the same relations to basic resources like land. In fact, Scott finds that peasant revolts drew on common moral understandings in militant attempts to re-establish the old order of reciprocities and subsistence guarantees which had been eroded by change. Alternatively, revolts involved separatism and attempts to withdraw from the forces of change. In these ways he finds that peasant justice is by nature conservative, preferring a reinstatement of old hierarchies over experimentations with new social orders.

Taussig's Devil as a Mediator between Economic Systems—Michael Taussig's anthropological approach is different from the others because of its concern with (a) the meanings forged by rural communities caught in the processes of economic change, and (b) the reflexive analysis of ideologies which, as it traces the transition from peasant to proletarian, also examines the advanced capitalist worldview of the observer's culture, and, thus, gives insight into the interconnections of the observer and observed.

Taussig studies the former peasants of Cauca, Colombia, whose lives have been transformed by capitalist relations of production and exchange in this century. These rural workers, standing at the periphery of the capitalist system in rural Latin America, are "market dominated" but not "market organized." Semi-proletarianized populations play an active role as interpreters of a capitalist reality which, while taken for granted by us, is alien and newly encountered by them. They critically evaluate modernity with pre-capitalist frames of reference.

What is particularly useful in this approach is its interactive picture of the forces that give a particular shape to capitalist expansion. Taussig sees change not just as a top-down Western imposition, but rather as an historical process, influenced and redirected by peasant responses and their sense of the desirable life. For instance, after abolition Colombia's ex-slaves in the Cauca Valley rejected the free market and wage labor on the haciendas, choosing instead to flee to remote areas and create separatist subsistence-oriented peasant communities. Their militancy deprived large haciendas of a cheap labor force, restricting the growth of the old estates and making them dangerously vulnerable to international market fluctuations well into the twentieth century.

Such militancy paralleled earlier symbolic subversions of colonial Christianity which had been promulgated by plantation owners to legitimize the status quo and depoliticize slaves. For their own part, the slaves and neighboring Indian populations were successful in syncretizing African and Indian readings of Christianity in new religious traditions which played on the colonials' fearful associations of blacks with the powerful devil, and plantation owners with the anti-Christ. The legacy of this history of resisting and transforming cultural and religious impositions continues today in the worldview of semi-proletarian agribusiness workers.

In the 1930s large scale commercialized agriculture and sugar production came into increasing conflict with separatist peasant culture:

> To some extent the peasants produced for the national market, but consumed few market commodities. They were neither easily able nor zealous in expanding a surplus. Without the clearly drawn lines of private property in the modern bourgeois sense, they were refractory to the financial institutions and inducements that met and attracted the ruling classes. The peasants' bond of kin and kind meant that capital accumulation was a virtual impossibility. Wealth, not capital, might be amassed, but only to be divided among the succeeding generations. Of course merchant capital could coexist with this form of social organization, but since national capital accumulation demanded an ever-increasing domestic market, peasants who continued to practice self-subsistence were an obstacle to progress. Whatever the intricate calculus of the emerging system, its initial push was to destroy a form of social organization embedded in a nonmarket mode of using and sharing land (Taussig 1980, 71).

While peasants lost the land base for a precapitalist life after the 1930s, they successfully resisted wholesale assimilation into the capitalist labor force and its vision of reality. Taussig believes that central to this resistance was the moral critique of capitalist relations of production which was implicit in a range of semi-proletarian beliefs. In only slightly veiled symbolism, former peasants described the moral ambiguity and unnaturalness for them of capitalist wage labor which offered workers much higher earnings but quite literally wore out their bodies in intensive plantation labor. Many preferred substantially lower wages in exchange for a slower work pace in traditional agriculture. The language they used to make sense of the cash economy and agribusiness was the moral language of pacts with the devil and sorcery directed at those who accumulated material goods.

Workers who earned more than others in piece rate wage labor were said to have made pacts with the devil (Nash 1979). These pacts had a high cost—an early and painful death—and limited advantages since the money so acquired could only be used to buy luxuries. Any capital investments made with these earnings, say in land or livestock, would be barren as would be the land that the laborer harvested while pacted. Pacts in effect denied semi-proletarians the chance to become capitalists through investment and sales at a profit.

Taussig holds that the best way to make sense of these beliefs is through the Marxist contrast between precapitalist production for use value (i.e., for subsistence) and capitalist production for exchange value (i.e., for profit and accumulation). The replacement of a system of production for use value by one that stressed exchange value had been judged by peasants as "neither natural nor good," but rather as "unnatural and evil." Thus, the devil represented the cost of alienation from earlier peasant patterns of valued equity, reciprocity, and mutual aid.

Colombian semi-proletarians created an analysis of capitalism that is radically different from our post-industrial worldview. Their themes of infertility and death for individuals who appear to benefit from the accumulation of wealth deny the modern Western assumption (or, in Taussig's vocabulary "fetishism") that "capital appears to have an innate property of self-expansion" (1980, 31). Nor did these former peasants speak of commodities as if they were disembodied from the people who produce them, as we conventionally do in talking about costs and profits as if they were entirely separate from the social process of production. Certainly they did not see the market economy and modern society as integral parts of the society and human nature which ought naturally to exist as they do.[8]

As we compare these approaches to economics and the moral order, it becomes clear that they are overlapping portrayals of powerful tensions in peasant life at different points along major trajectories of change. For Migdal, the conflict is between the coercive egalitarianism of traditional communities and the individual who wants to make self-contained decisions about economic accumulation. For Scott, the tension is between the traditional, mutually-binding responsibilities of patrons and clients and the impersonal nature of the market economy in which contracted relations do not necessarily carry other obligations for employers concerning workers' welfare.[9] Finally, Taussig combines elements of both approaches in his discussion of the basic dissonance, for proletarianized peasants, of different modes of production and the worldviews they engender.

Whether or not one is convinced of Taussig's discovery of an indigenous Marxist critique of capitalism in practices like the devil contract, Taussig has made a major contribution in his view of moral deliberation as a symbolic construct, one that is experienced not only through tensions between individuals and communities but more immediately through particular symbolic languages. Taussig's devil is good to think with, a key to one culture's shaping of tensions, transformations, and alienations. Ironically, what is missing in Taussig, because of his focus on a limited set of collective representations, is a fuller sense of the individual and community as changing social and cultural constructs.

Migdal and Scott suffer from different and more serious limitations because neither begins with a particular culture's phrasing of moral concerns. Rather, they see focal points of moral conflict as originating in structurally-created differences in interests and cultural values. Thus, the meaning systems through which the world is experienced are of less immediate interest to their analysis than the social organization of everyday life. Nevertheless, they give us a clearer sense of the ways social change creates individualism and transforms community. I want now to bring these two sets of concerns together as I add central questions from Gamwell's discussion of Western liberalism and from my own work on Guatemalan Indians' insightful and complex understandings of change.

II

Gamwell's essay in this volume raises the following questions for anthropological consideration:

1. Do moral deliberations about the economic order come to the fore primarily in modern society where economics is differentiated from other social spheres?

2. Is a distinctive characteristic of modern society its individualized autonomy (often termed "freedom") in belief, will and action as opposed to the heteronomy of traditional worldviews and institutions?

3. Is the traditional versus reformist debate of Western liberalism foreshadowed by similar debates as developing countries move toward a consumer-oriented capitalist economy?

To the extent that Western liberal capitalism implicitly becomes the singular yardstick by which to evaluate other political and moral orders, there is some risk in these formulations. In addressing questions from Gamwell's analysis of liberal capitalism and the debate over its traditional and reformist variants, I want to turn to my own materials on Guatemalan Indian populations in the 1970's. In so doing, I am not looking for Guatemala to mirror our descriptions of liberal democracy in the United States. Rather, I am interested in the extent to which our findings on Third World societies complicate the assumptions we make about what the West represents.

The anthropological contribution must be an indirect and relativizing one. So we must ask, for cultures on newer post-colonial routes of change and modernization: What issues stand at the center of their debates about cultural values? How do peasant populations—in this ethnographic example, Guatemalan Indians of the 1970's before the current crisis—talk about the appropriate relation of the individual to the community in a world that is rapidly changing? What symbolic languages do they use to express their changing conceptions? What do they discover in the process of formulating and testing these languages?

Guatemala: When History Haunts the Free Individual—For Gamwell and many others, the defining features of modern political liberalism are the identification of economics as a separate sphere and the person as an autonomous decision-maker in a political order that values individualized freedom and liberty. What is clear from the Guatemalan Indian materials is that colonial histories of injustice and dependent development have compelled a different moral discourse with distinctive assumptions about the nature of individual decision-making. Further, Indian moral preoccupations challenge Gamwell's assumption that there is something unique about modern society—specifically the differentiation of economics from other social systems—that allows it to engage in moral debates about the economic order. Moral deliberation in the Guatemalan case would appear to be as much a result of cultural contact as it is a consequence of the particular configuration of a society. This suggests that it might be more useful to see economics and politics as dimensions of all social life, rather than as bounded and specialized domains.

What we find in Guatemala is a great deal of moral deliberation about injustice. It is clear that culture contact with its attendant clashes and adjustments created grounds for major ethical reflection and introduced, at various times in colonial and contemporary history, new symbol systems through which reassessments of central cultural values have occurred. The resulting Indian understandings are not narrowly economic, but rather interweavings of economic, political and cultural concerns (Warren 1978).

From an external perspective one could see the Guatemalan case as an archetypal transition from traditional to modern. In the town of San Andrés Semetabaj, for example, a singular, communal Indian worldview has been challenged over the last thirty years by a younger generation which embraced individualistic religious doctrines, cultural assimilation, and work opportunities outside accepted ethnic divisions of labor. The results look more like Migdal's model than Scott's, for there has been no effective resistance, no militant desire to reinstate an older order as economic change and the political experiments of the national revolutionary period of 1945-54 weakened the power of traditional peasant elders. In towns like San Andrés, rival secular and religious groups and a generalized loss of commitment to the Indian power structure weakened the grip of the traditional worldview (costumbre) and its most important institutional structure (the civil-religious hierarchy), both of which had expressed Indian notions of community. Change provoked a local blowup, a fragmentation of the Indian community, and then a begrudging accommodation to new factionalism and pluralism, replacing the earlier monopoly of the communal system.

What was lost in the process? Since the sixteenth century Indians had been embedded in a bi-ethnic society which structurally subordinated them. In response, they sought and found a symbolic separation in traditional religion. Ritual guides (camol beij) stood at the apex of the hierarchy, respected because of their specialized knowledge of the communal order. Individuals were expected to participate in community activities, yet how they participated, why they engaged in particular activities, and which divinities they believed in was up to each person and their own voluntad ("will"). The ritual guides stood for the valued transcendence of the communal order over the pluralism of individual motivations rather than for a powerful mediation of experience by religious elites. The old order enforced an egalitarian ethic within the peasant sector, requiring the wealthy to make substantial contributions to community rituals and festivals. Greater prestige came through community service in the civil religious hierarchy which redirected surpluses and required major time investments in communal affairs. Age and service, not wealth, were the foci of respect. Small amounts of communal lands gave each family a base to build on for economic security, but families needed access to additional inherited private land for self-sufficiency.

Another loss from the traditional order was the power of pacts with the devil to capture Indian realities. Unlike Taussig's Colombian example, the Guatemalan pacts mediated *ethnicities*—the differences between Mayan Indians and whites (or "Ladinos" as they are called)[10]—not different forms of economic production. Indian pacts involved a pledge of the individual's soul for wealth, creating a debt to be paid by eternal suffering and work for the Ladino devil after death. The cultural fear underlying these pacts was that unusual wealth would result in a tragic exploitation of Indians by other Indians, replicating the same patron-laborer formula that governed inter-ethnic divisions of labor. Significantly, pacts were not pictured as products of free choice or volition (*voluntad*), but rather as the results of a person's immutable luck-destiny (*suerte*). Change, in this and other related beliefs, was portrayed as beyond individual control and as threatening to both the individual who became like a non-Indian and the community which suffered as a result.

Since the 19th Century, Indians increasingly lost land to Ladino settlers who became landlords and plantation owners with privileged positions politically and economically. Indian resistance was richly symbolic; in myth and ritual they defined a world in which individuals were denied autonomy due to Spanish and Ladino domination which categorically deprived individuals of the chance to make important moral decisions (see Warren 1985). Indian belief asserted that cultural separatism, with an emphasis on the communal order, was the antidote to subordination and the loss of individual moral decision-making.

Challenging the worldview of the communal order was the goal of groups like Catholic Action which organized regular meetings of local Indian converts and catechists in San Andrés in the 1950s.[11] Initially, no one realized what a dramatic change these new converts would make in belief and Indian identity. The convert-oriented orthodoxy introduced a new egalitarianism which was radical for its trans-ethnic universalism and insistence that individuals make crucial choices. Catholic Action rediscovered the submerged individual of the old order and introduced a new religious language for evaluating internal states and external behaviors. They worked for equal secular treatment of Indians and Ladinos as individuals, mirroring their belief in the spiritual equivalence of all persons.[12] They also analyzed the state and its development policies in these new terms.

When we look at Indian worldviews during this transition, a deeper level of debate is revealed. The traditional Indian worldview most directly worried about the dialectic between Indian separatism and Indian subordination. Only in an undercurrent form did the individual become an issue in beliefs about sorcery and pacts with the devil. The major issues were communal because racism and exploitation were portrayed as categorical and unchangeable, creating injustice that would only be rectified in the next world.

In the modern debate the issues have been transformed. On the one hand,

Indian worldview is concerned with the capacity of the individual to freely choose identities and paths of action (including when and how ethnicity is individually important, with the possibility of situationally passing as a non-Indian). These individual choices about identity are felt to flow directly from the belief in the equivalence of all Indians and Ladinos. On the other hand, Indians recognize that the history of Guatemalan racism means that equivalent rights and treatment of all individuals will not result in equitable outcomes, which in this case would mean an erosion of Ladino power and relative wealth. Equivalent treatment before the law or access to agricultural cooperatives does not in practice narrow the economic gap created by tremendous disparities in land holdings.

The Indian converts to a Westernized worldview in the mid-1970s found themselves caught in a liberalism which identified larger problems than it could resolve. Catechists and political activists found themselves advocating policies that they realized would neither philosophically nor pragmatically resolve the problem of historically-based inequities. As they found out through experiences in the new bi-ethnic development projects, the maximization of individual rights and equal treatment would only perpetuate the existing economic differences between the ethnic groups.

Taussig is right that subordinate communities resist capitalist expansion; but he has a limited notion of how this occurs. In Guatemala, it was precisely when Indians confronted the world as *individuals*, independently of the traditional communal order, that they began to understand (a) the contribution which traditional Indian separatism made to masking subordination and (b) the legacy of ethnic domination which neutralized the impact of liberal national reforms promising equal individual access and rights before the law. Where Taussig argues that the language of liberal capitalism erodes historical awareness, I find a cultural recovery by Guatemalan Indians of the historical processes that shaped their world (see Warren 1978). Their experiments with liberal philosophy ended in frustration in the 1970s, but the failure was all the more powerful for the deeper lessons it brought.

III

In this essay I have undertaken an exploratory analysis of the cultural context of debates about the moral order, specifically about the relation of the individual to the community, in peasant society. Rather than pursuing the specialized domains of political theory and philosophically weighing the consequences of alternative formulations, this approach has abstracted models directly from cultural systems in action. This, of course, is not solely a factual task. As comparative social scientists, we make sense of recaptured experiences with the aid of *our* understandings of the generalized patterns basic to the confusing currents and eddies of change.

Most of us have seen capitalist expansion as an example of economic change overwhelming older communal orders and unleashing individual aspirations and new class-based inequities. Yet as has been clear from this presentation, however economics may shape the raw material for debate, it does not mechanically create its terms. Scott, Taussig, and my own work show a much more interactive response on the part of peasants who forge their own understandings, test them, and find grounds for questioning the individualism and established liberalism of their own modernizing countries.[13] This model of change assumes that capitalist expansion created new problems for peasants, who as they transformed their understandings of a changing world, shaped new responses and developed new forms of moral reflection.

In answering the questions posed by Gamwell's discussion of liberal capitalism, this essay has questioned some of the terms and presuppositions of his analysis. It would appear that the conventional "traditional/modern" and "heteronomous/ autonomous" dichotomies for classifying societies hide more than they reveal of the *processes* of cultural change that accompany the expansion of international capitalism. Change is not a linear process, moving inevitably from heteronomy to individual autonomy, and while it is possible to generalize about broad patterns of change for peasant populations, we learn more about the relation of economics and the moral order through the particularities of individual cases. For Guatemala, change has been an encounter in which liberal, religious languages stressing individual autonomy have been embraced, tested and only partially accepted by peasants in the face of an historically ascribed group identity and national governments which have shown a greater commitment to established economic liberalism than to democracy.[14]

For Western scholarship, the question of individual autonomy centers on whether the fundamental principles of thought and practice are or are not properly legislated by the individual mind and will. The anthropological perspective adds to this question the issues of who mediates experience and meaning, who interprets important choices in the face of the conflicts and tensions of change, and how cultures cast the work of mediation. In Guatemala the shift in mediation is twofold. The shift in personnel is from the ritual guides—who gained their positions through age, service and knowledge, and mediated by example—to the Catholic Action catechists—who gained their position through literacy in Catholic orthodoxy and argued that individuals must make important decisions for themselves. Both mediators believed in important areas of individual choice, but it was Catholic Action that gave new viability to the idea of choice as the central individual moral act. Change has not so much invented "autonomy" as it has led to a significantly new understanding of individual autonomy and choice in the face of a history of domination.[15]

Notes

1. An early version of this paper was delivered at the University of Chicago conference on "Religion and the Economic Order: Historical Relations and the Normative Task" in April of 1984. My thanks to Frank Reynolds, Bruce Grelle, and David Krueger for useful feedback

on this analysis and to Susan Bourque for insightful background on liberalism and politics. At Princeton, Natalie Davis, Amelie Rorty, and Patricia Sloane have particularly stimulated my thoughts in this area.

2. Dependency theorists and their critics have traced the outline of this development. See, for example, Stavenhagen (1975), Wallerstein (1976), Wasserstrom (1983), and for a post-dependency approach that also examines the West, Nash and Fernandez-Kelly (1983).

3. Gamwell formulates the tensions in the following terms: "If the inclusive public problem for established liberalism is the appropriate distribution of economic resources and benefits, the inclusive economic issue for reformed liberalism involves the preconditions for the maximal public world, and the difference is the consequence of different convictions regarding human individuality and human freedom" (p. 64). Sturm finds conflict in the built-in "tension between democracy and capitalism, for one is fundamentally a principle of public governance, while the other is a principle of private control" (p. 103). In his social democratic resolution there would be wide public involvement in such issues as the quality of life and the distributions of resources.

4. For modern industrial capitalism, Taussig (1980) notes another pattern of dehistoricizing core concepts.

5. In this summary discussion of Migdal, I have not presented the full range of community types he analyzes but have focused rather on the freeholding communities. His discussion of settlements controlled by lords represents an important contrast and a very different pattern of change, given that cultural domination is already immediately present.

6. Alternatively, in resource abundant areas, they promoted worldviews that devalued the accumulation of surpluses.

7. See Nash (1967/68; 1979) and Warren (1978) for contrasting analyses. No doubt some of the differences in the Colombian, Guatemalan and Bolivian cases are due to the various histories and stages of capitalist development that these countries represent. But there are very significant differences in methodological and theoretical approaches as well, as my critique of Taussig details.

8. In many ways, Taussig's work on the Cauca Valley fails to pursue the *political* consequences of belief. For instance, sorcery is self-directed at inequities within the workers' stratum; it is not used against the owners of agribusinesses because it is felt that they do not believe in sorcery and, in the event that they did, would only pay more powerful shamans to counteract it. Taussig concludes, "The proletarian neophytes have lost a class enemy susceptible to magical influence, but they stand to win a new world in their realization of that enemy's disbelief" (1980, 111). I wonder if this is the only inference one could make from this material. Certainly, one could just as effectively argue that these beliefs depoliticize semi-proletarians.

9. Susan Bourque has pointed out to me that Scott and Migdal are, in their contrasting findings, reenacting an old debate between Burke's notion of the security of traditional obligations and responsibilities in the conservative, traditional order versus Locke's concept of modernity as releasing individual energies which were never realized or were severely restricted in traditional society.

10. For an interactive analysis of Ladino ethnicity, see Hawkins (1984).

11. This is not the only interpretation of Catholic Action. Lengyel (1979) argues that religious factionalism serves to formalize already existing individual differences in wealth, external orientations, and attitudes toward non-traditional authority. Wasserstrom (1975) and Falla (1978) have gone a step further, asserting that Catholic Action represents the organization of class interests of a new, Indian elite.

12. The worldviews which are reshaped in these transitions are dealt with in much greater detail in Warren (1978). The liberalism of the Indian converts to Catholic Action was conceptually developed in a set of contrasts used to describe the conflicting natures of the person and the world: soul/body, spiritual/material, and internal/external. This language differed substantially from the will/luck-destiny contrast through which the traditional Indian worldview defined the person.

13. The Guatemalan government is a good example of a state which balances strong commitments to established economic liberalism with great ambivalence about expanding political participation and democracy. For their part, Indians have experienced a desire to widen their political participation in part because of their experiences with twentieth century liberal ideologies.

14. The one very important source of information that I have had to ignore in this summary treatment is the history of nineteenth century liberalism in Latin America. Liberal national

policy sought to "civilize" Indians by encouraging them to become economically active in the cash economy. To this end Indian lands were introduced as a commodity into the market. The result was an influx of non-Indian settlers into rural areas and the impoverishment of Indians who lost their lands to a market they did not fully understand. Thus, as the Indians of San Andrés recaptured the significance of nineteenth century history for their economic position, they were in effect critiquing the direct consequences of early liberal national policy in Guatemala.

15. Liberal approaches to the study of peasants, like Popkin (1979), stress individual risk-taking in balancing short and long-term interests in the face of change. Yet they often fail to see individual autonomy as culturally constructed and subject to significant reformulation with change.

References

Alexander, Herbert E. 1976. *Financing Politics,* Washington: Congressional Quarterly Press.

Amjad-Ali, Charles and W. Alvin Pitcher (eds.). 1984. *Liberation and Ethics: Essays in Religious Social Ethics in Honor of Gibson Winter,* Chicago: Center for the Scientific Study of Religion.

Appleby, Joyce. 1978. *Economic Thought and Ideology in Seventeenth Century England,* Princeton: Princeton University Press.

——— 1984. *Capitalism and a New Social Order: The Republican Vision of the 1790's,* New York: New York University Press.

Arendt, Hannah. 1982. *On Revolution,* Westport, Conn.: Greenwood Press.

Assmann, Hugo. 1975. *Theology for a Nomad Church,* Maryknoll, N.Y.: Orbis Books.

Augustine. 1950. *The City of God* (trans.) Marcus Dods, New York: Modern Library.

Baillie, John (ed.). 1946. *Natural Theology,* London: Geoffrey Bles.

Barber, Bernard. 1977. "Absolutization of the Market: Some Notes on How We Got from There to Here", in Gerald Dworkin (ed.), *Markets and Morals,* Washington, D.C.: Hemisphere Publishing Corp.

Bastien, Joseph. 1978. *Mountain of the Condor: Metaphor and Ritual in an Andean Ayllu,* St. Paul: West Publishing Co.

Bauer, P.T. 1984. *Reality and Rhetoric: Studies in the Economics of Development,* Cambridge: Harvard University Press.

Baum, Gregory. 1979. "The First Papal Encyclical," *The Economist,* 17:4 (June).

Becker, Gary S. 1976. *The Economic Approach to Human Behavior,* Chicago: University of Chicago Press.

Bell, Daniel. 1976. *The Cultural Contradictions of Capitalism,* New York: Basic Books.

Bellah, Robert. 1970. *Beyond Belief,* New York: Harper & Row.

Bendix, Reinhard and Guenther Roth. 1971. *Scholarship and Partisanship: Essays on Max Weber,* Berkeley: University of California Press.

Benne, Robert. 1981. *The Ethic of Democratic Capitalism: A Moral Reassessment,* Philadelphia: Fortress Press.

Bennett, John. 1936. *Christianity and Our World,* New York: Association Press.

——— 1946. *Christian Ethics and Social Policy,* New York: Charles Scribner's Sons.

——— 1947. *Social Salvation* (first published 1935), New York: Charles Scribner's Sons.

——— 1954. *Christian Values and Economic Life* (ed.), New York: Harper.

——— 1956. *The Christian as Citizen* (first published 1955), London: Lutherworth Press.

——— 1958. *Christians and the State,* New York: Charles Scribner's Sons.

——— 1966. *Foreign Policy in Christian Perspective,* New York: Charles Scribner's Sons.

——— 1975. *The Radical Imperative—From Theology to Social Ethics,* Philadelphia: Westminster Press.

Berger, Peter. 1974. *Pyramids of Sacrifice: Political Ethics and Social Change,* New York: Basic Books.

Berger, Peter et al. 1979. "A Politicized Christ," *Christianity and Crisis,* March 19, 1979.

Bernstein, Richard J. 1978. *Restructuring Social and Political Thought,* Philadelphia: University of Pennsylvania Press.

——— 1983. *Beyond Objectivism and Relativism,* Philadelphia: University of Pennsylvania Press.

Bloch, Ernst. 1970. *A Philosophy of the Future,* New York: Herder & Herder.

Bock, Paul. 1974. *In Search of a Responsible World Society: The Social Teachings of the World Council of Churches,* Philadelphia: Westminster Press.

Boulding, Kenneth. 1953. *The Organizational Revolution: A Study in the Ethics of Economic Organization,* New York: Harper.

——— 1970. *Beyond Economics: Essays on Society, Religion, and Ethics,* Ann Arbor: University of Michigan Press.

Bowen, Howard. 1953. *Social Responsibilities of the Businessman,* New York: Harper.

Bramson, Leon. 1961. *The Political Context of Sociology,* Princeton: Princeton University Press.

Braudel, Fernand. 1981-1984. *Civilization & Capitalism: 15th -18th Century,* **3 vols.,** New York: Harper & Row.

Brentano, Lujo. 1916. *Die Anfänge des modernen Kapitalismus,* Munich: Akademie der Wissenschaften.

Bricker, Victoria. 1981. *The Indian Christ, the Indian King: The Historical Substrate of Maya Myth,* Austin, Texas: University of Texas Press.

177

Brodrick, James. 1934. *The Economic Morals of the Jesuits, an Answer to Dr. H.M. Robertson*, London: Oxford Univ. Press.

Brown, Robert McAffee. 1981. *Making Peace in the Global Village*, Philadelphia: Westminster Press.

Brunner, Emil. 1937. *The Divine Imperative*, Philadelphia: Westminster Press (first published by Lutherworth Press).

1943. *Justice and the Social Order*, New York: Harper & Brothers.

Brus, Wlodimierz. 1972. *The Market in a Socialist Economy*, London: Routledge, Kegan & Paul.

1980. "Political Systems and Economic Efficiency," *Journal of Comparative Economics*, No. 4.

Camara, Dom Helder. 1971. *Revolution Through Peace*, New York: Harper & Row.

Carnoy, Martin and Derek Shearer. 1980. *Economic Democracy*, Armonk, N.Y.: M.E. Sharpe.

Carnoy, Martin and Derek Shearer, with Russell Rumberger. 1983. *A New Social Contract: The Economy and Government After Reagan*, New York: Harper & Row.

Cliffe Leslie, Thomas E. 1888. *Essays in Political Economy, second edition*, Dublin: Hodges, Figgis, and Co.

Cobb, John B., Jr. and W. Widick Schroeder. 1981. *Process Philosophy and Social Thought*, Chicago: Center for the Scientific Study of Religion.

Cohen, Joshua and Joel Rogers. 1983. *On Democracy*, New York: Penguin Books.

Cole, G.D.H. 1953. *History of Socialist Thought, Vol. 1, The Forerunners, 1789-1850*, New York: St. Martin's Press.

Coleman, John. 1982. *An American Strategic Theology*, New York: Paulist Press.

Cunningham, William. 1904. *An Essay on Western Civilization in its Economic Aspects, Vol. II*, Cambridge: Cambridge University Press.

1914. *Christianity and Economic Science*, London: J. Murray.

Curran, Charles. 1982. *American Catholic Social Ethics: Twentieth Century Approaches*, Notre Dame: University of Notre Dame Press.

Dahl, Robert. 1956. *A Preface for Democratic Theory*, Chicago: University of Chicago Press.

Dewey, John. 1951. "Creative Democracy—The Task Before Us," in M. Fisch (ed.) *Classic American Philosophies*, New York: Appleton-Century-Crofts.

1954. *The Public and its Problems* (first published 1927), Chicago: The Swallow Press.

1963. *Liberalism and Social Action* (first published 1935), New York: Capricorn Books.

Dickinson, Richard D.N. 1975. *To Set at Liberty the Oppressed: Toward an Understanding of Christian Responsibilities of Development/Liberation*, Geneva: World Council of Churches.

Domhoff, G. William. 1970. *The Higher Circles*, New York: Random House.

1978. *The Powers That Be: Processes of Rising Class Domination in America*, New York: Vintage Books.

Dorr, Donal. 1983. *Option for the Poor: A Hundred Years of Vatican Social Teaching*, Maryknoll, New York: Orbis.

Douglas, Mary. 1983. "The Effects of Modernization on Religious Change" in Mary Douglas & Steven M. Tipton (eds.) *Religion and America*, Boston: Beacon Press.

Duff, Edward. 1956. *The Social Teaching of the World Council of Churches*, New York: Association Press.

Dupre, Louis. 1983. *Marx's Critique of Modern Culture*, New Haven: Yale University Press.

Eagleson, John and P. Scharper, (eds.). 1979. *Puebla and Beyond*, Maryknoll, New York: Orbis.

Edgeworth, Francis Y. 1881. *Mathematical Psychics: An Essay on the Application of Mathematics to the Moral Sciences*, London: Kegan Paul.

Egbert, Donald Drew and Stow Persons. 1952. *Socialism and American Life, 2 vols.*, Princeton: Princeton University Press.

Everett, William W. 1977. "Vocation and Location: An Exploration in the Ethics of Ethics," *The Journal of Religious Ethics*, 5/1, 1977, 91-115.

Falla, Ricardo. 1978. *Quiche Rebelde*, Guatemala: Editorial Universitaria de Guatemala.

Fanfani, Amintore. 1955. *Catholicism, Protestantism, and Capitalism* (first published 1935), New York: Sheed & Ward.

Fenno, Richard F., Jr. 1973. *Congressmen in Committees*, New York: Little, Brown & Co.

Fischoff, Ephraim. 1944. "The Protestant Ethic and the Spirit of Capitalism: The History of a Controversy," *Social Research*, XI, 61-77.

Fisher, Irving. 1918. "Is 'Utility' the Most Suitable Term for the Concept It is Used to Denote?", *American Economic Review*, June.

Fitch, John A. 1957. *The Social Responsibility of Organized Labor*, New York: Harper.

Fribourg Union. 1886. *Minutes of meeting.*

Friedman, Milton. 1953. "The Methodology of Positive Economics" in *Essays in Positive Economics,* Chicago: University of Chicago Press.

1962. *Capitalism and Freedom,* Chicago: University of Chicago Press.

Fullerton, Kemper. 1959. "Calvinism and Capitalism: An Explanation of the Weber Thesis" in Robert W. Green (ed.) *Protestantism & Capitalism: The Weber Thesis and Its Critics,* Boston: D.C. Heath & Co.

Galbraith, John Kenneth. 1970. *The Affluent Society* (first published 1958), New York: New American Library.

1972. *The New Industrial State* (first published 1967), New York: New American Library.

1973. *Economics and the Public Purpose,* Boston: Houghton Mifflin Company.

Gamwell, Franklin I. 1984. *Beyond Preference: Liberal Theories of Independent Associations,* Chicago: University of Chicago Press.

Geertz, Clifford. 1965. *The Social History of an Indonesian Town,* Cambridge: MIT Press.

1973. *The Interpretation of Cultures,* New York: Basic Books.

Gerth, H.H. and C. Wright Mills. 1946. *From Max Weber: Essays in Sociology,* New York: Oxford University Press.

Gewirth, Alan. 1962. "Political Justice," in Richard E. Brandt (ed.) *Social Justice,* Englewood Cliffs, N.J.: Prentice-Hall.

Giddens, Anthony. 1971. *Capitalism and Modern Social Theory,* Cambridge: Cambridge University Press.

1979. *Central Problems in Social Theory,* Berkeley and Los Angeles: University of California Press.

1982. *Profiles and Critiques in Social Theory,* Berkeley and Los Angeles: University of California Press.

Gilder, George F. 1978. *Visible Man,* New York: Basic Books.

1981. *Wealth and Poverty,* New York: Basic Books.

Glasner, Peter. 1977. *The Sociology of Secularization: A Critique of a Concept,* Boston: Routledge & Kegan Paul.

Greeley, Andrew. 1967. *The Catholic Experience,* Garden City, New York: Doubleday.

1984. "American Catholicism: 1909-1984," *America,* Vol. 150 (June 23-30).

Green, Mark, James M. Fallows, and David R. Zwick. 1972. *Who Runs Congress?,* New York: Bantam Books.

Green, Robert W. (ed.). 1959. *Protestantism and Capitalism: The Weber Thesis and its Critics,* Boston: D.C. Heath & Co.

Greenstone, J. David. 1982. "The Transient and Permanent in American Politics: Standards, Interests, and the Concept of 'Public'," in J. David Greenstone —(ed.), *Public Values and Private Power in American Politics,* Chicago: University of Chicago Press.

Gremillion, Joseph. 1975. *The Gospel of Peace and Justice,* Maryknoll, New York: Orbis.

Grenholm, Carl-Henric. 1973. *Christian Social Ethics in a Revolutionary Age,* Uppsala: Verbum.

Gustafson, James M. 1971. *Christian Ethics and the Community,* Philadelphia: Pilgrim Press.

1974. *Theology and Christian Ethics,* Philadelphia: Pilgrim Press.

1978. *Protestant and Roman Catholic Ethics: Prospects for Rapprochement,* Chicago: University of Chicago Press.

Gutierrez, Gustavo. 1973. *A Theology of Liberation: History, Politics and Salvation,* Maryknoll, N.Y.: Orbis Books.

Gutierrez, Gustavo and Richard Shaull. 1977. *Liberation and Change,* Atlanta: John Knox Press.

Habermas, Jürgen. 1975. *Legitimation Crisis,* Boston: Beacon Press.

Hall, Donald R. 1969. *Cooperative Lobbying—The Power of Pressure,* Tucson: University of Arizona Press.

Hamilton, Richard. 1972. *Class and Politics in the United States,* New York: Wiley.

Harrington, Michael. 1980. *Decade of Decision: The Crisis of the American System,* New York: Simon & Schuster.

Hartshorne, Charles. 1953. *Reality as Social Process,* Glencoe, IL: The Free Press.

Hartz, Louis. 1955. *The Liberal Tradition in America: An Interpretation of American Political Thought Since the Revolution,* New York: Harcourt, Brace and World.

Hauerwas, Stanley. 1982. "Work as Co-Creation: A Remarkably Bad Idea," *This World,* 3 Fall.

Hawkins, John. 1984. *Inverse Image: The Meaning of Culture, Ethnicity and Family in Postcolonial Guatemala,* Albuquerque: University of New Mexico Press.

Hayek, Friedrich. 1954. "History and Politics," in Hayek (ed.) *Capitalism and the Historians*, Chicago: University of Chicago Press.

    1961. *The Road to Serfdom*, Chicago: University of Chicago Press.

    1976. *Law, Legislation and Liberty. Vol. 2: The Mirage of Social Justice*, Chicago: University of Chicago Press.

Hefner, Philip. 1976. "The Foundations of Belonging in a Christian Worldview," in Philip Hefner and W. Widick Schroeder (eds.) *Belonging and Alienation: Religious Foundations for the Human Future*, Chicago: Center for the Scientific Study of Religion.

Heilbroner, Robert. L. 1966. *The Limits of American Capitalism*, New York: Harper & Row.

    1970a. *Between Capitalism and Socialism: Essays in Political Economics*, New York: Vintage Books.

    1970b. *The Economic Problem, Second Edition*, Englewood Cliffs, N.J.: Prentice-Hall, Inc.

    1976. *Business Civilization in Decline*, New York: W.W. Norton & Co.

    1980. *The Worldly Philosophers* (first published 1953), New York: Simon & Schuster.

Heimann, Eduard. 1961. *Reason and Faith in Modern Society: Liberalism, Marxism, and Democracy*, Middletown, Conn.: Wesleyan University Press.

Hempel, Carl G. 1965. *Aspects of Scientific Explanation*, New York: Free Press.

Heyne, Paul. 1968. *Private Keepers of the Public Interest*, New York: McGraw-Hill.

    1977. *The World of Economics*, St. Louis: Concordia Publishing House.

    1978. "Economics and Ethics: The Problem of Dialogue" in W. Widick Schroeder and Gibson Winter (eds.) *Belief and Ethics: Essays in Ethics, the Human Sciences, and Ministry in Honor of W. Alvin Pitcher*, Chicago: Center for the Scientific Study of Religion.

Hicks, John R. and R.G.D. Allen. 1934. "A Reconsideration of the Theory of Value", *Economica*, February and May.

Higgins, George G. 1980. "Religion and Economic Policy: A Catholic Perspective," in Eugene J. Fisher and Daniel F. Polish (eds.) *Formation of Social Policy in the Catholic and Jewish Traditions*, Notre Dame: University of Notre Dame Press.

    1982. "Foreword" to *On Human Work: A Resource Book for the Study of Pope John Paul II's Third Encyclical*, Washington, D.C.: U.S. Catholic Conference.

Hildebrand, Bruno. 1848. *Die Nationaloekonomie der Gegenwart und Zukunft*, Frankfort: Literarische Anstalt.

Hirschman, Albert O. 1977. *The Passions and the Interests: Political Arguments for Capitalism before its Triumph.*, Princeton: Princeton University Press.

Hobhouse, L.T. 1964. *Liberalism* (first published 1911), London: Oxford University Press.

Hollenbach, David. 1979. *Claims in Conflict: Retrieving and Renewing the Catholic Human Rights Tradition*, New York: Paulist Press.

Hook, Sidney. 1936. *From Hegel to Marx: Studies in the Intellectual Development of Karl Marx*, New York: Reynal & Hitchcock.

Hopkins, Charles H. 1940. *The Rise of the Social Gospel in American Protestantism, 1865-1915*, New Haven: Yale University Press.

Horowitz, Robert. 1963. "John Dewey," in Leo Strauss and Joseph Cropsey (eds.) *History of Political Philosophy*, Chicago: Rand McNally.

Horvat, Branko. 1982. *The Political Economy of Socialism*, Armonk, N.Y.: M.E. Sharpe.

Houthakker, Heinrich H. 1950. "Revealed Preference and the Utility Function", *Economica*, May.

Hoyt, Elizabeth (ed.). 1954. *American Income and its Uses*, New York: Harper.

Hudson, Winthrop. 1949. "Puritanism and the Spirit of Capitalism," *Church History*, XVIII, March, 3-16.

Hughes, H. Stuart. 1977. *Consciousness and Society*, New York: Vintage Books.

Hunter, Floyd. 1959. *Top Leadership U.S.A.*, Chapel Hill: University of North Carolina Press.

Hutchison, T.W. 1965. *The Significance and Basic Postulates of Economic Theory* (First published 1938), New York: Augustus M. Kelly.

Hyma, Albert. 1955. *Renaissance to Reformation*, Grand Rapids: William B. Eerdmans Publishing Co.

Isbell, Billie Jean. 1978. *To Defend Ourselves: Ecology and Ritual in an Andean Village*, Austin: University of Texas Press.

Jevons, William Stanley. 1865. *The Coal Question*, London: Macmillan.

Johann, Robert. 1966. *The Pragmatic Meaning of God*, Milwaukee: Marquette University Press.

Jones, Richard. 1831. *An Essay on the Distribution of Wealth*, London: John Murray.

Kariel, Henry S. 1977. *Beyond Liberalism, Where Relations Grow*, New York: Harper & Row.

Keynes, John Neville. 1917. *The Scope and Method of Political Economy, fourth edition*, London: Macmillan.

Kitch, M.J. 1967. "Introduction: Max Weber and R.H. Tawney," in Kitch (ed.), *Capitalism and the Reformation*, London: Longman, Green & Co., Ltd.

Knight, Frank H. and Thornton W. Merriam. 1945. *The Economic Order and Religion*, New York: Harper.

Knight, Frank H. 1947. *Freedom and Reform*, New York: Harper & Brothers.

——— 1976. *The Ethics of Competition and Other Essays* (first published 1935), Chicago: University of Chicago Press.

Kraus, J.B. 1930. *Scholastik, Puritanismus und Kapitalismus*, Munich and Leipzig: Duncker Humblot.

Kristol, Irving. 1978. *Two Cheers for Capitalism*, New York: Basic Books.

Kucheman, Clark. 1966. "Professor Tillich: Justice and the Economic Order", *The Journal of Religion*, Vol. 46 No. 1, 165-183.

Lange, Oskar. 1935. "Marxian Economics and Modern Economic Theory", *Review of Economic Studies*, June.

——— 1938. "On the Economic Theory of Socialism," in Benjamin Lippincott (ed.) *On the Economic Theory of Socialism*, Minneapolis: University of Minnesota Press.

Lee, Robert. 1969. *The Promise of Bennett: Christian Realism and Social Responsibility*, Philadelphia: J.B. Lippincott.

Lefever, Ernest W. 1979. *Amsterdam to Nairobi: The World Council of Churches and the Third World*, Washington, D.C.: Ethics and Public Policy Center.

Lengyel, Thomas. 1979. "Religious Factionalism and Social Diversity in a Mayan Community," *Wisconsin Sociologist* 16:81-90.

Lindblom, Charles E. 1977. *Politics and Markets*, New York: Basic Books.

Lindquist, Martti. 1975. *Economic Growth and the Quality of Life: An Analysis of the Debate Within the World Council of Churches, 1966-1974*, Helsinki: The Finnish Society for Missiology and Ecumenics.

Lindsay, A.D. 1943. *The Modern Democratic State*, London: Oxford University Press.

Little, David. 1969. *Religion, Order, and Law*, New York: Harper.

Long, Edward Jr. and Robert Handy (eds.). 1970. *Theology and Church in Times of Change: Essays in Honor of John Bennett*, Philadelphia: Westminster.

Lovin, Robin W. 1984. *Christian Faith and Public Choices: The Social Ethics of Barth, Brunner, and Bonhoeffer*, Philadelphia: Fortress Press.

Lowi, Theodore J. 1969. *The End of Liberalism*, New York: W.W. Norton and Company, Inc.

Löwith, Karl. 1982. *Max Weber and Karl Marx*, London: George Allen & Unwin.

Löwy, Michael. 1976. *Pour une Sociologie des Intellectuels Revolutionaires*, Paris: Presses Universitaires de France.

MacIntyre, Alasdair. 1981. *After Virtue: A Study in Moral Theory*, Notre Dame: University of Notre Dame Press.

MacMurray, John. 1961. *Persons in Relation*, London: Faber & Faber.

Manning, D.J. 1976. *Liberalism*, New York: St. Martin's Press.

Maritain, Jacques. 1947. *The Person and the Common Good*, New York: Charles Scribner's Sons.

——— 1951. *Man and the State*, Chicago: University of Chicago Press.

Marx, Karl and Friedrich Engels. 1978. "The Communist Manifesto," (first published 1848), in C.B. Macpherson (ed.) *Property: Mainstream and Critical Positions*, Toronto: University of Toronto Press.

McConnell, Grant. 1966. *Private Power and American Democracy*, New York: Knopf.

McCormick, Richard. 1982. "Notes on Moral Theology, 1981," *Theological Studies*, 43:1 (March).

McKenzie, Richard B. and Gordon Tullock. 1981. *The New World of Economics: Explorations into the Human Experience, third edition*, Homewood, IL: Richard D. Irwin.

Meland, Bernard E. 1953. *Faith and Culture*, New York: Oxford University Press.

——— 1976. *Fallible Forms and Symbols: Discourses on Method in a Theology of Culture*, Philadelphia: Fortress Press.

Migdal, Joel S. 1974. *Peasants, Politics, and Revolution*, Princeton: Princeton University Press.

Míguez Bonino, José. 1975. *Doing Theology in a Revolutionary Situation*, Philadelphia: Fortress Press.

——— 1983. *Toward a Christian Political Ethics*, Philadelphia: Fortress Press.

Mill, John Stuart. 1874. *Essays on Some Unsettled Questions of Political Economy, second edition*, London: Longmans, Green, Reader and Dyer.

1875. *A System of Logic: Ratiocinative and Inductive*, 2 vols., London: Longmans, Green, Reader and Dyer.

Mises, Ludwig von. 1951. *Socialism*, New Haven: Yale University Press.

1960. *Epistemological Problems in Economics*, Princeton, N.J.: Van Nostrand.

Moltmann, Jürgen. 1974. *The Crucified God*, New York: Harper & Row.

1977. *The Church in the Power of the Spirit*, New York: Harper & Row.

Muelder, Walter. 1953. *Religion and Economic Responsibility*, New York: Charles Scriber's Sons.

1959. *Foundations of the Responsible Society*, Nashville: Abingdon.

1972. "Communitarian Christian Ethics: A Personal Statement and a Response," in Paul Deats, Jr. (ed.), *Toward a Discipline of Social Ethics*, Boston: Boston University Press.

1983. "Issues in the Dialogue between Theology and the Social Sciences" in *The Ethical Edge of Christian Theology: Forty Years of Communitarian Personalism*, Toronto: Edwin Mellen Press.

Munby, Denys. 1956. *Christianity and Economic Problems*, London: Macmillan & Co. Ltd.

1961. *God and the Rich Society: A Study of Christians in a World of Abundance*, London: Oxford University Press.

1966 (ed.). *Economic Growth in a World Perspective*, New York: Association Press.

1969 (ed.). *World Development: Challenges to the Churches*, Washington, D.C.: Corpus Books.

Nash, June. 1967/68. "The Passion Play in Maya Indian Communities," *Comparative Studies in Society and History* 10:318-325.

1979. *We Eat the Mines and the Mines Eat Us: Dependency and Exploitation in Bolivian Tin Mines*, New York: Columbia University Press.

Nash, June and Maria Patricia Fernandez-Kelly (eds.). 1983. *Women, Men and the International Division of Labor*, Albany: State University of New York at Albany Press.

Nelson, Benjamin. 1969. *The Idea of Usury*, Chicago: University of Chicago Press.

Neuhaus, Richard John. 1984. *The Naked Public Square*, Grand Rapids, Michigan: Eerdmans.

Niebuhr, Reinhold. 1932. *Moral Man and Immoral Society*, New York: Charles Scribner's Sons.

1942. "Religion and Action," in Ruth Nada Anshen (ed.) *Science and Man*, New York: Harcourt, Brace and Company.

1944. *The Children of Light and the Children of Darkness*, New York: Charles Scribner's Sons.

1949. *The Nature and Destiny of Man*, 2 vols., New York: Charles Scribner's Sons.

Nisbet, Robert. 1966. *The Sociological Imagination*, New York: Basic Books.

Noonan, John. 1957. *The Scholastic Analysis of Usury*, Cambridge: Harvard University Press.

Norman, Edward. 1979. *Christianity and the World Order*, Oxford: Oxford University Press.

Novak, Michael. 1982a. "Creation Theology—John Paul II and the American Experience," *This World*, 3 (Fall).

1982b. *The Spirit of Democratic Capitalism*, New York: American Enterprise Institute/Simon & Schuster.

1984. *Freedom with Justice: Catholic Social Thought and Liberal Institutions*, San Francisco: Harper & Row.

Nove, Alec. 1983. *The Economics of Feasible Socialism*, London: George Allen & Unwin.

Nutter, Warren G. and Henry A. Einhorn. 1969. *Enterprise Monopoly in the United States*, New York: Columbia University Press.

O'Brien, David and Thomas Shannon. 1977. *Renewing the Earth*, Garden City, New York: Image Books.

Obenhaus, Victor. 1965. *Ethics for an Industrial Society*, New York: Harper.

Okun, Arthur. 1975. *Equality and Efficiency: The Big Tradeoff*, Washington, D.C.: The Brookings Institution.

Oldham, J.H. (ed.). 1937. *The Oxford Conference (Official Report)*, Chicago: Willett, Clark & Co.

Ollman, Bertell. 1976. *Alienation: Marx's Conception of Man in Capitalist Society (second edition)*, Cambridge: Cambridge University Press.

Olson, Mancur. 1971. *The Logic of Collective Action*, Cambridge: Harvard University Press.

1982. *The Rise and Decline of Nations: Economic Growth, Stagflation, and Social Rigidities*, New Haven: Yale University Press.

Pareto, Vilfredo. 1896. *Cours d'economie politique*, Lausanne: F. Rouge.

1971. *Manual of Political Economy (first published 1906)*, New York: A.M. Kelley.

Pateman, Carole. 1970. *Participation and Democratic Theory*, Cambridge: Cambridge University Press.

Paulhaus, Norman J. 1980. "Social Catholicism and the Fribourg Union," in Joseph L. Allen (ed.), *American Society of Christian Ethics Selected Papers 1980*, Missoula Mont.: Scholars Press.

Pawlikowski, John T. 1982. *Christ in the Light of the Christian-Jewish Dialogue*, Ramsey, New Jersey: Paulist Press.

Peacock, James. 1968. *Rites of Modernization: Symbolic and Social Aspects of Indonesian Proletarian Drama*, Chicago: University of Chicago Press.

Popkin, Samuel L. 1979. *The Rational Peasant: The Political Economy of Rural Society in Vietnam*, Berkeley: University of California Press.

Potter, Ralph B., Jr. 1972. "The Logic of Moral Argument" in Peal Deats, Jr., (ed) *Toward a Discipline of Social Ethics: Essays in Honor of Walter Muelder*, Boston: Boston University Press.

Rachfahl, Felix. 1909. "Kapitalismus und Kalvinismus", *Internationale Wochenschrift für Wissenschaft, Kunst und Technik*, Nos. 39-43.

Ramsey, Paul. 1967. *Who Speaks for the Church? A Critique of the 1966 Geneva Conference on Church and Society.*, Nashville: Abingdon.

Rauschenbusch, Walter. 1907. *Christianity and the Social Crisis*, New York: Macmillan.

1912. *Christianizing the Social Order*, New York: Macmillan.

1917. *A Theology for the Social Gospel*, New York: Macmillan.

Rawls, John. 1971. *A Theory of Justice*, Cambridge, Mass.: Harvard University Press.

Robbins, Lionel. 1937. *An Essay on the Nature and Significance of Economic Science*, second edition, London: Macmillan.

Robertson, H.M. 1933. *Aspects of the Rise of Economic Individualism*, Cambridge: Cambridge University Press.

Rothbard, Murray N. 1979. *Individualism and the Philosophy of the Social Sciences*, San Francisco: Cato Institute.

Ryan, John A. 1906. *A Living Wage: Its Ethical and Economic Aspects*, New York: Macmillan.

1916. *Distributive Justice* (revised 1927, 1942), New York: Macmillan.

Sahlins, Marshall. 1976. *Culture and Practical Reason*, Chicago: University of Chicago Press.

1981. *Historical Metaphors and Mythical Realities*, Ann Arbor: University of Michigan Press.

Salamon, Lester M. 1975. *The Money Committees*, New York: Grossman.

Samuelson, Paul. 1938. "A Note on the Pure Theory of Consumer's Behavior", *Economica*, February.

1952. "Economic Theory and Mathematics: An Appraisal", *American Economic Review*, May.

1963. "Problems on Methodology: Discussion", *American Economic Review*, May.

1965. "Some Notions on Causality and Teleology in Economics", Daniel Lerner (ed.), *Cause and Effect: The Hayden Colloquium on Scientific Method and Concept*, New York: Free Press.

1967. *Economics: An Introductory Analysis*. Seventh Edition, New York: McGraw-Hill Company.

Samuelson, Paul (ed.). 1973. *Readings in Economics*, New York: McGraw-Hill Company.

Samuelsson, Kurt. 1961. *Religion and Economic Action: A Critique of Max Weber* (first published 1957), New York: Harper & Row.

Sandel, Michael. 1982. *Liberalism and the Limits of Justice*, Cambridge: Cambridge University Press.

Schroeder, W. Widick. 1982. "Evolution, Human Values, and Religious Experience: A Process Perspective," in *Zygon*, Vol. 17, No. 3 (Sept), pp. 267-291.

Schultz, Theodore W. 1971. *Investment in Human Capital*, New York: Free Press.

Schumpeter, Joseph A. 1950. *Capitalism, Socialism, and Democracy (third edition)*, New York: Harper & Row.

1975. *Capitalism, Socialism and Democracy (first published 1942)*, New York: Harper.

Scott, James C. 1976. *The Moral Economy of the Peasant*, New Haven: Yale University Press.

Scriven, Michael. 1959. "Truisms as the Grounds for Historical Explanations" in Leonard I. Krimerman (ed.), *The Nature and Scope of Social Science*, New York: Appleton-Century-Crofts.

Sée, Henri. 1927. "The Contribution of the Puritans to the Evolution of Modern Capitalism," in Green (ed.) *Protestantism and Capitalism*, Boston: D.C. Heath & Co.

Segundo, Juan. 1976. *Liberation of Theology*, Maryknoll, N.Y.: Orbis Books.

1984. *Faith and Ideologies*, Maryknoll, N.Y.: Orbis Books.

Shils, Edward. 1972. *The Intellectuals and the Powers*, Chicago: University of Chicago Press..

Shonfield, Andrew. 1969. *Modern Capitalism*, New York: Oxford University Press.

Shoup, Laurence H. and William Minter. 1977. *Imperial Brain Trust*, New York: Monthly Review Press.

Sidgwick, Henry. 1962. "The Scope and Method of Economic Science" in R.L. Smyth (ed.) *Essays in Economic Method* (first published 1885), London: Gerald Duckworth and Co.

Sik, Ota. 1976. *The Third Way*, London: Wildwood House.

Silk, Leonard. 1976. *The Economists*, New York: Basic Books.

Smith, Adam. 1937. *An Inquiry into the Nature and Causes of the Wealth of Nations* (First published in 1776), New York: Modern Library.

Smith, David H. 1970. *The Achievement of John C. Bennett*, New York: Herder & Herder.

Smith, James D. and Stephen D. Franklin. 1974. "The Concentration of Personal Wealth, 1922-1969," *American Economic Review*, May.

Sölle, Dorothee. 1977. *Revolutionary Patience*, Maryknoll, N.Y.: Orbis Books.

1983. *The Arms Race Kills Even Without War*, Philadelphia: Fortress Press.

Sombart, Werner. 1913. *The Jews and Modern Capitalism* (first published as *Juden und das Wirschaftsleben* in 1911), London: T.F. Urwin.

1916. *Der Moderne Kapitalismus* (first published in 1902), Munich and Leipzig: Duncker Humblot.

1967. *The Quintessence of Capitalism* (first published as *Der Bourgeois* in 1915), New York: H. Fertig.

Stackhouse, Max L. 1972. *Ethics and the Urban Ethos: An Essay in Social Theory and Theological Reconstruction*, Boston: Beacon Press.

Stammer, Otto (ed.). 1971. *Max Weber and Sociology Today*, New York: Harper.

Stassen, Glen H. 1977. "A Social Theory Model for Religious Ethics," *The Journal of Religious Ethics*, 5/1, 9-39.

Stavenhagen, Rodolfo. 1975. *Social Classes in Agrarian Societies*, Garden City, NY: Anchor Press.

Stigler, George. 1982. *The Economist as Preacher*, Chicago: University of Chicago Press.

Stigler, George J. and Gary S. Becker. 1977. "De Gustibus Non Est Disputandum", *American Economic Review*, March.

Stone, Ronald H. 1980. *Paul Tillich's Radical Social Thought*, Atlanta: John Knox Press.

Strauss, Leo. 1953. *Natural Right and History*, Chicago: University of Chicago Press.

Stumme, John R. 1977. "Introduction" in Paul Tillich, *The Socialist Decision*, New York: Harper & Row.

Sturm, Douglas. 1974. "The Priority of the Philosophical Question: A Response to David Little on Max Weber," *The Journal of Religious Ethics*, 2/2, 41-52.

Sullivan, William M. 1982. *Reconstructing Public Philosophy*, Berkeley: University of California Press.

Swingewood, Alan. 1977. *The Myth of Mass Culture*, Atlantic Highlands, N.J.: Humanities Press.

Taussig, Michael. 1980. *The Devil and Commodity Fetishism in South America*, Chapel Hill: University of North Carolina.

Tawney, R.H. 1920. *The Acquisitive Society*, New York: Harcourt, Brace and Howe.

1926. *Religion and the Rise of Capitalism*, New York: Harcourt, Brace & Co.

Thomas, M.M. and Paul Albrecht. 1967. *Christians in the Technical and Social Revolutions of Our Time—World Conference on Church and Society (Official Report)*, Geneva: World Council of Churches.

Thurow, Lester. 1980. *The Zero-Sum Society*, New York: Basic Books, Inc.

Tillich, Paul. 1966. "Rejoinder", *The Journal of Religion*, 46, 1, 184-196.

1977. *The Socialist Decision* (first published 1933), New York: Harper & Row.

Tischner, Jozef. 1984. *The Spirit of Solidarity*, San Francisco: Harper & Row.

Tocqueville, Alexis de. 1954. *Democracy in America, Volume I*, New York: Vintage Books.

Todorov, Tzvetan. 1984. *The Conquest of America: The Question of the Other*, New York: Harper & Row.

Tribe, Laurence H. 1973. "Technology Assessment and the Fourth Discontinuity: The Limits of Instrumental Rationality", *Southern California Law Review*, June.

Troeltsch, Ernst. 1931. *The Social Teaching of the Christian Churches*, 2 vols., London: George Allen and Unwin.

Tucker, Robert C. 1972. *Philosophy and Myth in Karl Marx*, Cambridge: Cambridge University Press.

Turner, Jonathan H. and Charles E. Staines. 1976. *Inequality: Privilege and Poverty in America*, New York: Goodyear Publishing Company.

Unger, Roberto M. 1975. *Knowledge and Politics*, New York: The Free Press.

U.S. Bishops. 1984. "Catholic Social Teaching and the U.S. Economy", *Origins* 14:22/23, 338-383.

Viner, Jacob. 1972. *The Role of Providence in the Social Order: An Essay in Intellectual History*, Princeton: Princeton University Press.

1978. *Religious Thought and Economic Society*, Durham: Duke University Press.

Wallerstein, Immanuel. 1976. *The Modern World-System Vol. 1: Capitalist Agriculture and the Origin of the European World-Economy in the Sixteenth Century*, New York: Academic Press.

1980. *The Modern World System Vol. 2: Mercantilism and the Consolidation of the European World-Economy*, New York: Academic Press.

1983. *Historical Capitalism*, London: Verso.

Walzer, Michael. 1968. *The Revolution of the Saints: A Study in the Origin of Radical Politics*, New York: Atheneum.

Ward, A. Dudley. 1953. *Goals of Economic Life*, New York: Harper.

1955. *The American Economy—Attitudes and Opinions*, New York: Harper.

Warren, Kay B. 1978. *The Symbolism of Subordination: Indian Identity in a Guatemalan Town*, Austin: University of Texas Press.

1985. "Creation Narratives and the Moral Order: Implications of Multiple Models in Highland Guatemala," in Robin Lovin and Frank Reynolds (eds.) *Cosmogony and Ethical Order*, Chicago: University of Chicago Press.

Wasserstrom, Robert. 1975. "Revolution in Guatemala: Peasants and Politics under the Arbenz Government," *Comparative Studies in Society and History* 17:473-478.

1983. *Class and Society in Central Chiapas*, Berkeley: University of California Press.

Weber, Max. 1958. *The Protestant Ethic and the Spirit of Capitalism*, New York: Charles Scribner's Sons.

Weiskopf, Walter A. 1977. "The Moral Predicament of the Market Economy," in Gerald Dworkin (ed.) *Markets and Morals*, Washington, D.C.: Hemisphere Publishing Corporation.

Whitehead, Alfred North. 1925. *Science and the Modern World*, New York: Macmillan.

1926. *Religion in Making*, New York: Macmillan.

1938. *Modes of Thought*, New York: Macmillan.

1961. *Adventures of Ideas* (first published 1933), New York: The Free Press.

1978. *Process and Reality* (first published 1929), New York: The Free Press.

Wicksteed, Philip H. 1899. "Political Economy and Psychology," in Palgrave's *Dictionary of Political Economy, 3 vols.*, London: Macmillan.

Wilcox, Walter W. 1956. *Social Responsibility in Farm Leadership*, New York: Harper.

Will, George F. 1983. *Statecraft as Soulcraft: What Government Does*, New York: Simon & Schuster.

Winter, Gibson. 1966. *Elements for a Social Ethic*, New York: Macmillan.

1970. *Being Free: Reflections on America's Cultural Revolution*, New York: Macmillan.

1981. *Liberating Creation*, New York: Seabury Press.

Wogaman, J. Philip. 1977. *The Great Economic Debate: An Ethical Analysis*, Philadelphia, Westminster Press.

Wolff, Robert Paul. 1968. *The Poverty of Liberalism*, Boston: Beacon Press.

Wong, Stanley. 1973. "The 'F-Twist' and the Methodology of Paul Samuelson", *American Economic Review*, June.

World Council of Churches. 1948. *The Message and Reports of the First Assembly of the World Council of Churches*, London: SCM Press.

1954. *The Christian Hope & the Task of the Church*, New York: Harper.

1955. *Evanston Speaks: Reports from the Second Assembly of the World Council of Churches, 1954*, Geneva: World Council of Churches.

1967. *World Conference on Church and Society (Official Report)*

Yzermans, Vincent A. (ed.). 1961."The Christmas Message" in *The Major Addresses of Pope Pius XII, Vol. 2.*, St. Paul: North Central Publishing Company.

Notes about the Contributors

Robert Benne is Jordan-Trexler Professor of Religion and director of the Center for Church and Society at Roanoke College, Salem, Virginia. He is the author of *The Ethic of Democratic Capitalism: A Moral Reassessment* (1981), *A Christian Critique of the American Dream* (with Philip Hefner) (1974), and *Wandering in the Wilderness* (1972).

Daniel Rush Finn is associate professor of economics, associate professor of social ethics and dean of The School of Theology, St. John's University, Collegeville, Minnesota. He is the author of *Toward a Christian Economic Ethic* (with Prentiss Pemberton) (1985).

Franklin I. Gamwell is dean and associate professor of social ethics at The Divinity School, The University of Chicago. He is author of *Beyond Preference: Liberal Theories of Independent Associations* (1984) and editor of *Existence and Actuality: Conversations with Charles Hartshorne* (with John B. Cobb, Jr.) (1984).

Bruce Grelle is an instructor in the religious studies department of St. Xavier College in Chicago.

David Krueger is director of the Center for Ethics and Corporate Policy in Chicago and is co-editor (with Don S. Browning) of *Religion and the Economic Order: Contemporary Tensions* (1982).

John Pawlikowski, O.S.M. is professor of social ethics at The Catholic Theological Union in Chicago. He is author of *The Challenge of the Holocaust for Christian Theology* (1982), and is editor of *Justice in the Marketplace: Collected Statements of the Vatican and the U.S. Catholic Bishops on Economic Policy, 1891-1984* (1985), and *Biblical and Theological Reflections on the Challenge of Peace* (with Donald Senior) (1984).

W. Widick Schroeder is professor of Religion and Society at the Chicago Theological Seminary. He is author of *Suburban Religion* (with Victor Obenhaus, Thomas P. Sweetser and Larry A. Jones) (1974), *Where Do I Stand?* (with Keith A. Davis) (1973), *Cognitive Structures and Religious Research* (1970) and *Religion in American Culture* (with Victor Obenhaus) (1964) and co-editor of *Pastoral Care and Liberation Praxis* (with Perry LeFevre) (1986), *Spiritual Nurture and Congregational Development* (with Perry LeFevre) (1984), *Process Philosophy and Social Thought* (with John B. Cobb, Jr.) (1981), *Belief and Ethics: Essays in Ethics, the Human Sciences, and Ministry in Honor of W. Alvin Pitcher* (with Gibson Winter) (1978), and *Belonging and Alienation: Religious Foundations for the Human Future* (with Philip Hefner) (1976).

Douglas Sturm is professor of religion and political science at Bucknell University, Harrisburg, Pennsylvania. He is author of "Contextuality and Covenant: The Pertinence of Social Theory and Theology to Bioethics" in Earl E. Shelp (ed.) *Theology and Bioethics* (1985); "Cosmogony and Ethics in the Marxian Tradition: Premise and Destiny of Nature and History" in Robin W. Lovin and Frank E. Reynolds (eds.) *Cosmogony and Ethical Order* (1985); and "Crisis in the American Republic: The Legal and Political Significance of Martin Luther King's 'Letter from a Birmingham Jail,'" *The Journal of Law and Religion*, vol. II, no. 2, 1984.

Kay Warren is associate professor of anthropology and director of the Program in Women's Studies at Princeton University. She is the author of *Women of the Andes: Patriarchy and Social Change in Two Peruvian Towns* (with Susan C. Bourque) (1981) and *The Symbolism of Subordination—Indian Identity in a Guatemalan Town (1978)*.

Cornel West is associate professor of the philosophy of religion at Yale Divinity School. He is editor of *Post-Analytic Philosophy* (with John Rajchman) (1985) and author of *Prophesy Deliverance! An Afro-American Revolutionary Christianity* (1982).

STUDIES IN RELIGION AND SOCIETY

edited by

Robert L. Moore, W. Alvin Pitcher,
W. Widick Schroeder and Gibson Winter

Other CSSR Publications in the Series:

Charles Amjad-Ali and W. Alvin Pitcher, eds.,
Liberation and Ethics: Essays in Religious Social Ethics in Honor of Gibson Winter (1985)

John B. Cobb, Jr. and W. Widick Schroeder, eds., *Process
Philosphy and Social Thought* (1981)

Philip Hefner and W. Widick Schroeder, eds., *Belonging and Alienation:
Religioius Foundations for the Human Future* (1976)

Paul E. Kraemer, *Awakening from the American Dream: The Human Rights
Movement in the United States Assessed during a
Crucial Decade, 1960-1970* (1973)

William C. Martin, *Christians in Conflict* (1972)

Robert L. Moore and Frank E. Reynolds, eds., *Anthropology
and the Study of Religion* (1984)

Victor Obenhaus, *And See the People* (1968)

W. Widick Schroeder, Victor Obenhaus, Larry A. Jones, and
Thomas Sweetser, SJ, *Suburban Religion: Churches
and Synagogues in the American Experience* (1974)

W. Widick Schroeder and Gibson Winter, eds., *Belief and
Ethics: Essays in Ethics, the Human Sciences and Ministry
in Honor of W. Alvin Pitcher* (1978)

Walter M. Stuhr, Jr., *The Public Style: A Study
of the Community Participation of Protestant Ministers* (1972)

Thomas P. Sweetser, SJ, *The Catholic Parish: Shifting
Membership in a Changing Church* (1974)

Lawrence Witmer, ed., *Issues in Community Organization* (1972)

Other Books in the Series:

Thomas C. Campbell and Yoshio Fukuyama, *The Fragmented
Layman* (1970)

John Fish, *Black Power/White Control: The Struggle
of the Woodlawn Organization in Chicago* (1973)

John Fish, Gordon Nelson, Walter M. Stuhr, Jr., and Lawrence Witmer,
The Edge of the Ghetto (1968)

W. Widick Schroeder and Victor Obenhaus,
Religion in American Culture (1964)

Gibson Winter, *Religious Identity* (1968)